INFLATION AND WAGES
IN
UNDERDEVELOPED COUNTRIES

Inflation and Wages in Underdeveloped Countries

India, Peru and Turkey
1939-1960

BILL WARREN

School of Oriental and African Studies
University of London

FRANK CASS

First published 1977 in Great Britain by

FRANK CASS AND COMPANY LIMITED
Gainsborough House, Gainsborough Road,
London E11 1RS, England

and in United States of America by

FRANK CASS AND COMPANY LIMITED
c/o Biblio Distribution Center
81 Adams Drive, Totowa, New Jersey 07512

Transferred to Digital Printing 2004

ISBN 0 7146 2266 4

To
Mabel, Rose
and
Shaun

Contents

List of Tables

List of Abbreviations

E.C.A.	Economic Commission for Africa
E.C.A.F.E.	Economic Commission for Asia and the Far East
E.C.E.	Economic Commission for Europe
E.C.L.A.	Economic Commission for Latin America
F.A.O.	Food and Agricultural Organisation
G.O.I.	Government of India
I.B.R.D.	International Bank for Reconstruction and Development
I.L.G.	Indian Labour Gazette
I.M.F.	International Monetary Fund
I.L.O.	International Labour Organisation
J.P.E.	Journal of Political Economy
O.E.P.	Oxford Economic Papers
R.B.I.	Reserve Bank of India
R.I.I.A.	Royal Institute for International Affairs
R.O.T.	Republic of Turkey
R.P.	Republica Peruana
Q.J.E.	Quarterly Journal of Economics

PREFACE to *Inflation and Wages in Underdeveloped Countries* by Bill Warren, to replace inadvertently incomplete Preface in the book.

PREFACE

The following contribution embodies a treatment of our problem which is extensive rather than intensive, as is adequately testified by the attempt to encompass within the bounds of a single study the relevant experience of three such countries as India, Peru and Turkey. This extensive treatment is the result of the comparative approach adopted, the advantages of which, it is hoped, will at least partly counterbalance the clear risk of superficiality.

I am extremely grateful for the unstinting help given to me by my supervisor, Professor Alan Brown, and Mr Maurice Dobb, during the PhD phase of my work and, later, from continuous discussion with my colleague of the School of Oriental and African Studies, T. J. Byres. I have also benefited from discussions with Peter Ayre, Jim Calvey, Alec Gordon, Biplab Dasgupta, Mike Safier and Profulla Sanghvi, and I am grateful too to Mrs Judy Barrett, whose typing, well beyond the call of duty, was a great help. I wish to thank my colleague Michael Hodd for his contribution of the statistical appendices to three country chapters. Naturally, no one but myself is responsible for any deficiencies in the final result.

The system of notation adopted requires a word of explanation. Notes are printed at the end of each chapter. Where reference is made to a work full details of which appear in the bibliography, the author's name only is cited in the notes, along with the pertinent page numbers. Where several works by the same author or institution appear, the date of the work referred to is included in the reference for identification purposes.

The analytic and policy issues posed by the relation of inflation to industrialisation in the less-developed countries have lost none of their importance or topicality since the problems first drew significant attention in the 1950s. While the present essay may be regarded primarily as a contribution to modern economic history, it also, therefore, has direct relevance to current experience, since inflation in the majority of the less-developed countries shows little sign of disappearing or subsiding. For this reason, I have felt it worthwhile to allow it to appear in published form despite the long interval between the completion of the research on which it is based and its present appearance, an interval arising from ill health and technical publishing problems beyond the writer's control.

June 1977
                                                Bill Warren
                                                London

CHAPTER I

INTRODUCTION:

The general theme of the movement of income shares during inflation and its relationship to the process of industrialisation is one which has attracted an immense literature in its own right and which represents a confluence of three quite distinct trends in economic thinking: that concerned with the determinants of income distribution in modern manufacturing industry; that concerned with the character of the inflationary process; and that concerned with the characteristics of the industrialisation process.

The justification for yet another venture into this much-explored jungle in this case springs from the fact that the advantages of comparative analysis of national experience have by no means been fully utilised, most of the attempts to date having been restricted to rather general efforts to correlate a number of variables over a large number of countries, generally in a somewhat aggregative fashion and with only cursory reference to historical or institutional dimensions.[1] Moreover, most such studies have attempted to relate inflation to changes in income shares *or* rates of economic growth taken separately, rather than to establish some more complex relationship between all three.

Accordingly, in what follows we have attempted the comparative analysis of the experience, during inflation, of income redistribution in manufacturing industry in no more than three countries, India, Peru and Turkey, over the two generally inflationary decades which commenced with the beginning of World War II. Despite the limited number of countries considered, no more than a very approximate attempt can be made in a study of this size to trace the channels and directions of causality, and no attempt at all is made to give quantitative precision to the relative importance of the different variables at work on the phenomenon under consideration.

Little is to be gained from yet another survey of the relevant economic literature on theories of income distribution, inflation and industrialisation, even supposing there were space enough for it. However, a few comments on the articulation of these three strands of economic thought with one another are required in order to clarify the issues on which we might expect our comparative data to throw light.

Theories of the relation of industrialisation to inflation (defined as a more or less prolonged rise in the general price level)are bedevilled by the fact that inflation is the net resultant of all the forces at work in the economy as reflected in the movement of the aggregate price level. This being so, it is by no means always clear whether the problem under examination relates to the effects of inflation *per se,* or, alternatively, to the effects of the conditions giving rise to inflation on industrialisation. It will, of course, never be easy to disentangle these different types of effect from one another in practice. Nevertheless, in principle, there is clearly a group of effects which may reasonably be construed as resulting from inflation, irrespective of the specific causes of the inflation as such; for example, the development of possible tendencies to de-monetise and thus indirectly to de-commercialise the economy; or propensities to invest in quick-yielding assets as opposed to those with a longer pay-off period; or, perhaps, the conjuring up by prolonged inflation of new institutional mechanisms to protect formerly unprotected sections of the community—with permanent effects on the economy.

When we turn to consider *the effects of the conditions giving rise to inflation* on the industrialisation process, a new complication is introduced by the possibility that, since inflation may result from a range of different conditions at different times and places, so the result may be a range of different kinds of inflation. In particular, relative price movements of certain broad categories of commodities may be quite different in different types of inflation. In such circumstances the very concept of 'inflation' as a variable to be considered in conjunction with 'industrialisation' may prove to be an example of what Dr Myrdal has called 'misplaced aggregation'.[2]

We thus have three levels of analysis: first, the effect of inflation *per se* on industrialisation, irrespective of the conditions giving rise to inflation; second, the effect of the conditions giving rise to inflation on the movement of relative prices (including factor prices) during inflation; and third, the effect of the conditions giving rise to inflation on industrialisation more generally.

In effect, the more formally-ordered hypotheses concerning the relationshop of industrialisation to inflation have been those concerned with the effects on industrialisation of relative price and cost movements during periods of *increase* in the aggregate price level, the general assumption being that there is a difference in the direction of relative price/cost movements as between situations of rising and falling aggregate price levels.

Two such hypotheses usefully serve both to throw light on the relationship of this level of analysis (effects of relative price/cost movements during a general price rise), to the other two levels of analysis (effects of the price rise *per se* and the more general effects of the conditions causing the price rise); and to illuminate the articulation between the theories of wage determination and income distribution, theories of inflation, and theories of industrialisation. These are the 'profit inflation' (wage-lag) or 'forced savings' theory of economic development, and the 'inflation barrier' thesis.

The view of inflation as an engine of development via forced savings, in which the rise of final prices (of manufactures), faster than prime costs, shifts resources into the hands of investing entrepreneurs and away from agriculturalists or wage-labourers, has a long patronage, stretching from Earl J. Hamilton, the distinguished economic historian, who has applied it to European economic development in the period of the great inflation of the 16th-18th centuries,[3] through John Maynard Keynes[4] to W. Arthur Lewis who has advocated deliberate inflation as a policy for today's underdeveloped economies.[5]

The 'inflation barrier' hypothesis, on the other hand, posits inflation as a process which will tend to *set a limit* to the level of accumulation that can be achieved.[6] As applied to underdeveloped countries, this view holds that at a certain stage in the process of raising the level of investment, the rise in prices, as resources become fully utilised, forces the entrepreneurs themselves to grant higher money wages in order to maintain the efficiency of their labour forces. The resulting inflationary spiral, in one way or another, limits a further shift of resources towards investment and thereby limits the rate of growth.[7]

The similarities between these two theories point us in the direction of their articulation with industrialisation theory, while their differences orient us towards their articulation with income distribution and wage determination theory.

At the root of both the 'profit inflation' and the 'inflation barrier' theories lie two assumptions: first, that inflation itself is the product of an aggregate excess of demand over supply of resources on the economy (or a competition for aggregate resources between consumption demand and investment demand); and second, that the principal obstacles to industrialisation are to be located on the supply rather than on the demand side. These points are not, of course, unconnected, since if inflation is characteristic of a situation in which investment and consumption demand are competing for the aggregate resources of the economy, then the nascent industrial sector is most unlikely to be restricted by the limitations of the market, or its slow growth.

Both these assumptions can, of course, be challenged. Evidence of substantial excess capacity in the modern manufacturing sector in many parts of the underdeveloped world; attempts to circumvent small national markets by regional arrangements and to reduce barriers to the penetration by underdeveloped countries of the markets of the industrialised market economies; the predominance of the market in many so-called 'planned' economies—all suggest alternative assumptions about the obstacles to industrial expansion. Similarly, the development of theories of inflation which postulate general price rise as being the result of cost pressures—whether the result of sectoral supply bottlenecks or of rising wages—leaves open the possibility that inflation need not be concomitant with aggregate pressure of demand on resources.

There is, however, a crucial difference between the 'profit inflation' and the 'inflation barrier' theories which in principle permits the latter to be reformulated in such a way as to be compatible with some version or other of a cost/structural theory of inflation. Whereas the 'profit inflation' theory is predicated upon an excess demand for manufactures, the 'inflation barrier' theory is predicated upon an excess demand for *working class consumer goods*, i.e. of what may be considered, at one remove, to be inputs into the modern manufacturing sector. Now if these inputs, or a substantial proportion of them, are produced under significantly different supply conditions from the outputs of manufacturing industry in general, then the 'inflation barrier' theory can without difficulty be reformulated in terms of a cost-structural theory of inflation, i.e. an inflation which does not necessarily presuppose an excess *aggregate* demand over supply in the economy. To be specific, such an inflation might originate in food supply bottlenecks in the agricultural sector which spread to the industrial sector via rising wage costs and which may act to retard the expansion of the manufacturing sector by a limitation of the market.[8]

The difference between the 'profit inflation' theory and the 'inflation barrier' theory emerge more clearly when we examine their articulation with theories of the determination of wages movements and income shares. In the former theory, the inflation raises the profit share because wages lag behind final prices, whereas in the latter theory it is the fact of the rise of wages *pari passu* with that of final prices (in the aggregate version of the theory) which both causes the inflation and sets a limit to the rise in the level of investment.

In both cases wages are assumed to be the only input or else the movement of non-labour input-costs (hereafter referred to as raw material costs) are assumed to be such that the same result would have been obtained in terms of changing shares of value added had all costs been labour costs. The 'profit inflation' theory may be based either on a general model which stresses the fact that the demand for labour is derived demand so that, on certain assumptions, prices of final goods may be expected to rise *before* prices of labour; or, alternatively, it may be based upon what are considered to be the specific characteristics of the market for labour and for manufactures at the specific time and place under consideration, i.e. certain assumptions about the contingent, as opposed to the inherent, character of these markets. In the latter case, the wage-lag hypothesis may be based upon either the specific demand-supply relationships in the two markets, or on the relative flexibility of response of wages and prices to changes in demand, or a combination of both. Typically, then, the wage-lag hypothesis will rest upon the fact that the demand for labour is derived whereas that for manufactures is not, upon a relatively greater excess of demand over supply for manufactures as compared with labour, and upon the supposed relative inflexibility of wages as compared to final prices in response to demand changes.[9]

By contrast, the 'inflation barrier' theory, implicitly rejecting the wage-lag as a phenomenon *during inflation,* does so not on the basis of postulating a relatively better market situation for labour than for manufactures, or on the basis of denying the derived character of demand for labour as opposed to that for manufactures, but by rejecting *any* view that wages are directly determined by market forces. Instead, the view is substituted that wages are in effect an administered price determined by the employer in the light of considerations of productive efficiency.[10] Both views, however, have in common that wages rise, if at all, in order to assure or improve the quality or quantity of the flow of labour inputs into manufacturing industry, i.e. the general wage increase is in a sense the result of the aggregated internal productive demands of the firms. It is possible, however, as versions of the cost-inflation theories imply, that external pressures on the firm of an institutional and/or social-political character may push up wages irrespective of the situation in the labour market, or indeed in the product market, thus permitting us to envisage a third possibility—that of an increase in labour's share of value added during inflation.

If the assumption is dropped that raw material costs do not vary in such a way as to disturb the income redistribution effect which would otherwise be achieved were labour the sole variable input, then a new range of possibilities opens up. In particular, Kalecki has developed a theory that the wages share of gross value added alters as a result of differing relative movements of raw material costs and labour costs, assuming constant percentage profit margins, so that, as raw material costs rise faster than labour costs, the result under a cost-plus pricing system with constant percentage gross profit margins is to raise final prices faster than wages, so that labour's share in value added declines.[11] It is not difficult to construct an alternative model incorporating the effects of the movement of raw material costs, in which the share of labour in value added might rise on the assumption that labour costs could rise *pari passu* with raw material costs (or even, perhaps, faster than them), while gross profit margins are permitted a degree of variability, with the effect that the labour share of value added might *rise* as rising material costs squeezed profit margins. Although both theories are consistent with the assumption of some version of cost-plus pricing, albeit with different degrees of flexibility of gross margins assumed, they differ more sharply in the assumption as to the relative flexibility of wage adjustment compared with raw material cost movements and/or the relative demand/supply conditions of the two inputs. In other words, we are back at another wage-price lag assumption.

An explanation of the movement of labour shares in value added in the modern manufacturing sector thus involves us in an analysis of the determinants of the relative movements of raw material costs, labour costs and final prices during inflation, and this in turn demands that we consider the characteristics of price formation in these markets taken separately.

In turn, this brings us deep into the field of wage determination and of the inter-sectoral relationships of agriculture and industry. It is around these two axes that our argument hinges. However, in so orienting our analysis, it must be borne in mind that we are necessarily focusing our attention on the relative price-cost characteristics of the inflationary process in relation to economic development. Nevertheless, these two aspects (wage determination and agricultural industrial inter-relations), if not interpreted narrowly, will lead us naturally to an examination of the two other levels of analysis we specified earlier. Thus, the analysis of wage determination during inflation raises the question of whether or not the inflationary process itself affects the factors normally regarded as parameters rather than variables in the wage-determination process, i.e. the institutional framework and political environment within which and through which money wage changes are brought about. And the analysis of inter-sectoral relationships between industry and agriculture, on which, together with international trade, rests the explanation of relative raw material cost/final price movements, inevitably forces us to examine the sectoral aspects of industrialisation, of which the price increase is in some sense no more than an outward sign.

In the words of Mr Dow, 'Everything is connected with everything else but some things more closely than others'.

APPENDIX

Data and Methods used in the Country Chapters

On the whole, the methods used in the Country Chapters speak for themselves. Although perhaps obvious, it should be stressed that the discussion of the general sources of inflation cannot but be somewhat cursory, given the limits of space. Moreover, heavy reliance has been placed on secondary sources in some cases.

The basic evidence around which the discussion centres is partly direct and partly indirect. Direct evidence is that available from the results (covering a series of years) of censuses and enquiries into the receipts and expenditures of firms in manufacturing industry above a certain size (variously defined). We have much evidence of this type, albeit of varying scope, for the whole of our period for Peru, for scattered years during the war and from 1950 onwards for every year in Turkey, and for the whole post-war period in India.

Where there is no direct evidence of this sort, as for wartime India, or where the coverage of the direct evidence is very limited in scope, as for Peru during the war and immediate post-war periods, or where the data covers only scattered years, as for wartime Turkey, indirect evidence has been utilised.[12] Indirect evidence is that given by indices of unit labour costs, prices of final articles and prices of raw materials—all for manufacturing industry. In order to judge the direction of income redistribution *per se,* or alternatively to check on the picture of income redistribution shown by incomplete or inadequate direct evidence, the simple criterion used has been that, where unit labour costs and raw material costs both lag behind final prices of manufactures, the share of profit in gross value added may be assumed to have risen; and where the reverse has happened, the share of profit in gross value added may be assumed to have declined. Fortunately, for the inflationary periods where no direct evidence was available, the ratios of unit labour costs to final prices and of raw material costs to final prices moved in the same direction over the periods as a whole, so that these ratios could be used to identify the direction of change of shares in gross value added without further ado. There was a partial exception to this in the case of wartime Turkey.

The ratios of unit labour costs to final prices and of raw material costs to final prices were of course at best extremely crude indications of the direction of income redistribution. Unit labour costs in some cases had to be calculated from

8

indices of money wages, employment and production, which were not always well aligned. Problems of alignment also arose when it came to comparing the resulting index of unit labour costs with final prices where no general index of prices of manufactures existed, not to mention the alignment problems arising from comparing the indices of raw material costs with those of prices of manufactures. In all cases where these alignment problems exist, they have been indicated in the text or end-notes so that the reader will be aware of the extent to which the conclusions derived from these ratios of unit labour costs and raw material costs to final prices and to one another must be considered as tentative.

More positively, the usefulness of the price/prime cost ratios as guides to the direction of income redistribution was checked by comparing the picture given by these ratios with that given by direct evidence for periods, when both types of evidence were available.

Insofar as the data on prices and prime costs also gave us information on the changes in unit labour costs compared with raw material costs, the direct data on expenditure on the latter compared with the wage bill permitted us again to check the reliability of the picture shown by the prime cost/ price data. The correspondence of the two sorts of data as regards the direction of change was remarkably good.

Apart from using the direct data to check the usefulness of the indirect data, the overall background material of the Country Chapters was utilised to interpret the prime cost/ price ratio, where problems of alignment of the various indices used resulted from foreign trade, e.g. where import prices affected the price index used of manufacturing articles, as in Turkey and India.

In comparing the movement of unit wage costs and that of unit material costs, we have had to be aware of the fact that the total and unit value of materials used by the manufacturing sector will have been affected not only by the movement of primary commodity prices, but also by wage costs and profit margins at lower stages of production, which may by definition be excluded from the manufacturing sector. By assuming that unit wage costs and gross margins at lower stages of production vary proportionately with unit wage costs and gross margins at higher stages, we were able to ignore this complication in principle. We were also able to ignore it in practice, since we were concerned with the direction rather than the extent of change in the ratios of unit labour costs to material costs and of the latter to final prices. Thus, if what may be called the 'made-up' element affects constituent items of a price index for industrial raw materials, this is likely to mean that our ratio of material costs to unit labour costs will underestimate the rise of 'true' or unprocessed raw materials relative to unit labour costs, but it is unlikely to affect the direction of change of the ratio. We also adopted the necessary simplifying assumption that raw material inputs per unit of final output did not vary significantly for the manufacturing sector as a whole over the relevant periods (Kalecki, 1965: p. 29). It was further assumed that increases in capital intensity of production were not reflected in a rise in the ratio of profits, plus overhead costs to proceeds, and thus in the ratio of prices to unit *prime* costs. For some historical evidence and analysis supporting this assumption, see Kalecki, pp. 17-23 and *passim*.

The presentation of the data in terms of relative move· ments of unit labour costs, raw material costs and final prices in the case of the indirect evidence, and in terms of relative movements of expenditure on raw materials, the wage bill and gross value of production or gross receipts in the case of the direct evidence, permitted us to see whether the increasing or decreasing share of labour was the result of a changing share of labour in total prime costs (gross margins remaining unchanged), or the result of both, or the result of one factor partly offset by the other. Further, this presentation showed which was the active factor in changing gross margins in circumstances where the ratio of unit labour costs to final prices moved in a different direction from that of raw material costs and final prices.

The presentation of the conclusions reached on the direction of income redistribution, linked to data on relative movement of prices of manufactures, raw material costs and unit labour costs, permits us to go on to examine the main causal factors in these relative movements. Attention is focused on changing profit margins and the agricultural/ industrial terms of trade during inflation and, next, attention is focused on the determinants of the money wage rise during inflation. The elements of an interpretation of the distributional changes outlined earlier are thus presented. In dealing with the agricultural/industrial terms of trade during inflation, we pay particular attention to the role of foreign trade both generally and as a factor modifying the influence of the agricultural/industrial terms of trade on profit margins in the industrial sector. Finally, we draw together the threads, summarising the data on the direction of income redistribution during inflation and the conclusions reached on the immediate causal factors which have brought about the changes outlined.

NOTES

1. See Bernstein and Patel; Phelps Brown and Browne; and Dorrance. There have, however, been some exceptional attempts to develop more detailed comparisons of a small number of countries (e.g. Maynard) and occasionally to introduce specifically institutional variables into the analysis (e.g. Smith).

2. Myrdal, Vol. 3, Appendix 3.

3. Hamilton, 1929, 1942 and 1952. For a critique, see Felix, pp. 443ff.

4. Keynes, Vol. 2, Ch. 30.

5. Lewis, 1954.

6. An alternative explanation might be that inflation sets a limit to the length of time over which a given level of investment can be maintained.

7. Robinson, pp. 48-56, 91, 95, 200, 237-8, 257, 327 and 356.

8. Kaldor, 1969, pp. 240-1.

9. One might add the weakness of trade unions in many parts of the underdeveloped world.

10. Thus also rejected, implicitly, is the hypothesis that prices of manufactures necessarily adjust to demand changes in a more flexible fashion than wages.

11. Kalecki, Ch. 2; for a fuller elaboration of Kalecki's argument, see below, pp.

12. Although for wartime India, the picture shown by the relative price/cost movements could be checked in a rough-and-ready way by comparing the movements of two not very well aligned indices, one for industrial profits and the other for the wage bill in organised manufacturing industry.

CHAPTER 2

INDIA: PRICES AND INCOME REDISTRIBUTION IN ORGANISED FACTORY INDUSTRY, 1939-61

The two decades between 1939 and 1961 in India witnessed a remarkably varied experience in the behaviour of the general price level (Table 2:1), with, in the wartime period, first a spectacularly steep price increase in the early years, followed by a levelling-off towards the end of the war; and then, post-war, an extremely irregular resurgence of the upward movement of prices up to the first Five Year Plan (1952-56), during which prices fell nearly continuously, a trend which was reversed in the renewed upsurge of prices during the second plan.

The experience of income redistribution during these various phases of the price change in the modern manufacturing sector has also been varied, but the variations of income shares did not correspond in any regular fashion with variations in either the direction (sign) or the magnitude of the price changes. Certainly, the wage share did not automatically decline as prices rose (or rise as prices declined), as might be anticipated from popular mythology and the dominant

13

TABLE 2:1
India: Percentage Changes in the All India Working Class Cost-of-Living
Index and the Wholesale Price Index of Manufactured Articles,
1939/40 to 1960/61[1]

(i) All India Working Class Cost of Living Index	(ii) Wholesale Price Index of Manufactured Articles
Annual Percentage Changes	
1939-40 — 3.0	+ 22.2
1940-41 + 10.3	+ 19.2
1941-42 + 35.5	+ 15.1
1942-43 + 96.8	+ 46.8
1943-44 + 0.4	+ 4.9
1944-45 0.0	— 5.4
1945-46 + 6.0	+ 2.7
1946-47 + 13.3	—
1947-48 + 11.8	+ 23.1
1948-49 + 2.8	+ 1.1
1949-50 + 0.8	+ 1.2
1950-51 + 4.3	+ 13.8
1951-52 — 2.1	— 4.8
1952-53 + 2.9	8.0
1953-54 — 4.8	0.0
1954-55 — 5.1	— 1.0
1955-56 + 9.9	+ 6.1
1956-57 + 5.9	+ 2.9
1957-58 + 4.4	0.0
1958-59 + 4.5	+ 1.9
1959-60 + 2.9	+ 10.0
1960-61 + 1.4	+ 5.0

Sources: (i) from I.L.G., Oct. 1955, and G.O.I. Labour Bureau, *Indian
Labour Statistics*, 1960 and 1965, (ii) from G.O.I., *Statistical Abstract*
issues for 1949, 1957-58, 1963 and 1964. The wholesale price index of
manufactures relates to finished goods, imported as well as indigenous.
Handloom products are omitted.

tradition of economic thought on this topic. Initially during
the war, such an anticipation would have been found justified,
with the steep price acceleration being accompanied by a
decline in labour's share of income originating in the organised industrial sector[2] (Tables 2:2 and 2:3). The decline was
only reversed towards the end of the war when prices stopped
rising. Overall, the share of profits throughout the war was
higher than at the beginning. Postwar experience, however,

was much less obliging. As prices resumed their upward movement postwar, labour's share of gross value added *rose*
significantly (Table 2:4) while as prices dropped during the
following years of the First Five Year Plan, labour's share of
manufacturing income steadily declined (Table 2:4 and 2:6).

Rounding off this confusing picture, we find the years of
the Second Plan, 1952-56, witnessing a renewal of (moderate)
price increases without any decisive movement of labour
shares either up or down (Tables 2:1 and 2:4).[3]

TABLE 2:2
India: Final Prices, Raw Material Costs and Unit Labour Costs in
Manufacturing Industry: Indices, 1939-54

	Wholesale Prices of Manufactured Articles	Wholesale Prices of Industrial Raw Materials	Unit Labour Costs	Ratio of Raw Material Costs to Final Prices	Ratio of Unit Labour Costs to Final Prices	Ratio of Unit Labour Costs to Raw Material Costs
1939	100	100	100	100	100	100
1940	122	117	101	96	83	86
1941	146	126	117	87	80	93
1942	168	155	151	92	90	97
1943	246	225	213	91	87	95
1944	258	237	234	92	91	99
1945	244	245	253	100	104	103
1946	251	271	279	108	111	103
1947	277	365	349	132	126	96
1948	341	431	383	126	112	89
1949	344	464	450	135	131	97
1950	348	503	424	145	122	84
1951	296	608	402	154	102	66
1952	278	454	396	120	105	87
1953	367	400	364	109	99	91
1954	376	447	337	119	90	75

Source: Indices of average money earnings, production, employment
and productivity, (and thus unit labour costs) in Table 2:5. Wholesale
prices as for Table 2:1.

TABLE 2:3
India: Wages and Profits, 1939-46

	Index of Total Factory Wage Bill	Index of Industrial Profits	Ratio of Wage Bill to Profits
1939	100	100	100
1940	109	138	79
1941	134	187	72
1942	161	222	73
1943	240	245	98
1944	271	239	113
1945	287	234	123
1946	288	229	126

Sources: For wage bill I.L.G. (October 1955 and November 1955 for indices of average money earnings and employment); for profits, M.H. Ghosh and S.C. Chaudhri, p. 779.

Note: The profit index covers only 8 industries, viz. cotton textiles, jute manufactures, cement, tea, iron and steel, sugar, paper and coal. Generally its coverage is extremely limited. Ghosh and Chaudhri, p. 779.

TABLE 2:4
India: The Share of Labour in Gross Value added in Organised Manufacturing Industry, 1946-1958

	Percentages
1946	44.2
1947	53.3
1948	49.9
1949	61.3
1950	57.1
1951	51.7
1952	59.8
1953	57.5
1954	55.0
1955	51.6
1956	51.0
1957	52.2
1958	49.9

Sources: Calculated from data in G.O.I. Ministry of Industry and Supply, First Census of Manufactures, India 1946, 1949; for later years census figures in Indian Labour Statistics.

TABLE 2:5
India: Share of Labour in Gross Value Added in
Manufacturing Industry, 1959-61

	Percentages
1959	48.7
1960	49.8
1961	48.1

Sources: Calculated from results of *Annual Survey of Industries*
(Eastern Economist Annual Number), 1965, 25 December 1964,
p. 1369, and *Statistical Abstract*, issues for 1963 and 1964. All 63
industrial groups are covered.

TABLE 2:6
India: Indices of Average Money Earnings, Employment, Production
and Productivity of Factory Workers, 1939-54

	Average Money Earnings	Production	Employment	Productivity
1939	100.0	100.0	100.0	100.0
1940	100.3	108.1	103.7	104.2
1941	111.0	114.3	120.6	94.8
1942	129.1	106.9	125.3	85.3
1943	179.6	112.2	132.8	84.5
1944	202.1	115.7	134.1	86.3
1945	201.5	112.5	141.5	79.5
1946	208.6	102.9	137.8	74.7
1947	253.2	99.1	136.6	72.5
1948	304.0	112.3	141.4	79.4
1949	340.3	108.4	143.3	74.6
1950	334.2	107.2	136.0	78.8
1951	356.8	120.4	135.7	88.7
1952	385.7	133.2	136.7	97.4
1953	384.6	140.8	133.1	105.8
1954	381.2	153.6	135.9	113.0

Sources: I.L.G. (October 1955) and I.L.G. (November 1955).

These indices are calculated from the results of the annual *Census of Manufacturing Industry*, which cover only 29 of the 63 groups into which manufacturing industry has been classified. However, these cover the major industries in the country. In the industries concerned, factories are defined as all concerns employing 20 or more persons or 10 or more persons and using power. Wage bill includes wages paid to workers, salaries paid to persons other than workers and money value of other benefits or privileges.

The Wartime Indian Inflation

During the Second World War, the Indian economy had
simultaneously to cope with the tasks of raising an army, providing for an increasing population, and adjusting, by import
substitution or otherwise, to the disappearance or very great
reduction in supply of many, often vital, imports. The low
living standards of the population as a whole, and the
constitutional, administrative and political difficulties of
increasing taxation, taken in conjunction with the suddenness
and magnitude of the increased demands on the economy,
necessitated the financing of governmental expenditure partly
by the creation of new money. Thus, of the total expenditure
on all accounts by the Indian Government over the seven
years 1939/40 to 1945/46, only 37 percent was met by
taxation.[4] These expenditures were principally direct
military expenditures, involving the cost of all forces in
India, both European and Indian, the cost of equipment and
supplies needed for them, and the cost of Indian troops and
Indian military supplies used outside India.

Borrowing was not, however, markedly successful as a
means of mopping up purchasing power. The value of small
savings declined steadily from 1939 to 1943,[5] and the
Government's attempts to float long-term loans achieved
little success until the later war years. After 1942/43, however, although the budget deficit in 1943/44 was the largest
since the war began (Table 2:9), borrowing policy began to
show better results, both as regards the volume of small
savings and the floating of long-term loans, and at the same
time, also for the first time since the war began, the proportion of Indian non-recoverable expenditure covered by
taxation did not decline, and in the following year, 1944/45,
actually rose.[6]

To the inflationary effects of military expenditures, war
conditions added those of a persistent wartime positive
balance of payments. This was the result of rising export
prices, a greater decline in the volume of imports than of
exports and a surplus on invisibles arising mainly from local
expenditures by allied soldiers in India (Tables 2:7 and 2:8).
The decline in both import and export volume was due to
the physical disruption of trade flows by sea warfare and
restrictions on shipping space. However, at the beginning of
the war a rise in the volume of exports contributed to the
payments surplus.

TABLE 2:7
India: Export, Wholesale, Import Prices and Terms of Trade,
1938/39-1944/45

	Export Price Index	Wholesale Price Index	Import Price Index	Terms of Trade (Import prices ÷ Export prices)
1938-39	100	100	100	100
1939-40	120	125	106	88
1940-41	130	115	127	98
1941-42	156	137	153	98
1942-43	185	171	193	104
1943-44	227	236	195	86
1944-45	240	244	188	78

Source: *Accounts for Seaborne Trade*, cited in Prest, pp. 77-80.

While the trade and payments surplus as a source of
demand pressure on the economy was important in the early
years of the war, the impact of military expenditures rapidly
assumed dominant and increasing significance in this role
(Table 2:9). Further, little effort was made to curb private
investment until 1943, when an ordinance was passed (17
May) restricting capital issues. Irrespective of the ordinance,
however, difficulties of obtaining imported machinery
limited private investment all through the war, as did the
complete neglect of civilian building. Thus, the value of all
kinds of machinery imported into India fell to R.S. 10.5
crores in 1942/43 from a 1938/39 level of 19.7 crores
(Singh, p. 181; one crore = 10 million rupees), despite the
considerable rise of import prices over these three years.

TABLE 2:8
India: Export and Import Quantum, 1938/39-1944/45

	Export Quantum	Import Quantum
1938-39	100	100
1939-40	105	102
1940-41	88	81
1941-42	93	74
1942-43	63	38
1943-44	54	40
1944-45	56	67

Source: As for Table 2:7.

TABLE 2:9
India: Budget Deficits and Trade Balances 1939/40-1945/46
(Millions of Rupees)

	Budget Deficit on Indian Account	Recoverable War Expenditure of Imperial Government	Total Effective Deficit	Balance of Trade (positive)
1939-40	—	40	40	483
1940-41	65	530	595	417
1941-42	127	1,940	2,067	797
1942-43	1,122	3,255	4,377	841
1943-44	1,898	3,779	5,677	931
1944-45	1,611	4,108	5,720	242
1945-46	1,450	3,471	4,920	234

Source: U.N. *Survey of Current Inflationary and Deflationary Tendencies,* 1947, p. 65.

Declining private investment was thus in this period an off-setting factor to the expansionary forces at work in the economy.

The supply response of the economy to these demands took the form of a fairly rapid rise of industrial production in the early years of the war, with some slackening in the rate of increase in the later war years following the drop in 1942/43 (Table 2:10).[7] Agricultural production, on the other hand, declined in the first years of the war.[8] Indeed, it was only in the two years from 1941/42 to 1943/44 that total agricultural production rose at all, an increase which quickly tapered away into the decline of the later war years.

With the demands on the economy from credit-financed military expenditures and from an increasing current surplus on the balance of payments which was even greater in 1943/44 than in the earlier years of the war,[9] and with the falling off of the production response of both agriculture and industry also in those years, the much greater amplitude of the price response in the earlier than in the later war years appears somewhat paradoxical.

The paradox is to be explained in part by the course of supply and demand of and for cotton piecegoods and food grains, which between them accounted for the bulk of consumption of most Indians.

TABLE 2:10
India: Index Numbers of Industrial and Agricultural Production,
1939-51

	Agricultural Production	Manufacturing Production
1939-40	100	100
1940-41	100	108.1
1941-42	95	114.3
1942-3	100	106.9
1943-44	104	112.2
1944-45	99	115.7
1945-46	91	112.5
1946-47	93	102.9
1947-48	98	99.1
1948-49	93	112.3
1949-50	100	108.4
1950-51	96	107.2

Sources: Agricultural production index from Mukerji, p. 8, and industrial production index, I.L.G., November 1965.

Although the rate of increase of industrial production as a whole slackened off after 1941/42, this was not true of cotton textile production, which after the 1941/42 drop actually speeded up.[10] This was a crucial element in the situation since, besides its importance as the single biggest industry, the textile industry (apart from the munitions group) felt more than any other the impact of military demands.[11] In addition, the textile industry had to cater at the same time to the needs of import substitution (with a decline in the imports of cotton piecegoods from 647 to 182 million yards between 1938/39 and 1941/42) and expanding export demand (total exports of cotton piece-goods rose from 177 million yards in 1938/38 to 771 million yards in 1941/42.[12]

Furthermore, at the same time as the marked expansion of textile exports was taking place, the overall volume of exports actually declined. It was thus of considerable importanct that from 1942/43, the export trade was thoroughly controlled,[13] so that the continued decline in the overall export quantum after that date involved a proportionately greater decline in exports of cotton piece-goods.

A somewhat similar picture applies to foodgrains in the foreign trade sphere, where again exports were not adequately controlled until 1942/43 (exports of foodgrains were forbidden from March 1943), so that in 1941/42 India was still exporting 770,000 long tons of foodgrains and pulses as compared with 828,000 long tons in 1938/39.[14] Analogously, in the import sphere, deliberate measures were taken in the later war years to increase imports of essential goods, so that, for example, the total imported (long) tonnage of foodgrains and pulses increased to 384,000 in 1943/44 from 186,000 tons in the previous year. More generally, the rate of rise of the volume of imported cereals after 1942/43 as a result of these measures was considerably faster than that of imports as a whole.[15]

If disaggregation of the overall indices of production, imports and exports helps to explain the paradox of prices rising fastest when aggregate demands on the economy were least and the aggregate supply response greatest, it is nevertheless not the whole explanation. Despite improvements in the supplies of textiles and foodgrains in the later war years, the per head availabilities of these commodities were nevertheless at the end of the war much lower than they had been at the beginning.[16] Moreover, the pre- and post- 1942/3 changes in the supplies of such crucial commodities as foodgrains and textiles, even if there were sufficient explanation, which there are not, themselves require explanation. It has already been seen that the changes in supplies of these commodities were in part the result of changes in government control over trading in these items. The changes in this field were only one aspect of the marked change in the nature and degree of government control over the whole economy which took place around 1942/43, and which were the decisive causes of the differing impact in terms of price change of the demands on the economy in the later as opposed to the earlier war years.

The first impact of military expenditures was at once large and haphazard, often with slight reference to local supply conditions or the needs of the civilian population or even to controlled prices. The result was, naturally, to bring production up against bottlenecks far more quickly than was technically necessary, to expand money incomes and raise prices at a rate unmitigated by effective efforts at control, and to permit, under these circumstances, the cumulative reinforcement of these problems by speculation, hoarding and other forms of private initiative.

However, the result of this policy, or lack of policy, in terms of, in part at least, very rapidly rising prices and incomes, was one of the principal reasons for its profound transformation. The main elements of this policy transformation, which took place in 1942/43, related to prices, production, trade and the curbing of excess purchasing power in the economy generally.[17] Price control was strengthened administratively, particularly by taking it out of the hands of the State Governments and transferring it to the Central Government, and was supplemented by co-ordinating it with other interventionary measures to affect production and distribution, imports and exports, as well as procurement of food. Not only was experience gained in where to place contracts, but the method of pricing them was also altered, with the effect of mitigating the rise of profits. In the field of production, deliberate efforts were made to remove some of the worst bottlenecks which had earlier manifested themselves, particularly by obtaining some co-ordination of the demands on skilled labour. Efforts were made with some success to rationalise the textile industry, and the control of imports was tightened up so that the generalised control of the early war years gave way to deliberate attempts to procure the most essential items.

The rising share of profits in gross value added during the Indian war-time inflation was the result of the lag of *both* raw material input costs and unit labour costs behind rising final prices so that labour shares declined as a consequence both of rising gross profit margins and of a declining share of wages in prime costs (Table 2:2). This does not appear to have been a case of a cost-induced inflation providing an opportunity for a widening of margins but rather a case of prices of manufactures rising independently of prime costs which were (at least in the case of raw materials) pulled up after final prices rather than pushing up final prices.[18] The steepness of the decline in the ratio of raw material costs to final prices is a strong indication of this, as is the evidence of the rapidity with which overcapacity working was achieved in manufacturing industry at the beginning of the war.

This implies an abandonment of the mark-up pricing policies which are known to be the normal pricing practice in the Indian organised sector[19] and indeed an apparent reversal of what is normally regarded as the typical relative supply elasticities of the modern manufacturing and the agricultural sectors respectively, and it was the circumstances causing this change which accounted for the rise in gross profit margins. That these exceptional conditions held was due to a quite unusual combination of circumstances springing from the special peculiarities of the impact of the war on the Indian economy, particularly as regards the size of the demands to which organised industry was subjected and as regards the impact of the war on the volume and commodity pattern of foreign trade.

As we have seen, the early years of the war saw the simultaneous disruption in the flow of imported manufactures, including capital and other intermediate goods, and in the flow of exported materials, in particular jute and cotton, as war conditions physically cut off foreign markets; there was in any case a degree of slack in the jute and cotton sectors just before the war. The natural result of this, combined with the sudden[20] and extremely large increase in military demand for manufactures, especially textiles and the products of the engineering industries, was to strain manufacturing capacity to the limits[21] at a time when importation problems made an expansion of such capacity very difficult and at a time when a comparable strain was not placed on the sectors producing raw materials.

The significance of this situation was twofold. Firstly, the normal process whereby increased demand for industrial products is, other things being equal, more or less immediately reflected in increased derived demand for raw materials, which in turn quickly runs up against the short-term limits of capacity of the primary producing sector sooner than the short-term capacity limits of the manufacturing sector are reached, was disrupted. Secondly, whatever long-term considerations are conducive to mark-up pricing, as opposed to a price policy based on maximum exploitation of the current market situation, are likely to have been seriously weakened owing to the extreme and sudden favourableness of the new situation for manufacturers.[22] An important aspect of this was, of course, the rapid attainment of full capacity working.

The rise in the wartime share of profits during inflation was, as we have already remarked, the joint product of both rising gross profit margins and a declining share of labour costs in total prime costs. This decline must fundamentally be attributed to the failure of trade unions and/or the government to exert adequate pressures to raise money wages *pari passu* with the rise in the cost of living,[23] a failure which was the combined result of the initial weakness of the trade union morement at the beginning of the war, the very rapidity and magnitude of the price rise and the restrictions under which the trade union movement operated during the war.[24] This failure to raise money wages in such a way as to maintain real wages need not by itself have reduced the labour share of total prime costs, but for the crucial fact that the rise in food costs and industrial raw material costs were both rooted in the supply inelasticities of the agricultural sector so that *both* tended to be very large and to move together. Moreover, whatever difference there was in the price rise of food costs as compared to raw material costs this would be much less than the difference between the rise of either compared to the rise in labour costs. This was because, with an enormous price acceleration compared with pre-war price changes, the process of adjusting the institutional forces operating to raise money wages to deal with the new situation would be bound to be slower than the operation of market mechanisms. The market mechanisms required no such adjustment but simply worked as before, albeit to greater effect as far as prices were concerned.

The Immediate Postwar Inflation, 1945/46-1950-51

The changeover to peacetime conditions simultaneously permitted a significant reduction in the size of budget deficits,[25] and a switch from an export to an import surplus (Table 2:11), as a result primarily of an increased volume of imports (Table 2:12). Despite this change and despite the fact that the import surplus in most of the years in this period outweighed the budget deficit, the price stability of the later war years gave way to a continuous price rise. The renewed rise in the general price level in these circumstances must fundamentally be attributed to increased pressures from consumer demand compared with the war period, and to a marked expansion of private investment immediately after the war, together with an upward push from both wages and material costs.

The lack of imported goods during the war and the diversion of production to military needs, together with confidence in the value of money in the later war years and the expectations of more prosperous peacetime conditions, combined to exert, in the immediate postwar period, a considerable pressure of consumer demand.[26] This was financed in part by the wartime accumulation of liquid assets in the hands of the wealthier classes in town and country and in the richer peasants and small traders.[27] The consumer demand financed from accumulated assets was stimulated by a decline in the propensity to save out of current income in the immediate postwar period, a decline arising from wartime shortages and the expectation of their alleviation.[28] An independent source of expansionary pressures was the rise of money wages, which between 1946 and 1949 rose faster than prices (Table 3:1). The direct quantitative significance of this was small. Thus, it is estimated that in 1951 the total industrial labour force was only about 5 percent of the total economically active population.[29]

TABLE 2:11
India: Budget Deficits and Trade Balances, 1946/47-1950/51
(Crores of Rupees)

	(i) Budget Deficit (−) or Surplus (+)	(ii) Balance of Trade Positive + Negative −
	(Percentages of National Income in brackets)	
1946-47	− 58	− 36
1947-48	−111	−154
1948-49	− 82 (−0.9)	− 96 (−1.1)
1949-50	− 44 (−0.5)	−167 (−1.8)
1950-51	12 (0.1)	+ 70 (+0.8)

Sources: Budget figures from R.B.I., *Reports on Currency and Finance* cited by Singh (p. 13). Trade balance figures from R.B.I., *Bulletin,* July 1949 and R.B.I. *Bulletin,* June 1956. National income figures from G.O.I., C.S.O., *Estimates of National Income, 1948-9 to 1958-9* (1960). Budget deficit figures are for the Central Government only.

TABLE 2:12
India: Export and Import Quantum, 1946-50
(1938 = 100)

	Import Quantum	Export Quantum
1946	80	66
1947	94	66
1948	94	58
1949	97	62
1950	83	66

Source: U.N.E.C.A.F.E., *Survey for 1951*, p. 345.

Postwar liquidity was also an important factor in financing the expansion of private investment in the immediate post-war period.[30] Industrial equipment had been seriously over-worked during the war years. The difficulties of securing necessary imports of machinery, raw materials and con-structional materials, together with the problems of partition and political and industrial strife, to some extent meant that the attempts to remedy the state of industrial equipment were constrained. However, there does nevertheless appear to have been sufficient success in doing so to bring about a marked rise of private investment in the postwar years. Thus, in the industrial sector capital goods were being acquired during the postwar years in appreciably larger quantities than

TABLE 2:13
India: Indices of Wholesale Prices, Export Prices, Import Prices and
Terms of Trade, 1946-50
(1948 = 100)

	Wholesale Price Index	Import Price Index	Export Price Index	Terms of Trade (Import prices ÷ Export prices)
1946	–	74	67	110
1947	81	85	89	96
1948	100	100	100	100
1949	104	97	104	93
1950	109	102	108	94

Source: U.N., E.C.A.F.E., 1951, pp. 344 and 494.

in the prewar years,[31] and the high rates of private invest-ment during 1947 and 1948, partly stimulated by the post-war relaxation of controls, were characterised as possible sources of inflation.[32]

The initial response of the productive apparatus of the economy to these demands was extremely poor in the case of industry, owing to the worn-out state of industrial equipment, to postwar dislocation and the problems arising from Partition, to declining labour productivity (see below), and to the difficulties (partly physical and partly financial) of acquiring sufficiently quickly adequate supplies of machinery, raw materials and spare parts from abroad needed for the expansion of home production. To these temporary difficulties of the industrial sector were added the more obstinate problems of agriculture. Neither agriculture nor industrial production in this period ever regained the peak production levels achieved around about 1943/44 and 1944/45 (Table 2:10). Agricultural production had declined by over 12 per cent in 1945/46 compared to its 1943/44 peak, and fluctuated erratically thereafter, showing no decisive improvement. Industrial production declined from its wartime peak in 1944/45 each year down to 1947/48. The upward jump of the following year was followed by a resumption of the downward trend till 1950/51 to a level over 7 per cent below the 1944/45 peak. On the other hand, within the agricultural sector cash crops responded well to the booming world demand of the immediate postwar period. Throughout most of the period, balance of payments difficulties prevented a sufficient volume of imports from completely eliminating inflationary demand pressures.

Overall, the expansion of monetary demand unmatched by increasing production was restricted in its effect on prices by the operation of government policy, and this, together with the variations both of demand pressure and of the production response, caused the price response to fluctuate throughout these postwar years.

The postwar price spurt of 1945/46 to 1946/47, and the subsequent deceleration of the price rise (broken in 1950/51, can be explained broadly in terms of the higher demands on the economy in the first postwar years, the somewhat poorer production response in those years compared to the later years and the change of government policy. The inflationary effects of accumulated wartime liquidity were naturally most forcefully felt immediately after the war. However, 1947 was the year of the biggest budget deficit of the postwar period, owing to the expenditures arising from Partition. By contrast, the problems of supply were, for obvious reasons, considerably greater in the first of the two postwar years than in the later ones[33] for the industrial sector. The relatively (to later years) more even performance of the agricultural sector was counter-balanced, at least as regards food, by the decontrol measures announced in late 1947. These decontrol measures, owing to the greater flexibility of agricultural prices, had a much greater effect on food grain prices than on the prices of those manufactures which were freed shortly after. The decontrol policy proved a failure and, after only eight months, control was re-established in October 1948, simultaneously with an all-round anti-inflationary programme. This programme continued into 1949 and, coinciding with improvements in industrial production, the decline in postwar liquidity, and the decline in the size of the budget deficits, led to a steady deceleration of prices which continued until the Korean war raised export incomes and import prices in 1950 and 1951.[34] To an extent, the inflationary effects of the Korean war in September 1950 were a continuation of those arising from the devaluation of 1949, which raised both import prices and export incomes. These effects were, however, fairly small.[35]

The continued, albeit slower, rise of prices of manufactures after 1947/48, taken in conjunction with the widespread excess capacity existing in the modern manufacturing sector just prior to the First Plan,[36] demonstrates that the continued failure of industrial production to show any marked improvement was in part the result, in certain years, of demand rather than supply factors and that rising costs were an independent source of price increases.[37] Demand pressures affected agricultural prices throughout nearly the whole period, but appear to have been most important for manufacturing immediately after the war.

The inflation of the early postwar years raised the labour share of income originating in organised industry in a fluctuating but unequivocal fashion (Table 2:4). This was the result of both unit labour costs and raw material costs squeezing gross profit margins as they rose faster than final prices.[38] However, the push from unit labour costs ended in 1949, after which date they began to decline (Tables 2:2 and 2:14).

Why, when raw materials costs to urban industry were rising, should the demand situation have been such that in this period the rise in prime costs (including, up to 1949, unit labour costs) was not fully passed on to prices? We have already remarked on the relative stability of gross percentage profit margins as shown in column (i) of Table 2:14—for the years from 1949 to 1958, when margins displayed a range of no more than four percentage points between the lowest and the highest values, with the highest variation between one year and the next being 2.1 percentage points, and we have argued that this is what we should expect normally to be the case with an oligopolistic industry using a mark-up pricing system. However, the years 1946-49 show a very marked degree of margin variation, with gross profit margins at 20.6 per cent in the former year and 11.5 per cent in the latter.

This exceptional situation would be consisten with the existence of a normal conventional margin if the period covering the years 1946-49 was one in which a particular

TABLE 2:14
India: Prime Cost Expenditures, Total Output Value and Gross Surplus
in Manufacturing Industry, 1946-58

	Gross Surplus as a Proportion of Total Value of Production	Ratio of Expenditure on Raw Materials and Fuel to Total Value of Production	Ratio of Wage Bill to Total Value of Production	Ratio of Wage Bill to Expenditure on Raw Materials and Fuel
	(Percentages) (i)	(Index) (ii)	(Index) (iii)	(Index) (iv)
1946	20.6	100	100	100
1947	16.0	105	112	107
1948	17.4	104	106	102
1949	11.5	112	111	99
1950	12.6	112	102	91
1951	13.5	114	88	77
1952	11.4	114	104	91
1953	13.5	109	112	103
1954	13.9	109	104	95
1955	15.4	108	101	94
1956	15.3	109	97	89
1957	14.1	112	94	84
1958	15.2	110	96	87

Sources: as for Table 2:4. *Total value of production* is the ex-factory value of products and by-products and the value of work done for customers. *Wages bill* as in Table 2:4. *Expenditure on raw materials and fuel* includes value of work done for factories by other concerns. *Gross surplus* is the difference between the total value of production and the sum of expenditures on raw materials, etc., plus the wage bill. Taken in the first column as a percentage of the total value of production, it is used here as an indicator of gross profit margins.

conjunction of circumstances was bringing about a once-for-all revision of previous entrepreneurial conventions on the appropriate size of profit margins.[39] Such a conjunction of circumstances (in the case of a downward revision of the conventional margin) is likely to be one in which an extremely rapid rise of prime costs takes place in a relatively tight demand situation. And this is precisely the situation which prevailed in the immediate postwar years in India. The marked and sudden change to relative stability of margins from 1949 onwards indicates that the period 1946-49 was indeed an exceptional time of margin displacement. And that the immediate postwar period was indeed a period of insufficient demand relative to capacity is testified by the widespread existence of excess capacity in the organised sector. Indeed, the First Five Year Plan relied to a large extent on the considerable excess capacity inherited from this (inflationary) period for fulfilment of its targets for industrial production.[40] Nor could this idle capacity be regarded as solely the end-product of a period of continuing excess demand, since the idle capacity was largely the result of the series of poor harvests from 1947 to 1952.[41] And here we have the crux of the matter. The development of excess capacity alongside rising prices can only be understood by reference to the simultaneous impact of rising agricultural prices on the cost and demand curves of the industrial sector. Since the demand for the products of Indian factory industry depends mainly on the agricultural sector,[42] a rise in agricultural prices may be expected to increase money demand for industrial produce as well as costs to urban industry. However, in the immediate postwar period, rising agricultural prices were the result of a fall in agricultural production compared with the later war years (Table 2:10). While a given rise in agricultural producer prices with the marketed surplus unchanged means that the rise in prime costs is more or less matched by the rise in money demand,[43] a rise in agricultural prices to the towns as a result of a decline in the marketed surplus means that, other things being equal, the rise in prime costs will be less than matched by an equivalent increase in rural demand. Rapidly rising food and raw material prices in the towns combined with reduced total agricultural production, implied a reduction in the marketed surplus[44] in the immediate postwar period[45] which involved a faster rise of raw material costs than of money demand from agriculture[46] for industrial products.[47]

Moreover, rising money wages also tended to exert pressure on margins in this period. This tendency was accentuated by the rise in relative food prices, due to the lag of agricultural production. Pressure on margins from rising labour costs was especially important between 1946 and 1949, when average money earnings rose by over 60 per cent in three years. Here again, the fact that about 60 per cent of the working class budget is devoted to food expenditures, the fact that demand for food tends to be price inelastic[48] so that food prices rise relative to prices of non-food wage-goods, together with the small proportion of the total market constituted by the organised urban labour force for its own products—all meant that rising wage costs per unit of output were not accompanied by a *pari passu* rise in demand per unit of capacity from wage earners.[49]

The discussion above has been conducted in terms of money wage changes. However, productivity changes have to be taken into account to get at the movement of unit labour costs.

In the normal course of events, a strict cost-plus pricing policy will imply that labour productivity changes do not affect relative shares, in an inflationary situation. With a degree of margin variability, however, productivity increase may affect relative shares. Since a large proportion of working-class income is spent outside the manufacturing sector, i.e. particularly on food, rising productivity will reduce costs per unit of output more than demand per unit of output, and declining productivity will have the reverse effect. Relative price movements as a result of changing productivity will reinforce these effects, which will partly determine whether or not rising total prime costs will succeed in reducing gross margins. Although productivity changes are thus clearly relevant to the income redistribution we are considering, they involve longer-period factors than are within the scope of this study. Nevertheless, there do appear to be certain short-term influences on and from productivity change which are related to the agricultural/industrial relationships we have been considering and which, at times, reinforce the tendency for a lagging agricultural sector to bring about declining margins during inflation.

Specifically, it appears that when production is declining or increasing only slowly, as in the war or immediate post-war years, productivity tends to decline and when production is increasing fast, productivity tends to rise. It will be recalled that the rate of growth of industrial production seems to have been to a marked degree a function of the movement of agricultural production, mainly via effective demand, but also partly via the existence or otherwise of supply bottlenecks including those associated with limitations of the capacity to import. Since this is so, it follows that the effects of the agricultural lag on production and thus on productivity will tend to be negative and thus to reinforce the difficulties faced by entrepreneurs in passing rising prime costs fully onto prices.

This, of course, will be a highly qualified effect, particularly insofar as other factors besides the behaviour of the agricultural sector will affect the rate of growth of industrial production, including those self-stimulating factors we will observe at work in the industrial sector during the Second Plan period, the supply bottlenecks arising from the physical impossibility of obtaining imports, especially of machines and equipment during the war, and the political and industrial conflict and disruption of the immediate post-war period.[50]

The rapid rise of money wages, faster than the rise of prices of manufactures, was the result of the efforts of the trade union movement to keep money wages rising in step with, or faster than, the cost of living, in which the most important item, food, rose faster than prices of manufactures. The trade union movement succeeded in raising money wages faster than the cost of living, and this joined with and contributed towards declining gross margins to raise labour's share. This success was the result of the stimulus to the trade unions given by the steep decline in real wages during the war period in conjunction with the political and institutional changes of the post-war period (and also the unionisation of the war period) which permitted more effective 'mobilisation' to raise money wages. Among the more important of such changes were the removal of wartime official restriction on trade union activity, the change to a more militant industrial policy by the communists, the phenomenal post-war increase in unionisation of the working class and of course trade union activity itself. Dominating all these changes was the post-war 'radicalisation' of the political situation connected with the upsurge of the national movement and, associated with it, the greatly increased social and economic expectations of the urban masses in particular.

The reasons for declining margins during the immediate post-war inflation, even to the extent of causing a permanent (or at least semi-permanent) and significant downward adjustment of the normal conventional margin, are thus fairly clear. The coming of peace brought a period in which decline and stagnation of agricultural output raised raw material costs directly and unit labour costs indirectly[51] to factory production. Since these rising costs were the result of bad harvests, the marketed surplus was declining so that the rise in money prime costs was not accompanied by a *pari passu* rise in demand. Moreover, although budget deficits, credit-financed private investment and pent-up customer demand from the war period exerted aggregate expansionary pressures in excess of available import surpluses and domestic supplies, the agricultural bottlenecks quickly diverted much of this expenditure away from industry, so that the resultant 'hard' market environment made it difficult to pass the associated rise in prime costs on to prices.

Inflation during the Two Five Year Plans, 1952-61

We may consider the two plan periods together, since they present instructive contrasts.

The first Five Year Plan period corresponds almost exactly to the only prolonged period of price stability and/or decline between 1939 and 1961. Paradoxically enough, this was a period when budget deficits far outweighed import surpluses and when indeed the former attained a level 45 per cent above the total volume of deficit financing planned,[52] while the import surplus was 61 per cent below the planned level.[53] Moreover, the rate of investment in factory entreprises, exclusive of expenditure on modernisation and replacement, is estimated to have risen from an annual average of 260 million rupees in the first two years of the plan period to 440 million rupees in the third year, 500 million rupees in the fourth year and 850 million rupees in the final year.[54]

That these demand pressures did not produce inflation was essentially due to the extremely positive supply response of the economy. Agricultural production rose by over 20 per cent between 1950/51 and 1955/56, so that grain output during the first plan appreciably surpassed the targets for 1955/56. Industrial production including mining increased by as much as 32.6 per cent over the plan years through 1956.[55] Real national income in 1955/56 was about 19 per cent above the level of 1950/51—well above the 11-12 per cent aim of the Plan.[56] This supply response was largely responsible for the reduction of the import surplus above anticipated levels, since imports of food and raw materials declined as home production rose.[57]

The favourable supply response of the economy was founded, in the industrial sector, on the considerable margin of excess capacity existing in the early 1950's, on overall government planning particularly via its effects on expanding production in heavy industry, and on the good harvests of the period with their stimulating demand effects on factory industry in the private sector, especially on those enterprises producing consumer goods.[58]

Favourable supply conditions in the economy as a whole thus dominated the movements of the price level during the First Plan period and, as may be seen in Table 2:16, to such a degree that Indian prices remained largely unaffected by the rising prices of the outside world in general, and the prices of Indian imports in particular in the last two years of the Plan.

TABLE 2:15

India: Index Numbers of Net National Output at Constant Prices and Industrial and Agricultural Production, 1950/51-1960/61 (1950/51 = 100)

	(i) Net National Output at 1948/49 Prices	(ii) Agricultural Production	(iii) Industrial Production (mining and manufacturing)
1950-51	100	100	100
1951-52	103	102	104
1952-53	107	106	106
1953-54	113	119	113
1954-55	117	122	122
1955-56	119	122	133
1956-57	125	129	137
1957-58	123	121	140
1958-59	129	140	152
1959-60	134	135	170
1960-61	144	146	181

Sources: (i) G.O.I. *Statistical Abstract*, 1957-58 and 1963-64; (ii) G.O.I. Ministry of Food and Agriculture, *Growth Rates in Agriculture* (1965) and G.O.I., Labour Bureau, *Indian Labour Statistics*, 1966 (1966); (iii) Malenbaum, p. 228, and Eastern Economist, Quarterly Bulletin, November 1962, p. 15.

Whereas during the First Plan, deficit financing was above plan levels and the import surplus below, in the Second Plan, deficit financing more or less achieved the levels planned, while the import surplus greatly exceeded planned levels. The result was that in aggregate terms over the whole plan period, the deflationary import surplus far outweighed inflationary budget deficits (Table 2:17). The contrast with the First Plan

period seems to be complete if we note that, while in the
First Plan period an excess of inflationary public deficits over
deflationary import surpluses produced no general price rise,
the excess of deflationary import surpluses over public
deficits in the Second Plan was coterminous with rising wholesale prices and cost of living indices (Table 2:1 and 2:17). Nor
does the paradox seem to be completely explained by the rise

TABLE 2:16
India: Indices of Whole Prices, Import Prices, Export Prices and the
Terms of Trade, 1952/53-1955/56

	General Wholesale Price Index	Import Price Index	Export Price Index	Terms of Trade (Import Prices ÷ Export Prices)
1952-53	100	100	100	100
1953-54	104	92	92	100
1954-55	99	80	89	91
1955-56	95	89	89	89

Sources: For import and export prices, G.O.I. *Statistical Abstract 1958-
59* (1960). For general wholesale price index, R.B.I., 1956.

in private investment in the Second Plan period compared
with the First, or by a reversal of the aggregate supply response of the economy over the period as a whole. Thus, while
it is true that private gross investment rose from 10.4 per cent
of the G.N.P. in the First Plan to 12.2 per cent in the Second,
in the corporate sector (and of course the government sector
discussed above) there was a savings deficit, the household
sector showing a surplus. Since money creation on account of
credit expansion to the private sector during the Second Five
Year Plan was only a third of that under the First Five Year
Plan (0.5 billion rupees as against 1.5 billion rupees),[60] and
since an increased share of the household sector's increased
saving was held in the form of corporate and co-operative
shares and securities (rising from 6.1 per cent of total household saving during the First Plan period to 7.1 per cent during
the Second),[61] there seems to be no reason to believe that the
increased private investment of the Second Term involved
more inflationary financing than the First. In fact, the total
expansion of the money supply was about half what had been
anticipated as necessary during the Second Plan to finance
the expected rise in national income, the transactions demand

from increasing monetisation of the economy and the demand for larger cash holdings,[62] especially in the rural sector.

TABLE 2:17
India: Budget Deficits and Trade Balances, 1956/57-1960/61

	Budget Deficit (−) or Surplus (+)	Balance of Payments on Current Account (Positive + Negative −)
	Crores of Rupees	
1956	− 15.9 (−0.1)	− 312.8 (−2.8)
1957	− 24.4 (−0.2)	− 431.4 (−3.8)
1958	− 47.8 (−0.4)	− 327.0 (−2.6)
1959	− 17.0 (−0.1)	− 185.6 (−1.4)
1960	− 15.8 (−0.1)	− 392.4 (−2.8)
	(Percentages of national income in brackets)	

Sources: Budget deficits and balance of payments current account figures from R.B.I., 1964. National income figures from G.O.I., *Statistical Abstract* for 1963 and 1964 and *National Income* 1948-49 to 1958-59.

Whereas the explanation of the price stability of the First Plan lay in the extremely positive supply response of the economy, the price rise of the Second Plan cannot be explained by a failure of the supply response in aggregate terms, for, while net national output increased by 18.5 per cent in 1948/49 prices during the First Plan, it increased by 21.5 per cent over the Second Plan, and while net national output per head rose by 8.2 per cent over the First Plan, it rose by 9.5 per cent over the Second.[63] Moreover, although the Suez crisis affected import prices and freight rates, these price rises affected mainly imported capital goods, and it can be seen from Table 2:18 that no steady upward pressure was exerted on the general domestic price level from import prices, which rose only sporadically and lagged behind internal prices.

It thus appears that whatever aggregate imbalances of savings and investment may have been important in individual years during the Second Plan, the contrasting experience of the First Plan strongly suggests that certain structural imbalances must have played a crucial role in the price rise. The crux of the matter seems to lie in the disappointing performance of the agricultural sector. Thus, whereas agricultural production increased at an annual average compound rate of 4 per cent over the First Plan Period, it increased by only 2.9 per cent during the Second Plan period.[64] Industrial production, on the other hand, although growing irregularly, nevertheless showed an aggregate performance superior to that of the First Plan, with a rise from 1955/56 to 1960/61 of 36 per cent as compared with a 33 per cent rise during the First Plan (Table 2:15). The rise in industrial costs as agricultural prices rose was in itself a direct inflationary factor, even with a satisfactory industrial supply performance.

TABLE 2:18
India: Wholesale Prices, Export Prices, Import Prices and the Terms of Trade, 1955/56-1960/61 (1955/56 = 100)

	(i) General Wholesale Price Index	(ii) Import Price Index	(iii) Export Price Index	(iv) Terms of Trade (Import Prices ÷ Export Prices)
1955-56	100	100	100	100
1956-57	106	104	105	99
1957-58	107	82	109	75
1958-59	113	105	104	101
1959-60	120	98	104	94
1960-61	129	103	114	90

Sources: (i) R.B.I. *Bulletin*, February 1965; (ii) (iii) (iv) *Eastern Economist*, December 1966, p. 1369.

The autonomous role of rising costs in pushing up prices revealed itself with the simultaneous[65] re-emergence of undercapacity working in the years of the Second Five Year Plan.[66] This somewhat paradoxical combination of price increases alongside surplus capacity during the Second Plan excited some comment.[67] The textile industry was notable for excess capacity working in 1956, 1958[68] and was still significant at the end of the Plan period. Not only did excess capacity become more prominent in textiles during the Second Plan period than the First, but also in, among others, the jute,[69] metallurgical[70] and chemical industries—especially superphosphates, which by 1955/56 were operating at only 35 per cent of their capacity.[71] While in part, excess capacity in this period was the consequence of scarcities of complementary goods and materials arising from balance-of-payments problems in 1957/58,[72] there can be no doubt that deficient demand played a crucial role, particularly in the case of the jute, textile and fertiliser industries. The lag of the agricultural sector has, however, also had serious indirect inflationary effects through the capacity to import. Increasing domestic absorption of slowly-growing

TABLE 2:19
India: Export and Import Quantum, 1955-60 (1958 = 100)

	Import Quantum	Export Quantum
1955	82	106
1956	98	102
1957	151	105
1958	100	100
1959	110	107
1960	107	101

Source: *Eastern Economist Annual Number*, December 1966, pp. 1388 and 1392.

home agricultural production has been largely responsible for the failure to expand India's exports[73] (Table 2:19).[74] Moreover, since the slow growth of home production has also failed to keep pace with domestic needs, a bad harvest can seriously disrupt industrial activity by causing a balance-of-payments crisis, thus limiting the imports of raw materials, semi-finished goods and fuel on which factory industry depends. 1957/58 was a good example of this, and although such a crisis has deflationary effects through the consequent reduction of activity, the continued recurrence of specific supply bottlenecks brought about by a precarious balance of payments does seem to have constituted an inflationary factor during India's Second Five Year Plan.

With declining price levels, the First Plan was a period of declining labour shares in organised industry, whereas with rising prices the Second Plan ushered in a period of roughly stable shares (Tables 2:4 and 2:5). Broadly speaking, the difference between the two periods, when considered in terms of relative price-cost movements, was the result of the difference in the behaviour of raw material costs (relative to final prices). The decline of labour's share during the First Plan (Table 2:4) was the result, taking the period as a whole, of stable final prices, irregularly and gently declining prices of industrial raw materials, and steadily declining labour costs—with a resulting rise in gross profit margins (Tables 2:2. 2:14 and 2:20). By contrast, the Second Plan period was one of irregular and indecisive change in gross profit margins (Tables 2:14 and 2:23) and the labour share of gross value added. This was the result of pressure on margins from raw material costs which were now rising and which pushed up final prices (Tables 2:23 and 2:20). However, the pressure on margins was substantially mitigated and the pressure of rising raw material costs reduced the profit share of manufacturing income only irregularly, if at all, as a result of the irregular decline of unit labour costs.

As with the immediate post-war inflation, the rise of raw material costs was rooted in the agricultural lag which we noted in our discussion of the contrast between the First and Second Five Year Plans.[76] However, by contrast with the earlier post-war inflation, agricultural output did increase over this period. On the other hand, the high growth rate of industrial production meant that, even with some increase in

TABLE 2:20
India: Final Prices, Raw Material Prices and Unit Labour Costs in
Manufacturing Industry, 1952-61

	Wholesale Prices of Manu- factured Articles	Wholesale Prices of Industrial Raw Materials	(Indices) Unit Labour Costs	Ratio of Unit Labour Costs to Final Prices	Ratio of Raw Material Costs to Final Prices	Ratio of Unit Labour Costs to Raw Material Costs
1952	100	100	100	100	100	100
1953	100	110	96	96	110	87
1954	100	104	92	92	104	88
1955	99	97	91	92	98	94
1956	105	113	94	90	108	83
1957	108	118	100	93	109	85
1958	108	115	97	90	106	85
1959	110	120	94	85	109	78
1960	121	139	92	76	115	66
1961	127	148	105	83	117	94

Sources: Table 2:21; wholesale prices from G.O.I. Labour Bureau, *Indian Labour Statistics*, 1962.

TABLE 2:21
India: Indices of Average Money Earnings, Production, Employment
and Productivity of Factory Workers, 1951-61

	Average Money Earnings	Manufacturing Production	Employment	Productivity
1951	100	100	100	100
1952	107	103	104	99
1953	108	106	102	104
1954	108	113	104	109
1955	113	123	107	115
1956	115	133	117	114
1957	121	137	122	112
1958	119	139	123	113
1959	122	150	125	120
1960	130	169	129	131
1961	139	180	135	133

Sources: Money wages and employment indices from R.B.I. *Bulletin*, April 1964; production index from G.O.I. Labour Bureau, *Indian Labour Statistics* 1962 and 1966.

the agricultural marketed surplus, the market environment for industrial products was not sufficiently easy to permit increased prime costs to be fully passed on to prices throughout the whole period.[77]

Nevertheless, pressure on margins was sporadic and variations in margins were small, unlike the immediate post-war inflations. This was partly because there were some years of particularly good harvests, especially in 1958/59 and 1960/61. A side-effect of this was that food prices rose less than raw material costs throughout the period[78] (and rather faster than prices of manufactures).[79] These favourable harvests were a factor in limiting, although they did not completely prevent, diversion of urban money expenditure away from the products of urban industry, as happened during the immediate post-war inflation. Moreover, although the expansionary effects of agriculture on industrial production were much smaller in this than in the previous period, this was partly offset by the tendency for the rapidly-expanding industrial sector to provide its own market to a much greater extent during the Second Plan than in the previous years.[80] This limited the tendency of expanding industrial capacity to outstrip demand, with the result that the demand effects of the agricultural lag were insufficient to prevent a rise in productivity in these years with a consequent easing of pressure on margins.

Decisive in preventing a swing back to a rising labour share of value added after the decline during the First Plan was the extremely poor response of money wages, which lagged behind the rising cost of living in the first few years of the

TABLE 2:22
India: Rising Cost Expenditure, Total Output Value and Gross Surplus in Manufacturing Industry, 1959-61

	Gross Surplus as a Proportion of Total Value of Production (Percentages)	Ratio of Wage Bill to Total Value of Production (Index)	Ratio of Expenditure on Raw Materials and Fuel to Total Value of Production (Index)	Ratio of Wage Bill to Expenditure on Raw Materials and Fuel (Index)
1959	17.1	100	100	100
1960	15.4	94	110	85
1961	15.7	89	122	73

Sources: Results of Annual Survey of Industries as given in *Eastern Economist*, December 1964, p. 1369, and G.O.I., *Statistical Abstract*, 1963 and 1964.

period. This was partly the result of the disappearance of the immediate post-war impetus to trade union activity, a result of a more stable political environment and the real wage gains of the preceding First Plan period. Also important was the increased control of the government over industrial relations since the first post-war inflation, control which was used with considerable skill to grant money wages sufficient to prevent a major explosion of discontent, but not large enough to prevent a slight real-wage decline. The increased disunity of the national trade union movement, compared with the first post-war inflation, contributed to a greater degree of government control over the situation.

The critical role of the agricultural sector is very clearly illustrated by the fact that, although money wages actually rose rather faster during the Second Plan than the First, the share of labour in value added declined during the First Plan, whereas it did not do so during the Second Plan. However, although the labour share of gross value added declined during the First Plan, real wages rose as a result of the movement of the terms of trade against agriculture (food prices and prices of manufactures), and this real-wage gain was in part the reason for the weakness of the impulse behind money-wage increases during the Second Plan.

Summary

In the wartime inflation, the share of labour in gross value added declined. In the inflation of the immediate post-war years, the share of labour in value added in organised manufacturing industry increased. In the inflation of the Second Five Year Plan, the share of labour in value added did not change decisively in either direction.

(i) *The Wartime Inflation, 1939/40-1942/43*

The shift towards profits during the wartime inflation resulted from the lag of rising raw material costs behind prices of manufactures and the lag of unit labour costs (and money wages) behind both. The unusual lag of raw material costs behind final prices was due to the rather special peculiarities of the impact of the war on the Indian economy. These were, on the one hand, simultaneously to cut off physically imports of manufactures and increase very significantly military demand on the modern industrial sector, and on the other, to cut off foreign markets for India's raw material exports. The strain on manufacturing capacity and the sudden and unorganised nature of military expenditures made prices of manufactures more than usually responsive to demand, so that they rose faster than prices of materials for which foreign demand had been physically cut off. The initial weakness of the trade union movement and the restrictions under which it operated during the war meant that the rise of money wages was unable to maintain real wages and did not, despite the productivity decline, raise labour costs as fast as final prices or as fast as raw material costs. Thus, the share of labour declined.

(ii) *The Immediate Post-war Inflation, 1945/46-1950/51*

Declining profit margins, together with rapidly rising money wages, ensured that the inflationary years of the immediate post-war period brought about a continuation of the shift back to an increasing labour share in gross value added which the later non-inflationary years of the war had already ushered in.

The inability of manufacturers fully to pass rising prime costs (the result of accelerating money wages, declining productivity and rising raw material costs) onto prices in this period, despite aggregate excess demand[81] in the economy, was the result of stagnant or declining agricultural production due to a series of bad harvests.[82] This agricultural failure absorbed aggregate excess demand pressures in rising food and raw material prices so that industry suffered from too slow a growth of effective demand, and excess capacity began latterly to emerge, while at the same time agricultural stagnation brought about rising raw material costs directly, and rising labour costs indirectly (as a result of rising food prices). Rising costs in a difficult market environment meant declining gross margins. The rapid acceleration of money wages was a consequence of the political and social pressures and institutional changes brought about by the real-wage decline of the war years, which were such as to create tremendous pressures to push up wages, despite the expanded labour surplus of the post-war period. Rising money wages and declining profit margins thus compressed the share of profits in gross value added.

(iii) *The Inflation of the Second Five Year Plan, 1956/57-1960/61*

The continuous decline of labour's share which took place during the First Plan period was brought to a halt in the Second Plan period, although there was no decisive movement in the other direction. This was primarily the result of declining gross margins due to rising raw material costs, together with a rather slow response to rising money wages to the rising cost of living.

The pressure of rising raw material costs on margins was again the result of structural elements in the inflation due to the lag of agricultural production which raised unit raw material costs, while industrial capacity and output increased sufficiently fast to absorb demand pressures. (Again, import restrictions meant that the role of import competition was negligible.)

However, gross margins declined only intermittently. This

was partly because agriculture did, in certain years, experience extremely good harvests, so that the agricultural failure was much more qualified than in the immediate post-war period. Moreover, since food production increased more than that of cash crops, and consequently food prices rose less than raw material costs and at about the same rate as prices of manufactures, there was a lesser diversion of consumer demand from manufactures, at the same time as manufacturing had in any case become slightly less reliant on the rural community for its markets. The result of both these factors was an offsetting productivity increase which lessened pressure of rising prime costs—in addition to the lesser stimulus to rising money wages which the slower rise of food prices (compared with the immediate post-war inflation) entailed.

If, despite the pressure of rising raw material costs on profit margins, labour's share of gross value added failed to increase as in the inflation of the immediate post-war period, this was decisively determined by the slow rise of money wages, which tended to lag behind final prices, and this in turn reflected the internal disunity of the trade unions and the temporary decline in the powerful social pressures behind the early post-war wage-increases.

NOTES

1.   Among the most serious weaknesses of the cost of living index is the non-representativeness of some of the price quotations on which it is based, particularly at certain periods, owing to rationing controls and the periodic non-availability of certain items during the war was such that even Government departments paid free-market prices occasionally. See Prest, p. 50. This last point is particularly important since the quotations taken are the official controlled prices, which naturally do not always reflect the prices at which commodities are available. The significance of this point is difficult to assess, since not only has the formal structure of controls, together with supporting policy measures, frequently been changed, but the effectiveness of their application has always been varied. Thus, controls over consumer prices were established during the early years of the war but were not effective until late 1943, and even then black market operations in food-grains and textiles remained significant (Prest, pp. 67-71).

Major changes in the degree of control were instituted thereafter on four occasions; in December 1947, when the war-time structure of price controls was almost completely dismantled; in October 1948, when the price increases of the preceding eight months induced a more or less complete return to the pre-December 1942 position, from June 1952 through 1953 and 1954 when, under the impact of rising internal food production and continuing imported supplies, various food controls and their associated administrative machinery were steadily dis-

mantled; and from 1955 through 1957, when the recommencement of
the rise of food-grain prices brought about the gradual re-introduction
of controls over distribution and sales of food grains through designated
retailers (fair price shops) at fixed issue prices. (See G.O.I., *Guide to
Official Statistics*, 1949, pp. 57 and 61). Arrangements were also made
for imports to meet special distribution needs. Use was also made in this
period of the method of release of Government stocks to the wholesale
market, together with various other measures. It is important to note,
however, that apart from the setting of maximum control prices for
rice in some surplus producing districts (linked with limited procurement of domestic surpluses) in 1957, official maximum prices were not
part of the post-1955 measures.

It may thus be surmised that the effect of the utilisation of controlled price quotations for the cost of living index will have tended to
result in an underestimation of the fall in or an overestimation of the rise
of real wages at times when prices were rising at all considerably, until
1952, i.e. from 1939/40 to 1942/43 and from 1945/46 to 1947/48, but
particularly in the former period; and that thereafter, distortion from
this source would be negligible.

2.   There are no census or survey-of-industry figures covering the
years prior to 1940, so we have to rely upon price/cost data for our
picture of income distribution trends in the period. However, it is
possible to check in an approximate fashion on the picture suggested by
the price/cost indices by calculating a ratio of the indices of the total
factory wage-bill and industrial profits as shown in Table 2:3, which
suggests, contrary to the implications of Table 2:2, that the decline in
the share of wages had begun to be reversed by 1942, i.e. before the
period of high inflation had ended. Table 2:2 suggests that the implied
rise in labour's share in 1942 was in the nature of an exceptional
incident, and that the shift back to labour did not properly get under
way until 1944, i.e. until the period of inflation was effectively over.
The latter interpretation seems the more likely, owing to the superior
quality of the statistics used in Table 2:2—the profits index is one of
the weakest of Indian statistical series—moreover, it is not well-aligned
with the wage-bill index, since, apart from the limitations of its coverage, it includes the coal industry whereas the wage-bill index does not.
Further, the estimates of the *Eastern Economist* (*annual number*, 31
December 1948, p. 1123) that wages as a proportion of total income
from organised industries declined from 31 per cent to 28 per cent
between 1939/40 and 1944/45, provide independent confirmation of
the picture suggested by Table 2:2 rather than that suggested by Table
2:3. Nevertheless Table 2:3 provides *proximate* confirmation of the
income redistribution trends implied by Table 2:2.

3.   Since the figures of Table 2:4 are not strictly comparable with
those of Table 2:6 and since in Table 2:20 the ratios of unit labour
costs to final prices declined, while the ratios of raw material costs to
final prices rose in 1958-59, we do not know the direction of change in
income shares in that year. In contrast to the First Plan Period, however, after 1956 the share of labour rose in as many years as it fell (in
the years for which we have information).

4.   As against this, however, provincial budgets closed with surpluses during war years (Singh, pp. 126 and 133). Expenditures 'on all accounts' included 'recoverable' expenditures on behalf of the British Government. Above a certain minimum level, the costs of troops and supplies inside India and the costs of all Indian troops and supplies deployed outside India were 'recoverable', i.e. were to be subsequently recouped by the British Government. Apart from the small proportion of recoverable expenditure financed by British sales of sterling securities and gold and British receipts of rupees from ordinary merchandise trading, the normal method used was to credit the Reserve Bank with sterling assets against the necessary expansion of credit. Indian non-recoverable government expenditure not covered by taxation or long-term loans was similarly financed by the creation of rupees against short-term assets. ``

5.   Singh's belief (Singh, pp. 123-4) in the Government's success in mobilising 'small' savings is not borne out by his own figures.

6.   From data in Prest, p. 62.

7.   Figures for individual industries indicate that, for the war period as a whole, many industries never regained the peak production figures of 1941, although this is not true of the vital cotton piece-goods industry (Prest, p. 37).

8.   Mukerji, pp. 97-103.

9.   Although, as indicated on p.   above, the proportion of government non-recoverable expenditures which were deficit-financed declined after 1942/3, and although the increase in the budget deficit and the positive trade balance taken together was smaller in 1943/4 over 1942/3 than in 1942/3 over 1941/2, the absolute increase was, nonetheless, large.

10.   Prest, pp. 35, 37, 41.

11.   Thus, up to the middle of 1942 the Government was taking 20 per cent of the cotton textile industry's total output for war purposes. A year later the proportion was 35 per cent (U.N. *Survey of Current Inflationary and Deflationary Tendencies*, 1947).

12.   The slackening of the production response in some other sectors of industry in the later war years may not have been critical in the sense that this slackening may itself have represented a response to reduced demand pressure on these particular sectors. Various alleviatory measures were introduced in 1944/5 to reduce military demands for munitions and manpower, and Prest argues that it is not unreasonable to suppose that the Indian economy was not overburdened during the war years, except possibly in 1942 and 1943. However, this may be, there were certainly strong expansionary pressures. The critical point was the precise manner of their impact on the economy.

13.   Despite the licensing system in operation in the earlier years,

private export trade was, in practice, largely uncontrolled prior to 1942/3.

14.   G.O.I., *Indian Information*, 1 June 1945, pp. 671-2.

15.   Knight, p. 297.

16.   Thus, total cereal supplies declined from an average of 337 lbs. per adult for the years 1937/8-1939/40, to 361 lbs. per adult in 1944/5 (*ibid.*, p. 298). Nor had the average level of food supplies per capita attained the average 1934-38 level in 1949/50, measured in kilograms per capita (U.N. *Economic Survey of Asia and the Far East*, 1950, p. 201). The real wage of an employee in organised industry in 1944 was only three-quarters of its 1939 level and, according to U.N. estimates, real per capita product in 1946 was less than half its 1938 level (*ibid.*, 1955, p. 3).

17.   In addition to the changes in this respect referred to, gold sales in 1943/4, although not large, took place at a critical period.

18.   The role of rising import prices during the early years of the inflation was small, since the drastic decline in the volume of imports in the early years of the war reduced the practical importance of this factor. In most war years, import prices in any case lagged behind domestic prices (Table 2:7). The principal effect of changes in foreign trade on the evolution of prices operated, in the case of the manufacturing industry, via the strain placed upon domestic capacity.

19.   As would in any case be expected from the oligopolistic structure of the modern manufacturing sector (Maranjan, pp. 151-5), and the admittedly rough data assembled in Table 2:14 showing an approximate stability of gross profit margins in less changeable times.

20.   Between August and September, 1939, the wholesale price index of manufactured articles rose by 45 per cent, that of industrial raw materials by 27 per cent. Prest remarks on the 'business as usual' atmosphere which prevailed in India just before the war and which militated against precautionary stock-piling (Prest, p. 182).

21.   Textile mills were frequently working 168 hours per week (Prest, p. 15), the number of weekly working hours was increased from 45 to 54 and then to 60 (Singh, p. 182).

22.   We have already seen how disorganised was the first impact of military expenditure. No doubt the British military and Indian Governments' pricing policy in the early war years was a further incentive to a price policy based on what the market would bear. It was only after 1941 that any attempt was made to apply pricing principles to contracts based on a cost-plus system. Even then, this applied only to organised industry. The fact that it was only after 1941 that the ratios of unit labour costs and raw materials costs to final prices for the first time failed to decline, lends further support to the view that normal pricing conventions had been abandoned over large sectors of organised

industry. The subsequent further decline of these ratios in 1942/43 may be attributed to the re-emergence of crisis conditions.

23.   As we shall see, it would not be accurate to add to this the postulate that market forces were neutralised in their effect on money wages by employer policy, since even if this were not the case, the evidence is that even if market forces operated, there were no generalised pressures of excess demand for *unskilled labour.*

24.   See Chapter 3 below for a more extensive discussion of the determinants of money-wage changes.

25.   The State Governments in this period, however, unlike the position in the wartime years, tended to show deficits (Singh, p. 133).

26.   In particular, there had developed a backlog of demand for durable consumer goods (U.N., E.C.A.F.E., *Economic Survey of Asia and the Far East, 1948,* New York, 1949, p. 190).

27.   U.N., *Inflationary Tendencies,* 1947, p. 70.

28.   *The Eastern Economist,* Annual Number, Vol. XI, No. 26, 31 December 1947, p. 1130.

29.   Myers, C.A., 1958, pp. 7-8. The industrial labour force in this estimate includes the plantation industries (tea, coffee and rubber), mining, construction, utilities, transport and communications, manufacturing and part of the employment in trade, banking and public administration.

30.   It has been estimated that, of the total new investment in the period 1946-51 by 492 public corporations, 57 per cent was financed by retained profits (G.O.I., *Report of the Taxation Enquiry Commission,* Vol. 1, 1953/54, New Delhi, 1955, p. 115). The remaining finance seems to have been largely provided through credit creation. The commercial banks were in this period able to increase their reserves at will (owing to the government's cheap money policy) by selling government securities to the Reserve Bank. The flow of private funds into productive investment in this period was limited by political and economic uncertainties.

31.   U.N., E.C.A.F.E., *Survey for 1950,* p. 122.

32.   U.N., E.C.A.F.E., *Survey for 1948,* p. 190, *Survey for 1950,* p. 156, U.N. *Inflationary and Deflationary Tendencies, 1940-48,* New York, 1949, p. 29.

33.   The average annual level of industrial production for the years 1948/49-1950/51 was higher than for the years 1946/47 to 1948/49.

34.   Singh, pp. 56-59; E.C.A.F.E., *Survey for 1950,* pp. 324-328, 492, 496.

35.   The inflationary export surplus of the last quarter of 1949 and

the first quarter of 1950 could not be attributed to devaluation alone. Particularly important in this connection were the government's import restriction measures, which coincided with devaluation. Apart from the 1949 devaluation and the Korean war boom, import prices played a relatively unimportant part in the movement of the Indian price level, lagging behind home prices during this period (Table 2:13).

36.   G.O.I., 1952, pp. 425-7.

37.   For a discussion of the sources and role of rising costs in pushing up prices of manufactures in the period, see below, pp.

38.   The proportion of total prime costs accounted for by labour costs first rose and then fell.

39.   This is what Phelps Brown has characterised as a 'displacement effect' (Phelps Brown, especially pp. 58-65).

40.   The degree of excess capacity in organised industry in India prior to the First Plan was considerable. The document of the First Plan remarked that 'It will be seen that in the scheme of priorities set out above an increase in the supply of consumer goods has under present conditions to come mainly from fuller utilisation of existing capacity. By and large the capacity of industries producing essential goods like cotton, textiles, sugar, salt, matches and soap is adequate for present requirements. In the case of consumer goods of secondary importance such as radios, bicycles, automobiles, electric fires, etc., the problem again is one of utilising existing capacity more fully' (G.O.I., *First Five Year Plan*, p. 427). Underutilisation of capacity was not confined to consumer goods industries. The planners also advocated 'Fuller utilisation of existing capacity in producer goods industries like jute and plywood' (*ibid.*, p. 425); and other industries mentioned as having adequate existing capacity for expansion of production were *vanaspati* and paints and varnishes (*ibid.*, p. 425). See also G.O.I. Planning Commission, 1955, pp. 175-6.

41.   However, rigorous import controls meant that competition from foreign manufactured consumer goods was not an important factor in causing idle capacity in the post-war years. On the other hand, balance of payments problems and problems arising from the changeover to a peacetime economy caused supply bottlenecks which were also responsible for some of the idle capacity of this period. Moreover, although the immediate post-war years were years of aggregate excess demand, this was largely siphoned off into rising food prices. As a result, some of the war-expanded manufacturing industries faced demand problems after the war. The crucially important cotton piece-goods industry had expanded to such an extent during the war that India became a post-war net exporter of textiles instead of being a net importer, as she had been pre-war.

42.   '. . . The decisive movements of the general index (of industrial production) correspond broadly with agricultural output. . . Whatever the generative power of industrial activity itself. . . the significance of

rural developments upon industrial production in India's essentially
market economy must always be borne in mind.

'Today India's production is dominated by the output of consumer
and light industry products. Less than 10 per cent of current industrial
output takes place in government plants. An even smaller percentage of
factory employment is in government industrial enterprises. Perhaps 75
per cent of Indian industry produces light and consumer goods for
private domestic and foreign markets' (W. Balenbaum, 1962).

43.   Allowing for the proportion of total prime costs constituted by
raw material costs and for the proportion of the total market for
industrial products accounted for by the rural sector.

44.   Of course if declining agricultural production is accompanied by
an increase in the power of the government and/or the wealthier rural
classes *vis-à-vis* the peasantry, this may mean that an increased proportion of total agricultural output finding its way to the towns offsets
to a greater or lesser degree the decline in agricultural production. Post-
war land reform measures and, with the possible exception of the years
1943-45, the ineffectiveness of agricultural taxation, indicates that these
are unlikely to have been important offsetting factors in periods of
decline or stagnation of agricultural production in India during the
inflationary periods. Subsequent discussion, in this and the other
country chapters, of declining total agricultural production will omit
mention of these possible offsetting factors unless they are known to
have been, in the actual situation, of major importance.

45.   There was, however, some offset from rising imports of food and
raw materials in these years (U.N., E.C.A.F.E., *Survey for 1950*,
pp. 320, 392).

46.   At the risk of a nearly circular argument, we may note that the
evidence of some excess capacity in factory industry in this period,
noted earlier, confirms this interpretation.

47.   The production indices of Table 2:10 do not suggest that agriculture lagged behind industry, whose production performance was
also poor in this period. However, it should be borne in mind that the
slow growth of industrial production was partly attributable to demand
factors originating in the agricultural sector, so that there is no reason
to suppose the industrial supply response to have been as inflexible as
that of agriculture.

48.   Palvis, pp. 31-32, cited by Hoover, p. 128.

49.   On the other hand, the price inelasticity of demand for food will
tend to be counterbalanced by the less than unitary income elasticity
of demand for food, since real wages were rising in this period. Income
elasticity of demand for food, drink and tobacco was estimated at 0.81
for urban consumers in 1952 (Palvis, p. 125).

50.   However, the decisive factor in the inflation of labour costs was
undoubtedly the wage increases. Slowness in replacing worn-out

capacity and continuing limitations on the capacity to import, together with increased absenteeism and shorter hours in industry, all contributed to the decline in productivity in post-war manufacturing. Reluctance to rationalise owing to possible political repercussions of increased unemployment may also have been a factor.

51. Unit labour costs from 1940 to 1949 actually rose slightly faster than money wages, owing to the decline in productivity in these years (Tables 2:2 and 3:1), partly the result of declining capacity utilisation, in turn partly the result of the obstacles to the expansion of demand set by stagnating agricultural output.

52. The Government explains this in terms partly of the shortfall in foreign loans and grants, also partly the reason for the shortfall of the import surplus (G.O.I. Planning Commission, 1957, p. 23).

53. The procedure used above and elsewhere in the text of the Country Chapters of balancing budget deficits (or surpluses) against import (or export) surpluses is taken from Malenbaum, Ch. XII, and is used as an expository device, particularly convenient because budget and trade figures are generally readily available and can thus be used as a focus for more limited data relating to other variables. Analytically, of course, the use of this device must be supplemented by consideration of other sources of demand pressure, by information on the supply response of the economy, both in aggregate and sectoral terms, on the movement of import prices, and on various other variables.

54. U.N., E.C.A.F.E., *Survey for 1957*, p. 75.

55. *Ibid.*, p. 229.

56. G.O.I., *National Income Statistics, 1948-49 to 1958-59.*

57. Between 1952 and 1955, the quantum index of food and raw material imports declined by 62 per cent and 1 per cent respectively (the latter figure including semi-manufactures and the former drink and tobacco) while imports of manufactures rose by 81 per cent (U.N., E.C.A.F.E., *Survey for 1959*, p. 231).

58. *Cf.* Malenbaum, p. 230.

59. U.N., E.C.A.F.E., *Survey for 1961*, p. 84.

60. *Ibid.*, p. 88.

61. These percentages are given only as an indication of the direction of changing household investment. In fact, a higher proportion of household savings will have been invested indirectly in the corporate sector, through insurance policies, provident funds, etc. Savings of the household sector (the other two sectors being government and corporate) rose from 76.2 per cent of the total saving during the First Plan to 77.6 per cent during the Second Plan, and from 5.0 per cent of the National Income during the First Plan to 6.6 per cent during the Second Plan (*R.B.I. Bulletin*, March 1965, pp. 330 and 332). Of course, foreign

saving also accounted for part of the corporate sector's increased investment.

62.   A rise in money supply of 66 per cent had been anticipated. The actual increase (taking the 1960/61 figure over the 1955/56 figure) was 30 per cent. Although the rise in national income fell short, by about a quarter in real terms, of the planned level, it is clear that the rise in money supply was fairly modest (U.N., E.C.A.F.E., *Survey for 1960*, p. 113; *R.B.I. Bulletin*, March 1965, p. 382).

63.   *Eastern Economist*, Annual Number, December 1966.

64.   U.N., E.C.A.F.E., *Survey for 1961*, p. 82.

65.   At the same time as the renewal of the inflation.

66.   As intended, the First Five Year Plan period did in fact witness a marked improvement in the degree of capacity utilisation in industry. However, with the falling off in agricultural output in the later years of the First Plan, renewed signs of under-capacity working became apparent, in consequence partly of deficiency of effective demand (U.N., E.C.A.F.E., *Survey for 1954*, p. 11).

67.   'But the rise in prices so far has not developed the usual character-istic of an inflationary movement. . . Moreover, whilst there is an up-ward pressure on the prices of food grains, signs of excess supply are evident in the case of other commodities such as cotton textiles. This tendency is likely to become more prominent as the investment under-taken in private industry leads to further increases in installed capacity'. (U.N., E.C.A.F.E., *Survey for 1957*, p. 81 (commenting on developments since early 1956).

68.   U.N., E.C.A.F.E., *Survey for 1958*, p. 13; G.O.I. Ministry of Commerce and Industry.

69.   Little, p. 29.

70.   Sastri, p. 32.

71.   Gulati; U.N., E.C.A.F.E., *ibid.*, p. 129.

72.   Little, p. 20; U.N., E.C.A.F.E., *Survey for 1957*, p. 8.

73.   The acceleration of the rate of population growth which has apparently been taking place in recent years may well have been an important supplementary reason for the contrast between the First and Second Five Year Plans via its effect on the demand for food (Byres, p. 94).

74.   U.N., E.C.A.F.E., *Survey for 1961*, p. 89.

75.   The indices of average money earnings, production and employ-ment (and thus productivity) from which the unit labour cost index was

calculated are given in Table 2:21. The result must be regarded as a much rougher approximation than the unit labour cost index for 1939 to 1954 based on the Labour Bureau's productivity and money earnings indices, since the production, employment and money earnings indices are less well aligned. Thus, the industrial classifications used by the Directorate of Industrial Statistics, which constructs the production index, are not quite the same as those used for the returns under the Factories Act, on which is based the employment index. Moreover, there are differences in the coverage of the statistics from which the money earnings and employment indices are calculated. In particular, the former excludes Railway Workshops and groups of industries that are seasonal in character, comprising foods, beverages, tobacco and gins and presses.

A further minor difficulty arises from the fact that the average earnings indices cover only workers earning less than 200 rupees montly, while the employment indices cover elements of salaried workers.

Since the unit labour cost index is used in conjunction with the wholesale price index of manufactures to check on the picture of income redistribution given by the Census of Manufacturing Industries and the Annual Survey of Industries, in which salaries are here classified as part of the wage bill, we ought really to have average money earnings figures which include salary earners. This would have the additional advantage of giving us consistency with the employment inded. However, indices of average money earnings, including salary earnings, do not much differ from indices of average earnings of manual workers only (as estimated from figures in G.O.I., *Indian Labour Statistics* for 1961 and 1962).

Apart from problems of alignment, the indices of money wages and employment themselves suffer from various defects. See *R.B.I. Bulletin*, April 1964, pp. 422-3; *Indian Labour Statistics, 1962*, pp. VIII-IX and XI-XII; *Indian Labour Statistics, 1965*, p. 36. Despite all this, there is no strong reason to suspect that the resulting labour cost index, in conjunction with the wholesale price index of manufactures, gives us a misleading idea of the relative movements of unit labour costs and final prices, especially as regards the direction of movement of this ratio taken over the broad periods which are our framework of discussion (as, indeed, is evidenced by comparison with the Census and Survey figures despite the very occasional year-to-year differences).

76.   Whereas the increase in agricultural output was approximately 66 per cent of that of industrial production during the First Plan, the corresponding figures was only 56 per cent in the Second Plan (Table 2:15. Government price and profit policy supplemented the effect of the agricultural lag in squeezing industrial profit margins (Malenbaum, p. 265).

77.   Competition from imported manufactures was of no significance in preventing increased margins, since practically the only manufactured articles allowed into the country in this period were plant, machinery and some intermediate goods (Little, p. 23). (It should be borne in mind that, although imports of manufactures were restricted, this was nevertheless a period when in aggregate terms the import surplus was far in excess of budget deficits in every year).

78. In the Second Plan, production of food crops, although falling short of production targets, outpaced that of non-food agricultural products (U.N., E.C.A.F.E., *Survey for 1961*, p. 82).

79. Between 1955/56 and 1960/61, wholesale prices of manufactured articles and wholesale prices of industrial raw materials rose by 24 per cent and 47 per cent respectively, while wholesale food prices increased by 40 per cent (*R.B.I. Bulletin,* March 1965).

80. This effect relates of course to the expansionary effect of the growth of different sectors within manufacturing upon one another. Insofar as these intersectoral effects were not operating, the more rapid the expansion of output and capacity in the modern industrial sector, the greater would be the pressure on margins with a given rate of increase of demand (Malenbaum, p. 299; U.N., E.C.A.F.E., *Survey for 1957*, p. 78).

81. Budget deficits, an increased volume of credit-financed private investment and rising consumption expenditures financed by liquid assets accumulated during the war, offset the deflationary effects of import surpluses.

82. Control of imports meant that competition from manufactured imports was of little significance in this period.

CHAPTER 3

THE MOVEMENT OF
MONEY WAGES IN INDIA,
1939-61

As we have seen, in the wartime inflation in India the lag of money wages[1] behind final prices and prices of raw materials helped reduce labour's share by permitting increased gross margins and reducing labour's share of total prime costs. In the immediate post-war inflation, money wages, rising faster than prices of manufactures, helped rising raw material costs to reduce gross margins. The result was that labour's share of gross value added rose despite the declining share of labour in total prime costs. In the inflation of the Second Five Year Plan, rising raw material costs reduced gross margins, and the rise of money wages was sufficient to ensure relative stability of labour's share, even though money wages were lagging behind final prices and raw material costs, and even though labour productivity was rising. The rate of rise of money wages was not, however, in this period sufficiently fast to cause a clear redistribution of gross factory income towards labour, even given the pressure of rising raw material costs on margins.

The behaviour of the price of labour is thus a necessary element in explaining the changes in the share of labour during inflation. This is particularly so if we bear in mind that declining margins do not necessarily mean a declining share of profit in gross value added.

Up to this point, the reader has been obliged to accept on trust the thesis that the rate of rise of money wages in relation to prices has been primarily a function of the relative 'push-fulness' of various institutional forces exerting pressure on the firms, and broadly unrelated to the state of the labour market throughout the different phases of the development of the Indian price level since 1939. We must now examine this thesis more closely, and we shall do so initially by a consideration of various possible processes whereby a generalised rise of urban money wages in the organised sector might take place.

Average money earnings rose nearly continuously between 1939 and 1961, a rise sufficient to cause a rise in real wages after 1943, so that the 1939 level of real wages was regained in 1952 (despite a fourfold increase in the cost-of-living index over the same period. There was a fluctuating rise of real wages up to 1955, a decline until 1958 or 1959, and a recovery thereafter (Table 3:1).

These changes have taken place quite independently of developments in the urban labour market which, since the end of the Second World War, has witnessed a substantial visible surplus of unemployed labour, the numbers of which, in all the principal industrial centres, have grown steadily year by year. Thus, for organised industry alone, the numbers of unskilled unemployed were estimated to have amounted, in 1953, to a total of 0.24 million out of a total labour force of 2.5 million, or about 10 per cent of the total.[2] A later estimate for 1956 put the total of urban unemployed at 2.5 million (with 2.8 million in the rural areas—the definition used is of unemployed *per se* and excludes under-employment.)[3]

Even the extraordinary demands of the war resulted in an increase in labour employed in all organised industries of no more than 721,690, while population grew at an annual average rate of a million a year[4] (Table 3:2). The brunt of the strain fell upon supplies of skilled labour[5] and scarcities of unskilled labour were a local rather than a general phenomenon.[6] In the most crucial of all industries, the cotton textile industry, Dr Morris's careful investigations show that in Bombay at least no difficulty was experienced in obtaining an adequate supply of unskilled labour.[7] Nor did the situation in Bombay differ appreciably from that in other centres.[8]

Perhaps the most decisive indication, however, of the non-relevance of market forces to wartime money wage increases was the tendency for skill differentials to narrow at precisely the period when the most severe strains were being exerted on the market for skilled labour,[9] while unskilled labour was in adequate supply. Since average earnings rose rapidly through the granting of cost of living or 'dearness' allowances, which were generally flat-rate increases, the unskilled lower-paid workers received larger percentage increases than the higher-paid workers. Thus, the ratio of fitters' earnings to those of the least skilled workers in the Tata Iron and Steel Company at Jamshedpur was 3.73 in 1939, and only 2.76 in 1952.[10]

TABLE 3:1
India: Indices of Money Wages, Cost-of-Living and Real Wages, 1939-61

	Cost of Living Index	Index of Average Money Earnings	Real Wage Index
1939	100	100	100
1940	97	105	108
1941	107	111	104
1942	145	129	89
1943	268	180	67
1944	269	202	75
1945	269	202	75
1946	285	209	73
1947	323	253	78
1948	361	304	84
1949	371	340	92
1950	374	334	89
1951	390	357	92
1952	382	386	101
1953	393	385	98
1954	374	381	102
1955	355	399	112
1956	390	406	104
1957	413	427	103
1958	431	420	97
1959	450	430	96
1960	458	459	100
1961	463	487	105

Sources: Cost-of-Living index as for Table 2:1; average money earnings 1939-54 from *Indian Labour Gazette*, October 1955, and for 1954-61 from R.B.I. *Bulletin*, April 1964, and *Indian Labour Statistics* 1965.

TABLE 3:2
India: Co-efficient of Industrial Absorption of the Population, 1939-45 and 1945-48

	Annual Increment in Population	Industrial Employment	Ratio of Industrial Employment Increment to Population Increment (Percentage)
1939-45	3,365	150.0	4.5
1945-48	3,072	22.8	0.7

Source: Prest, pp. 80, 72.

There are, it might be added, certain more general considerations of a historical character, which are bound, in any case, to suggest caution in attributing, in the case of India, any generalised increase of money wages to a 'classical' process of competitive bidding up of wages by competing employers. And these relate to the characteristics of labour policy as it developed and became standardised by custom and interest in colonial territories, i.e. the adoption of 'mercantilist labour policies', as Myrdal calls them, the crux of which has been to hold money wages steady, while expanding the labour force, by adopting whatever administrative-cum-political mechanisms might be necessary to shift the supply curve of labour sufficiently to the right. The social economic and ideological origins, and historical phases of this policy have been summarised by Myrdal,[11] and all we need note here is that this tradition was continued by various measures in those specific sectors where labour was scarce during the Second World War. Thus, contrary to management's normal policy, children were employed in the Bengal Mills;[12] women were employed underground in the mines (entailing the relaxation of the legislation prohibiting such a practice;[13] labour supply committees were set up to settle conflicting claims for unskilled labour;[14] attempts were made to locate the building of airfields in accordance with local availability of labour;[15] and for skilled labour various training and labour-sharing schemes were established.[16]

None of the above, of course, is meant to suggest that competition for labour never occurred during the war. As stated previously, local scarcities did occur, but the crucial point is that the methods used appear to have been predominantly of a type which would permit wage discrimination and thus avoid a generalisation of wage increases. Thus, with reference to the 'scramble for labour' in certain war industries, the Labour Investigation Committee reported that 'This scramble has shown itself in such activities as sending out recruiting agents to entice away labour employed by other employers by promises of tips and advances. . .'[17] That is, the methods used did not imply a general process (or part of one) of bidding up money wages but, rather, the partial discriminatory raising of money wages (if at all) of a minority of workers employed.[18]

There is a paradox posed by a large percentage differential in urban-rural earnings greater than can be accounted for by the difference in urban-rural living and transfer costs and alongside an urban labour surplus. One suggested explanation is that the average level of real earnings for urban manufacturing workers is determined not by the average level of real earnings obtainable by the individual worker in agriculture, but by the average level of real earnings obtainable by the *family* in agriculture. This is held to be due to the fact that the employer is primarily interested in a stable labour force which can be obtained only by paying a wage sufficient to enable the individual wage earner to transfer and keep his family in the city. Such a wage must at least be equal to the average earnings of the family in agriculture. Since the earner/dependent ratio tends to be lower in the cities than in the country, the supply price for urban employment has to be higher than the average earnings in the rural areas by an amount sufficient to compensate for the 'adverse' earner-dependent ratio.[19]

Thus, a large urban-rural earnings gap, adequate to attract family labour in sufficient quantities from agriculture, is consistent with a large surplus of labour in the urban areas, provided this surplus is composed of lone, non-family migrants. On certain assumptions, i.e. a continuous excess demand for stable labour in the urban areas, this hypothesis can readily be adapted to explain a continuous, generalised rise of money wages in the urban areas such as we have been examining. How convincing is such an explanation? Its validity rests upon three important assumptions (among others). These are:

(1)   that labour turnover is entirely or principally a product of employing semi-rural workers in urban industry, and not of factors internal to urban industry;

(2)   that the number of labourers complete with families in the towns is insufficient for the requirements of urban industry;

(3)   that the response of employers to scarcity of stable labour will be the offer of higher money wages.

There is no doubt that high labour turnover is not entirely a result of urban/rural socio-economic relationships, and may even be principally a product of conditions internal to urban industry alone in underdeveloped economies, attributable fundamentally to a wide range of conditions of employment in circumstances of rapid change.[20] Moreover, it appears to be the case that in India there has been a surplus of permanent town-dwelling labour, complete with families.

Even if labour turnover is entirely a product of internal urban industrial conditions, and even if there is an urban surplus of family-provided labour, money wages may still be raised in the attempt to combat high turnover, simply as one method of retaining the workers' loyalty. Such a procedure is, however, less likely than if the problem were simply one of attracting family-provided labour from agriculture, since it is likely to be self-defeating, due to similar measures by competitors. In other words, the notion of labour turnover as primarily the result of the village nexus has embedded within it a neat once-for-all solution via raising money wages which is no longer applicable when the problem of labour turnover is considered to be a more complex phenomenon involving the internal conditions of urban industry.

We do not intend to imply that the village nexus plays no part in causing high labour turnover in the urban economy. It does. However, our concern is to point out that labour turnover in urban industry in underdeveloped countries is partly, and even in certain cases, dominantly, a product of conditions internal to urban industry and, to the extent that this is so, solutions to the problem by means of offering higher money wages are likely to be and to appear to be more self-defeating than when the problem is simply one of attracting family labour from agriculture.

More important, however, is the problem of the degree of instability itself since, if we are to explain a generalised rise of money wages in the modern urban sector as the consequence of an effort to maintain or expand an adequate supply of stable labour, we shall have to show the existence of a problem of instability. Has there been such a problem?

Naturally, insofar as the build-up of surplus urban labour has progressed, labour turnover due to the village nexus has declined, quite apart from the effect of employment insecurity in reducing labour turnover. As early as 1946, the Labour Investigation Committee in its Report commented as follows:

'When the Royal Commission on Labour reported in 1931, the working class was neither sufficiently organised nor properly stabilised. In recent years, however, there has been a greater concentration of the working class population in industrial areas and this has led to the rise of an industrial proletariat in most cities which is prepared to stick to the town to a greater extent than before to fight for its legitimate rights and to seek livelihood in urban rather than rural area. . . the labour force in principal industrial cities like Bombay, Calcutta, Cawnpore, etc., is getting more and more stabilished.'[21]

Since this was written the process has, naturally, been accentuated, so that by the early 1950's Myers was able to record turnover rates in the Bombay cotton textile industry well below those for the United States.[22] Again, Dr Morris's valuable study, utilising length of service data (for both the Bombay cotton textile industry and the individual mill), leads him to the conclusion that 'even quite early in the industry's history there was a significant proportion of the work force which had developed a long-term attachment to employment in the cotton textile industry if not to employment in a single mill. Over time this proportion rose substantially.'[23] Moreover, R.C. James has pointed out that the 1940 and 1955 length-of-service data compared very favourably with the United States experience.[24]

It thus appears that between 1939 and 1961 factory industry in general at all times experienced no difficulty in obtaining unskilled labour *per se,* and that such labour was in growing excess in the post-war period. Again, the supply of stable labour,[25] with the possible exception of the war years, has been steadily increasing, and this appears not to have been the result of rising money wages since, as with unskilled labour *per se,* labour stability *preceded* rising money wages.[26]

We may now turn to the last assumption of Dr Mazumdar's theory—that employers, to prevent labour turnover, will raise money wages. Employers have, however, analagously to their reaction to skilled labour scarcities, preferred to deal with the problem by other means than offering higher money wage rates. These means have been particularly the provision of better housing facilities (often associated with various social welfare facilities), wages in kind—often food, stabilising industrial relations by promoting either legitimate or 'tame' trade unions or workers' associations, and providing graded pay, promotion and long-service schemes. Such measures provide the basic physical facilities necessary to move a family from agriculture or to retain it in urban conditions of desperate housing shortage, and/or the appropriate social and economic conditions to give the worker a material advantage in staying with the firm.

Analogous to the 'stability explanation' of the supply price of urban labour is the 'efficiency theory', analogous in the sense that both may be characterised as variants of a 'high wage' explanation of what employers do. The 'efficiency theory' holds that in an underdeveloped economy, rising prices so threaten the efficiency of the workers via reduced living standards that 'employers themselves offer a rise in money wages to counteract a rise in prices'.[27] A variant of this view is that which considers the minimum real wage to be set by some kind of minimum subsistence standard, the maintenance of which requires the raising of money wages as prices of wage-goods rise. This may be considered a *variant* of the strict efficiency theory, insofar as it implies the possibility of a decline in physical efficiency before reaching the nadir of minimum physical subsistence, after which money wages must rise. Insofar, however, as the rise of money wages at this point is taken to be motivated by considerations of efficiency, it must be considered a straightforward efficiency theory.[28]

Two principal objections may be lodged against this type of theory. On the one hand, changes in the physical efficiency of the factory worker for health reasons and as measured in terms of his output are likely to be neither sudden nor obvious to the individual employer. On the other hand, the reaction of the employer to high labour costs due to in-efficiency is likely to take some form other than the raising of money wages, and traditionally has done so. That changes in the real wages of the factory worker are unlikely to bring about sudden and/or obvious changes in his physical efficiency is most obvious when we consider the concept of the physical subsistence minimum. It is, presumably, in the region of this minimum that the employer is most likely to raise money wages to maintain efficiency. Yet this 'standard. . . is not a fixed level since the amount of subsistence will depend on how arduous or how extensive the work is', and it may be very low, sufficient only for the bare physical needs of the present, and not for maintaining a normal working life or for rearing a family.[29] The very fact that it is not a 'fixed level' means that changes in the *current* physical efficiency of the worker (which is what interests the employer except in the case of skilled and semi-skilled workers, who are in any case in much less danger of malnutrition than the unskilled) are the less likely to result from changes in real wages in the short run. The worker will, consciously or unconsciously, attempt to maintain the same output achievement as before.

His job and his earnings are likely to depend upon it.[30] Only over time will the strain tell. A larger proportion of the family budget will be spent on the wage-earner, thus undermining the efficiency of the rising generation. A larger proportion of the food bought will be stomach-filling and energy-giving in a purely temporary fashion—the body-building foods, the 'long-term' foods will be neglected, and so on. The point is clear. The effects of malnutrition on physical efficiency, undeniable though they are, are likely to take effect only gradually over time. And the very lapse of time necessarily makes malnutrition as an independent cause of high labour costs so much the less likely to impinge on the employer's notice. This is particularly so in cases where other causes of high and/or rising labour costs are obvious, such as lack of training and high turnover rates. On the other hand, the raising of money wages represents a perfectly obvious, definite and current rise in labour costs. The employer is unlikely to cure an almost invisible, unmeasurable (at least for him) and non-current rise in labour costs, which all his competitors are likely to be suffering to much the same extent, by means of a perfectly visible, current and measureable rise in labour costs which will by no means necessarily be equally suffered by his competitors.

Turning to the employer's reactions to high labour costs due to inefficiency traceable to a low real wage, we need only say here that historically the most general reaction to this problem has been on the one hand to keep labour costs low by keeping money wages low, and on the other to introduce labour-saving machinery.

Indeed, the general unwillingness or inability[31] of employers to pay a money wage which will ensure a reasonable minimum standard of subsistence is one of the principal reasons for the prevalence of minimum wage-fixing machinery in underdeveloped countries. It is difficult to believe in the compulsion of a minimum real wage necessary for physical subsistence when, for example, the miserable pittance on which Indian urban workers in manufacturing industry lived in 1939 was reduced by over 30 per cent in four years.

This argument is not intended to imply that manufacturers in underdeveloped countries never take a long view of the problem of labour costs. Indeed, the literature gives many examples of advanced employers and it is apparent that, in organised industry at least, a long-term view of labour problems is becoming increasingly accepted. Advanced employers in organised industry are certainly much less exceptional than they were before the war.

However, the point here is that the advanced employers, by and large, are advanced, not in respect of long-term views as to the physical health of their labour force, but in respect of improving the skill and reducing the turnover of their labour force, and in respect of the 'normalisation' of labour relations. That this should be so is due to the fact that the problems of skill, turnover and labour relations are all problems which present themselves to the employer in an acute and obvious form and are moreover, within limits, all problems, the attempted solutions of which are not unlikely to lead to definite and visible results. Such is to a much lesser extent the case with the problem of the physical health of the worker.

Of these problems, skill, turnover and labour relations, we consider only labour relations to be a significant factor in the rise of money wages and insofar as an advanced employer does raise wages for the sake of good labour relations, this is directly traceable to institutional pressures, and needs, therefore, no further consideration here.

To summarise: the view that employers raise money wages in order to maintain the physical efficiency of the workers voluntarily, without any external pressure, is unconvincing not only because it is not in the tradition and therefore psychology of employers to do so, but also because they can have very little conscious idea of the effects of a rise in the cost of living on physical efficiency, while they do have a definite idea of the effect of the raising of money wages on costs.

To postulate a positive correlation between productivity levels (and changes) and real wage levels (and changes) does not in itself imply any particular causal mechanism nor even any specific direction of causality. In particular, unless some third variable is introduced, such as in the two theories discussed above, physical health or stability, a postulated or actual correlation between high wage levels and high productivity levels need not imply an economic mechanism at work, since the tautologies of orthodox theory equate wages with marginal productivity and not average productivity. (Thus wages in competitive markets will be equal—discounting non-monetary advantages and disadvantages—and so will marginal productivities, but not average productivities.) How-

ever, it is possible to conceive of an institutional mechanism
linking wage levels and productivity levels via the effect of
high productivity on profits.

Thus, it may be that while the rise of money wages cannot
be explained in terms of conditions in the labour market, it
can nevertheless be explained in terms of conditions in the
product market, i.e. while money wage changes are related to
'bargaining power', bargaining power is itself a direct function
of industrial prosperity.[32]

However, inspection of Tables 3:3 and 3:4, while suggest-
ing that industrial prosperity may indeed be an influence
affecting the rate of rise of money wages, suggests nevertheless
that it is a less important influence than the movements of
the cost of living index. Thus, both Tables 3:3 and 3:4
inspection shows that changes in the cost of living index in
any one year tend to be associated in the same year with.
variations in the rate of rise of average money earnings in the
same direction (by the same direction is meant rises and/or
accelerations[33] of the rate of rise on the one hand, and
declines and/or decelerations of the rate of rise on the other).

TABLE 3:3
India: Percentage Changes in Average Money Wages in Manufacturing
Industry, the Cost-of-Living Index and Industrial Profits, 1939-50

	Cost-of-Living Index	Average Money Earnings	Profits
1939-40	− 3.0	+ 5.0	+38.0
1940-41	+10.3	+ 5.7	+35.5
1941-42	+35.5	+16.2	+18.7
1942-43	+96.8	+39.5	+10.4
1943-44	+ 0.4	+12.2	− 2.5
1944-45	0.0	0.0	− 2.1
1945-46	+ 6.0	+ 3.4	− 6.0
1946-47	+13.3	+26.1	−16.2
1947-48	+11.8	+20.2	+35.4
1948-49	+ 2.8	+11.8	−30.0
1949-50	+ 0.8	− 1.8	+35.7
1950-51	−	+ 6.9	−

Sources: Cost-of-Living index as in Table 2:1; money wages from
Indian Labour Gazette, October 1955; profits from Ghosh and
Chaudhri, p. 779. The profits index is extremely limited and covers
mining as well as manufacturing, while the index of average money
earnings covers manufacturing only.

This was so in 10 out of 10 cases in Table 3:3 for the years 1939/40 to 1949/50, and in 9 out of 10 cases for the years 1947/48 to 1957/58 in Table 3:4. However, if we take changes in profits instead of the cost-of-living index, the corresponding figures are three cases out of 10 for 1939/40 to 1949/50, and 3 cases out of 10 between 1947/48 and 1957/58. On the other hand, taking variations in profits in one year as against changes in money wages in the following year, we find that movements of the former do tend to be followed more often than not by movements in the same direction as the latter (in 6 out of 10 cases between 1939/40 and 1949/50 and in 6 out of 9 cases between 1947/48 and 1957/58). It is significant that the lagged relationship of money wage changes with profit changes, even though better than the simultaneous relationship, was nevertheless markedly less pronounced than that between changes in the cost-of-living index and changes in average money wages in the same year.[34]

These same relationships are consistent with the view that institutional forces external to the individual firm or industry, as distinct from a process of competitive bidding for labour by employers, have been the decisive factors in the rise of money wages more or less in line with the cost-of-living; that the prosperity of industry has some effect on the 'ability' of such factors to raise money wages more or less in line with the cost-of-living; but that the institutional forces are influenced in their ability so to raise wages by factors other than industrial prosperity. In particular, the immediate post-war rise of money wages in the face of the continuous decline of profits from 1943/44 to 1946/47, and the low or even negative rate of rise of money wages in the First Five Year Plan, while profits showed relatively large percentage gains, illustrate the limited influence of industrial prosperity on money wage changes.

Thus, we have a relationship in which changes in the direction of movement (as defined) of one variable are directly related to changes in the direction of movement of the other,[35] but not a relationship (as may be seen from inspection) in which the size of the change in one variable is related to the size of the change in the other. This is the kind of non-linear relationship we should expect if money wage changes were indeed linked to changes in the cost of living, not in a mechanistic way, but rather by means of institutional factors, the ability of which to raise money wages in line with the cost of living was bound to vary considerably over a period of years.

TABLE 3:4
India: Percentage Changes in Average Money Wages, the Cost-of-Living Index and Gross Profits in Manufacturing Industry, 1947/48-1957/58

	Average Money Wages	Cost of Living Index	Gross Profits (i)	(ii)	(iii)
1947-48	+18.0	+11.8	+38.5	–	–
1948-49	+10.2	+ 2.8	−31.6	–	–
1949-50	− 3.1	+ 0.8	+14.3	–	–
1950-51	+12.7	+ 4.3	+36.5	+28.1	+32.4
1951-52	+ 4.2	− 2.1	−23.2	−23.2	−34.6
1952-53	+ 3.4	+ 2.9	+11.9	+10.7	+16.5
1953-54	− 0.7	− 4.8	+18.0	+14.1	+20.5
1954-55	− 1.3	− 5.1	+20.8˙	+20.5	+23.4
1955-56	+ 3.3	+ 9.9	+13.8	+ 9.4	+11.4
1956-57	+ 3.2	+ 5.9	− 1.5	− 8.1	−20.0
1957-58	− 3.1	+ 4.4	+ 7.2	+11.2	+13.5

Sources: Cost-of-Living Index as in Table 2:1; average money wages and gross profits from Census of Manufacturing Industry figures given in *Indian Labour Statistics*, 1961 and 1962; gross profits (ii) and (iii) from *Statistical Abstract* 1957-58, 1963, 1964. Gross profits (i) is simply gross surplus as defined in Chapter 2 and here serves as a guide to profit changes in manufacturing industry alone. Gross profits (ii) and (iii) cover tea, coffee and rubber plantations, coal mining and electricity, trading and shipping, as well as manufacturing.

We may now consider rather more closely the cost of living orientation of money wages (Table 3:5), and the institutional pressures behind it. The rise of money wages divides naturally into five main periods. These periods are: the wartime rise of money wages; the end-of-war pause; the post-war rise up to 1949; the irregular movement during the First Five Year Plan and the rather more decisive upward movement of the Second Plan period. With minor variations, these periods correspond almost exactly to the periods into which the movements of the cost-of-living index fall.

As the cost of living rose in a steeply accelerating fashion between 1940 and 1943, the index of money wages accelerated after it, and when the rise of the cost-of-living index practically halted in 1943, the index of money wages decelerated, in its rise. The appearance is not deceptive. The evidence shows that money wages did rise during the war, *in direct response* to the rise in the cost-of-living index, and that the rise was brought about by pressure brought to bear upon employers. Karnick's description of the process is typical of many:

TABLE 3:5
India: Percentage Changes, Average Money Wages and the Cost-of-Living Index, 1939-61

	Money Wages	Cost-of-Living Index
1939-40	+ 5.0	− 3.0
1940-41	+ 5.7	+10.3
1941-42	+16.2	+35.5
1942-42	+39.5	+96.8
1943-44	+12.2	+ 0.4
1944-45	0.0	0.0
1945-46	+ 3.4	+ 6.0
1946-47	+21.1	+13.3
1947-48	+20.2	+11.8
1948-49	+11.8	+ 2.8
1949-50	− 1.8	+ 0.8
1950-51	+ 6.9	+ 4.3
1951-52	+ 8.1	− 2.1
1952-53	− 0.3	+ 2.9
1953-54	− 1.0	− 4.8
1954-55	+ 4.7	− 5.1
1955-56	+ 1.8	+ 9.9
1956-57	+ 5.2	+ 5.9
1957-58	− 1.6	+ 4.4
1958-59	+ 2.4	+ 4.5
1959-60	+ 6.7	+ 2.9
1960-61	+ 6.1	+ 1.4

Sources: Cost-of-Living Index as in Table 2:1; money wages indices from *Indian Labour Gazette*, October 1955, and R.B.I. *Bulletin*, April 1964.

'The first impact of the war on the workers and the Trade Union Movement was the rise in prices and the scarcity of commodities. . . The mercantile community took advantage of war to indulge in large-scale hoarding and profiteering. . . The first to react strongly to this situation were the textile workers of Bombay. They embarked on a general strike in April 1940 demanding an adequate dearness allowance to compensate against the rise in prices. The demand voiced by the textile workers of Bombay became

a general demand of all workers at all places and of all
trades and industries. During the period of the war it
became necessary for workers to place the demand
before the employers and the Government as prices kept on
rising. . . It was only in a few places and a few industries
that machinery was evolved for the automatic adjustment
of wages.'[36]

Moreover, during the war, 'workers in places in which either
legal machinery or collective bargaining has existed have been
able to secure much greater relief than others.'[37]

TABLE 3:6
India: Indicators of Industrial Unrest, 1938-61

	Number of Stoppages	Number of Workers Involved	Number of Man-Days Lost
1938	399	401,075	9,098,708
1939	406	409,075	4,992,795
1940	322	452,539	7,577,281
1941	359	291,054	3,330,503
1942	694	772,653	5,779,965
1943	716	575,088	2,342,287
1944	658	550,015	3,447,306
1945	820	747,530	4,054,499
1946	1629	1,961,948	12,717,762
1947	1811	1,840,784	16,562,666
1948	1259	1,059,120	7,837,173
1949	920	605,457	6,600,395
1950	814	719,883	12,806,704
1951	1071	691,321	3,818,928
1952	963	809,242	3,336,961
1953	772	466,607	3,382,807
1954	840	477,138	3,372,630
1955	1166	527,767	5,697,848
1956	1203	715,130	6,992,040
1957	1630	889,371	6,429,319
1958	1524	928,566	7,797,585
1959	1531	696,616	5,633,148
1960	1583	986,268	6,536,517
1961	1357	511,860	4,918,755

Sources: Karnick, p. 260, and *Indian Labour Statistics*, 1965. A
radical change in coverage of these statistics took place after 1965
owing to reorganisation of states.

Some illustration of the pressure upon employers is afforded by the fact that during the war years the figures for the number of stoppages were almost at peak levels (unknown since 1921). Between 1940 and 1943, the years of the highest rate of price rise, the number of stoppages more than doubled rising from 322 to 716.[38] Even so, Ramaswamy remarks that 'If the number of working days lost in 1943 was not heavy, it was because of the anxiety of the industrialists to avoid disputes which might undermine production and their willingness to meet the demand of labour—as far as possible.'[39]

The pressure on employers was accompanied by an increase of 30 per cent in the number of registered trade unions between 1939/40 and 1944/45 and an increase of 75 per cent in the membership of those submitting returns.[40] These organisational efforts were not in vain. In 1945, for example, rather more than 50 per cent of strikes were successful.[41]

The pause in the rise of money wages between 1943 and 1945 is naturally explained by the pause in the rise of the cost of living index.

When the price rise was resumed in 1945 (to continue until 1951) this was the signal for the most severe trade union pressure to raise money wages. It is important to note that, by 1945, labour costs had already risen higher than prices, compared with the 1939 level. Further, as we have seen, the industrial profits index had declined in every year between 1943 and 1949, with the exception of 1947/48 (Table 3:3). It is thus the more remarkable that, except for the first year and 1949/50, money wages were able to rise at a rate sufficient to raise real wages in every year of this immediate post-war inflationary period. Ability to pay can have had little to do with the rise of money wages.

The forces behind the money wage rise are easily illustrated. After the price stability of 1943/45, the cost-of-living index recommenced its upward course between 1945 and 1946. Accordingly, between 1945 and 1946 alone, the number of stoppages almost doubled, rising from 820 in 1945 to 1,629 in 1946 (Table 3:6), 40 per cent of them being concerned with questions of wages and dearness allowance,[42] and the number of workers involved more than doubled, rising from 747,530 in 1945 to 1,961 in 1946.[43] 1947 was a year in which 'industrial unrest reached unprecedented levels',[44] and in 1948, 'the factors mainly responsible for the rise in the earnings of industrial workers were. . . the upward trend in the cost of living, the intense industrial unrest and the awards of the adjudicators, Industrial Courts, Industrial Tribunals in granting higher wages and allowances in a large number of disputes referred to them during the year.'[45]

The immediate post-war period experienced 'a phenomenal growth in the number of trade unions and their membership',[46] 1947/48 alone witnessing a 50 per cent increase in the number of trade unions over the previous year, which itself witnessed a 75 per cent increase over the year before.[47]

The general slowing up of the price rise after 1948 reduced the rate of rise of money wages after 1948/49, and the period of irregular price movement of 1951 to 1955 was also one of irregular money-wage movement, sufficient, however, to raise real wages somewhat in this period.

The recommencement of a steady rise of the cost-of-living index in 1955/56 saw also the end of the irregular money-wage movement of the interregnum of the 'fifties, and the recommencement of the steady rise of money wages.

The varying rates of rise of money wages in the post-war period may be seen to correspond roughly with the indicators of industrial unrest. The slackening of the rate of rise of money wages in the interregnum of the 'fifties may be seen, from Table 3:6, to correspond to a marked falling-off in this period, compared to the situation prior to 1950, of the number of stoppages and the number of man-days lost through stoppages. Further, all three indicators of pressure to raise money wages only began to climb again with the recommencement of the rise of the cost-of-living index in 1954/55, after which industrial unrest mounted steadily (Table 3:6), although with a falling-off in the later years of the Second Plan.

There is, thus, a rough correlation between the movements of money wages, of the cost-of-living index and of industrial conflict or (particularly during the war) potential conflict), consistent with the view that institutional forces have pushed up money wages in an effort to maintain or raise real wages.

The role of external pressures in raising money wages is perhaps more clearly demonstrated by consideration of their success in achieving their object, namely, the raising or defending of real wage levels. In this connection, we may ask the following questions:

(a)   Why did real wages decline during the wartime inflation up to 1943, and fluctuate indecisively in the inflation of the late 'fifties, but rise in the immediate post-war inflation?

(b) More generally, can any relationship be observed between the rate of rise of prices and the rate of rise of real wages (e.g. should we expect that the faster the price rise, the more difficult it was to raise real wages)?

Taking the first question, the contrast between the decline of real wages in the 1940-43 inflation and the rise of real wages in the immediate post-war inflation is attributable to the fact that the institutional forces which were (at the beginning of the war) operating to raise money wages were relatively 'ill-equipped' to handle the situation; but by the time the immediate post-war inflation got under way in 1946, they had become more fully mobilised. In fact, the 1945-51 period also witnessed a marked mobilisation of the institutional forces operating to raise money wages. In more concrete terms, as we have seen, the immediate post-war inflationary period was marked by an immense upsurge in trade union organisation compared with the immediate pre-war period, in terms both of the numbers of registered trade unions and of their membership. In fact, so great was the contrast post-war with the situation when the war began that the authors of *Labour in India* go so far as to say of the Indian Labour Movement that 'its continuous history as an organised movement dates only from the Second World War'.[48] If to this we add the consideration that the post-war period started with real wages 25 per cent below the 1939 level, itself miserable enough, and if we further bear in mind the accumulated, if not wholly successful, experience of the wartime in raising money wages following a rising cost of living, it is scarcely surprising that there should have been a much more immediate and much more successful response of money wages to the post-war re-emergence of the price rise. The trade unions were also helped by the removal or slackening of such wartime restrictions on trade union activity as the Defence of India Rule 81-A.[49] The considerably superior strength of the post-war upsurge of industrial unrest compared to that of the wartime may be gauged by the indicators of Table 3:6.

It is, perhaps, more surprising that the inflation of the later 1950's should have witnessed a fairly prolonged initial decline in real wages after the real wage rise of the inflation of the 1940's (although it could not, of course, be expected to continue indefinitely without completely destroying the trade unions). In both inflations there was pressure on margins from prime costs. The difference is attributable to a combination of changes within the labour movement,[50] the exhaustion of the post-war political impetus, the gains already achieved in the following period (real wages increased by 26 per cent between 1950 and 1955) and rapid action by the Government, which in the intervening years had played a steadily increasing role in regulating the wage-bargain.[51] This government action was sufficient to prevent a major decline of real wages and so to stave off to some extent the kind of nation-wide industrial conflict which was so successful in raising real wages in the 1940's.[52]

Turning to the second question, and ignoring real wage gains in a situation of declining prices as in the First Plan period (which requires no discussion), we may note that there is no necessary observable connection between the rate of rise of prices and the ability to make real-wage gains. The 1955-59 inflationary years were much milder than the 1946-49 inflationary years, yet the latter were years of substantial real-wage gains, whereas the former were years of real-wage decline. And the reason is not far to seek. The institutional set-up cannot be regarded as a constant framework within which other factors operate. On the contrary, the operation of other factors, specifically the price rise, has had the most profound effect upon the institutional parameters.[53]

We must, however, qualify the general sense of this discussion by saying that, other things being equal, we may safely presume that, at least at the beginning of an inflationary period, before institutional forces operating to raise money wages have become fully mobilised, the faster the rise in the cost-of-living index, the more likely are real wages to decline, if only because it takes time to exert pressure. Emphasis, however, remains on the qualifications to this statement.

Let us briefly recapitulate the basic reasons why institutional forces have been able to raise money wages.

In spite of the advance of working-class organisation we have noted in the period under review, the Indian trade union movement has many serious weaknesses, and may still be compared to an island surrounded by a sea of surplus labour. 'Rival unionism, weak union finances, outside leadership in unions, aversion to industrial conflict, emphasis on legislation and governmental machinery for settlement of disputes,'[54] are some of its typical features.

If, under these circumstances, money wages have risen, it is natural to look at the increasing degree of state intervention in the wage-determination process. Dr. Morris, in his study of the relationship of government and the unions to the changing wages and conditions of the Bombay mill-hands, has highlighted the crucial part played by the state in relation to this, the most important agglomeration of workers in organised industry in the country. 'The policy of the Congress Ministers since 1937', he says, 'has also been to provide to the mill-hands the substantive wage-welfare concessions which in Western countries have traditionally been obtained through unions bargaining collectively with employers. Since that time, every arrangement for keeping step with the rising cost of living, every significant wage increase, every annual bonus, every major standardisation of work relations—has been granted through the agency of the state and as a result of the intervention of the state. No genuine collective bargaining developed before the war; none developed after independence. The role of the state in shaping the wage-welfare status of the mill-hands has been strengthened and made more formal.'[55]

The same pattern holds for the workingclass as a whole. 'For the same reasons the pattern we have described for Bombay has also manifested itself on an India-wide basis. Although few in number compared to the total working population, the industrial workers are by virtue of concentration of force, potentially the country's most powerful political group. Further, they occupy an absolutely critical position in a country dedicated to economic development. Since 1946 an increasingly formal and officially-determined pattern of labour discipline has been established on a national scale. At the same time national government has become the arbiter of the wage-welfare benefits that flow to the labour force.'[56]

To the above analysis we need only add that the exercise by government of its 'wage-welfare' role is itself a function of the independent industrial activity of the working class which we have examined, since such independent activity is itself an indicator of the potential political consequences of governmental inaction.[57]

APPENDIX

Wage Relationships in India

Earnings/prices relationship

Testing the hypothesis that earnings are related to prices over the period 1939-1961 (twenty-three observations) a linear relationship showed evidence of autocorrelation which was removed by taking first differences, giving the equation.

$$\Delta E = 0.325 \Delta p + 12.235$$
$$\quad\quad (0.115) \quad\quad (3.781)$$
$$R^2 = 0.284 \quad\quad D.W. = 1.80$$

Where E is an index of earnings
P is the cost-of-living index.

The coefficient of Δp is significant at the 5 per cent level, and the hypothesis is supported.

Earnings/profits relationship

Testing the hypothesis that earnings are related to profits over the period 1939 to 1958 (twenty observations) a linear relationship showed evidence of autocorrelation. When this was removed by taking first differences, the coefficient of the profit term was not significant at the 5 per cent level. Experience in testing whether earnings were related to profits lagged a period was exactly similar. We conclude that there is no evidence that the level of earnings is affected by the level of profits in India.

Mechanism relating earnings and prices

The hypothesis that trade union activity is stimulated by price rises and that earnings are raised by union activity was tested by use of three union activity variables (1) number of strikes; (2) number of workers involved in strikes; and (3) number of days lost in strikes.

The linear relationship between each of the three union variables and prices over the period 1939-1961 (twenty-three observations) showed evidence of autocorrelation, and when this was removed by first differences, the level of prices was not significant at the 5 per cent level in explaining the level of union activity. The linear relationship between earnings and each of the three union activity variables showed evidence of autocorrelation, and when this was removed by first differences, the level of union activity was not significant at the 5 per cent level in any of three cases in explaining the level of earnings.

However, it was felt that relating *levels* of prices and earnings to *levels* of Union activity was a rather implausible hypothesis. It implies that as the price trend rises, the level of union activity would continually increase. A more likely mechanism would be that the *level* of union activity would be related to the *percentage increase* in prices and that the *percentage increase* in earnings would be related to the *level* of union activity. Earnings and prices were transformed by $100 (X_t - X_{t-1})/X_{t-1}$ to give percentage changes. All the relationships between the level of union activity and percentage change in prices showed evidence of auto-correlation, and when this was removed by first differences, the equations obtained were:

$$\Delta S = \underset{(2.727)}{2.696} \ \Delta \dot{p} + \underset{(62.250)}{55.522}$$

$$R^2 = 0.048 \qquad \text{D.W.} = 1.61$$

$$\Delta W = \underset{(3.580)}{5.398} \ \Delta \dot{p} + \underset{(81.695)}{26.434}$$

$$R^2 = 0.107 \qquad \text{D.W.} = 1.71$$

$$\Delta D = \underset{(38.891)}{54.099} \ \Delta \dot{p} + \underset{(887.620)}{62.983}$$

$$R^2 = 0.092 \qquad \text{D.W.} = 2.32$$

Where S is number of strikes
$\quad\quad$ W is number of workers involved in strikes
$\quad\quad$ D is days lost in strikes
$\quad\quad$ $\dot{p}$ is percentage change in cost-of-living index

Although the coefficient of the price term is not significantly different from zero at the 5 per cent level, it does look as though there is some evidence of a relationship between union activity and the change in prices, though this is only tentatively supported by the results.

Turning to the relationship between percentage change in earnings and the level of union activity variables, again the equations showed evidence of auto-correlation, and when this was removed by first differences, the results were as follows:

$$\Delta \dot{E} = \underset{(0.008)}{0.017} \ \Delta S - \underset{(2.228)}{0.936}$$

$$R^2 = 0.210 \qquad \text{D.W.} = 2.312$$

$$\Delta \dot{E} = \underset{(0.005)}{0.016} \ \Delta W - \underset{(2.018)}{0.396}$$

$$R^2 = 0.329 \qquad \text{D.W.} = 2.059$$

$$\Delta \dot{E} = \underset{(0.0006)}{0.0011} \ \Delta - \underset{(2.237)}{0.028}$$

$$R^2 = 0.172 \qquad \text{D.W.} = 2.11$$

Where $\dot{E}$ is the percentage change in the earnings index. Here, one coefficient, that of workers involved in strikes, is significant at the 5 per cent level, and the coefficient of the other two union activity variables are close to the 5 per cent level. There would appear to be a fair amount of evidence that the rate of change of earnings is affected by the level of union activity.

Conclusions

(1)   There is evidence of a strong relationship between earnings and prices.

(2) There is no evidence of a relationship between earnings and profits or profits lagged.

(3) There is tentative evidence that the link between movements of earnings and prices is made by union activity: the relationship between earnings and union activity being rather more strongly supported by the figures than the relationship between union activity and prices. The results involving the union activity variables are encouraging as a rather simple hypothesis was tested—it is possible that if a more complex hypothesis involving a trend variable of union strength (e.g. degrees of unionisation) and a variable of union activity (e.g. days lost per union member) that the influence of collective bargaining could be more firmly established. A more sophisticated method of removing auto-correlation (e.g. estimating the regressive scheme from the residuals) might confirm the influence of union activity more strongly.

NOTES

1. We are dealing with money wages and not unit labour costs.

2. The total was estimated to be made up on 0.162 million wholly unemployed and 0.076 million seasonally unemployed (Gupta, pp. 40 and 47).

3. G.O.I., Planning Commission, *Second Five Year Plan*, pp. 110-11.

4. Ramaswamy, p. 135.

5. Prest, p. 80.

6. *Indian Labour Gazette*, March 1944, p. 215.

7. Even between 1940 and 1945, when average daily employment on all shifts rose by 52 per cent, the industry reported that the supply of labour was, in general, extremely adequate for its needs (Morris, 1965, p. 61). Dr. Morris adds that 'the sole exception to the general adequacy of labour occurred in 1942 when Japanese military successes caused a brief panicky exodus of people from Bombay' (*ibid.*, p. 61, note 82).

8. It might, of course, be argued that the adequate labour supply was itself the *result* of the wartime rise of money wages, and is thus evidence of the role of market factors in wage determination. However, this interpretation cannot be sustained, since the evidence is clear that *from the beginning of the war* the unskilled labour supply was adequate to the demands made upon it. Moreover, the evidence is that the outflow of labour to the cities was in the main the result of 'push' rather than 'pull' forces. See G.O.I., *Labour Investigation Committee*, p. 8, and G.O.I., *Royal Commission on Labour*, p. 114.

9. U.N., *Processes and Problems of Industrialisation in Underdeveloped Countries*, p. 139.

10. Kotler, p. 284, cited in Myers, p. 47.

11. Myrdal, Vol. II, pp. 966-73.

12. G.O.I., *Labour Investigation Committee*, p. 365.

13. Prest, p. 30.

14. *Ibid.*, p. 73.

15. *Ibid.*, p. 61.

16. *Ibid.*, pp. 30, 61 and 72-3.

17. G.O.I., *Labour Investigation Committee*, p. 101.

18. It is, perhaps, significant that in the Punjab the classes in the towns to suffer most severely from the price rise were 'the lowest classes of menials and servants' (Geren, cited in Prest, p. 45), i.e. those whose wages might be expected to rise most with a general recruiting of un-skilled labour (owing to the possibility of discrimination—see Kaldor, 1959, pp. 292-3) and those whose wages might be expected to rise least if money wages were rising through the agency of trade union and/or government pressure.

19. Mazumdar, p. 332.

20. Morris, 1965, p. 90; G.O.I., *Labour Investigation Committee*, pp. 106-8; Thorner, p. 121.

21. G.O.I., *Labour Investigation Committee*, p. 18.

22. Myers, p. 47. Dr. Myers himself suggests that the data are not strictly comparable 'because extended absence (counted as part of absenteeism in India) would lead to discharge in the United States (and count as part of labour turnover)' (Myers, pp. 47-8). However, Morris has given convincing reasons to believe that the Bombay cotton textile absenteeism rates used by Myers overestimate 'true' absenteeism (Morris, 1965, pp. 92-6).

23. Morris, 1965, p. 90.

24. James, cited in Morris, 1965, p. 90.

25. We are referring here to labour committed to urban industry. How-ever, Morris' evidence shows increasing labour stability for the individual firms as well as for the industry after 1927/8 (Morris, 1965, p. 90, note 23). Of course, this does not relate to all Indian manu-facturing industry.

26. G.O.I., *Royal Commission on Labour*, p. 114.

27. Robinson, p. 49.

28. We are not concerned here with non-efficiency reasons for the rise

in money wages to compensate for a threatened or actual decline in real wages.

29. Dobb, 1956, p. 134. See also the comment that 'unfortunately experience has shown that human beings can adapt themselves, at a low level of vitality and with their power impaired, to an insufficient ration, and scarcely realise that they are underfed' (Ackroyd, pp. 3-4). Moreover, Dr. Sanghvi has pointed out, utilising data collected by the Agriculture Labour Inquiry in India, that there are many levels of subsistence corresponding to degrees of vitality and varying life spans (Sanghvi, p. 87).

30. Even if workers are suffering in the same way, so that substitution of one worker for another would make little or no difference to efficiency, his job would still *appear* to depend on it.

31. 'Inability' from the point of view of the individual employer faced with alert competitors.

32. Kaldor, 1959, p. 293.

33. By analysing the direction of movement in terms of accelerations or decelerations where there is no simple contrast between a fall in one year followed by a rise in the next (or vice versa), we avoid the difficulty arising from the fact that we are dealing with a predominance of rises.

34. The lagged relationship between cost of living changes and money wages was equally pronounced as that between profit changes and money wages in the period 1939/40 to 1949/50. On the other hand, the lagged relationship between cost-of-living changes and money-wage changes for the period 1947/48 to 1957/58 was much less pronounced than that between profit changes and money-wage changes.

35. i.e. a relationship between the direction of the cost-of-living changes and money-wage changes (unlagged)—and also between the direction of profit changes and the direction of money wages (lagged), which is less important than the first.

36. Karnick, pp. 98-9. For similar accounts of the wartime rise of money earnings in organised industry stressing the role of the cost-of-living index and of external pressures on the employers (although with differences of emphasis in some cases), see Ramaswamy, pp. 134-5; G.O.I., *Labour Investigation Committee*, pp. 365-6; Morris, 1955, p. 299.

37. G.O.I., *Labour Investigation Committee*, p. 365.

38. Ramaswamy, p. 135.

39. *Ibid.*, p. 32.

40. G.O.I., *Ministry of Information*, p. 49.

41. *Ibid.*, p. 48.

42. Ramaswamy, p. 135.

43. Karnick, p. 200.

44. *Indian Labour Gazette*, February 1950, p. 548.

45. *Ibid.*

46. *Indian Labour Gazette*, September 1949, p. 15.

47. *Ibid.*, August 1949, pp. 77-8.

48. G.O.I., *Ministry of Information*, p. 45.

49. The communist support of the war effort represented a rather different type of 'restriction' of which the post-war period saw a relaxation. The Communist Party was influential in the leadership of the All-India Trade Union Congress, the only national trade union body at the time, as well as among the rank and file.

50. By the fifties, in place of the unity which had formerly prevailed on a national level, there now existed well-established rival national bodies (*cf.* G.O.I., *Ministry of Information*, p. 50). It is significant that the most important new trade union body, the INTUC (Indian National Trade Union Congress), was set up by the governing Congress Party and was quickly recognised by the Government as the most representative organisation of labour in India. Moreover, this event occurred simultaneously with the 1947 Trades Disputes Act, and it may safely be presumed that both occurred as a policy reaction to the (largely successful) activity in raising money wages on the part of the Communist-supported All-India Trade Union Congress (AITUC).

51. *Cf.* Myers, p. 141. The decisive changes in this respect were the Industrial Disputes Act of 1947 and the Industrial Truce Resolution of the same year. The former embodied a continuation of many of the wartime restrictions on trade unions, empowered the government to refer any dispute to arbitration, and forbade strikes during the period when an award was in force.

52. Giving the General Report of the Coimbatore session of the All-India Trade Union Congress, S.A. Dange, speaking of the period from 1954 to 1960, said: 'The Delhi Tripartite, the minimum wage resolution, the Wage Boards, the Second Pay Commission hoped to stave off a big strike wave, reorganise the wage structure and secure a peaceful growth for industry and the Plan. The hopes were not without foundation. The strike wave did calm down to a certain extent in expectation of the Board's fulfilling some of the claims of the workers, especially on wages. The hopes were not belied, though not fulfilled to expectations' (Dange, pp. 32-3).

53. 'The period following the Second World War of 1939 to 1945 witnessed a spiral of soaring prices and rising wages which gave a further impetus to the trade union movement resulting in a phenomenal

growth of [the number of trade unions and] their membership' *Indian Labour Gazette*, September 1949, p. 151.

54. Thomas, p. 1731.

55. Morris, 1955, pp. 305-6.

56. *Ibid.*, p. 307.

57. The complex and changing inter-relationship between, on the one hand, cost of living changes, unionisation and political changes and, on the other, government, politics and trade unions naturally suggests that the attempts to show unilinear and mechanistic relationships between the degree of unionisation and the rate of change of money wages are bound to fail. Thus, we may expect a positive relationship between price and wage increases, but it would be surprising to find a close one between degree of unionisation and wage levels. *Cf.* Fonseca, Ch. VII.

CHAPTER 4

INFLATION AND INCOME REDISTRIBUTION IN PERU, 1939-58

Unlike India, there was no break in the price rise in Peru, inflation being continuous from 1939 to 1958 (Table 4:1).

TABLE 4:1
Peru: Percentage Changes in the Cost-of-Living Index and the Clothing
Price Index, 1939/40-1957/58[1]

	(a) Cost of Living Index	(b) Clothing Price Index
1939-40	+ 7.0	+ 8.0
1940-41	+ 8.4	+ 8.3
1941-42	+12.9	+19.7
1942-43	+ 9.9	+13.6
1943-44	+13.9	+16.4
1944-45	+11.6	+41.1
1945-46	+ 9.3	+ 9.5
1946-47	+29.0	+24.3
1947-48	+31.0	+17.4
1948-49	+15.1	+15.4
1949-50	+12.1	+ 5.9
1950-51	+10.1	+13.4
1951-52	+ 6.9	+ 5.6
1952-53	+ 9.2	+ 2.8
1953-54	+ 5.4	+ 3.2
1954-55	+ 4.8	+ 3.3
1955-56	+ 5.3	+ 4.1
1956-57	+ 7.4	+ 4.6
1957-58	+ 8.0	+ 7.6

Sources: *R.P. Boletin de Estadistica Peruana*, Year 1, No. 1, 1958, and Year 3, No. 4, 1960.

This continuous price rise may be divided, somewhat arbitrarily, into the following periods:
(i)   the wartime period, 1939/40 to 1944/45, a period of irregular, fairly steep, price rise.[2]

(ii) the immediate post-war period, 1945/46-1948/49, a period of substantially steeper price rise than the last, divided naturally from the succeeding period by the devaluation of November 1949 and the subsequent stabilisation policy.

(iii) the period of the 1950's, 1949/50-1957/58, a period of nearly continuously decelerating price rise until 1954/55 (beginning with a high rate of rise and ending with a not insignificant rise of 5 per cent). After 1954/55 the price rise slowly accelerated.

The clothing price index which we have used as a very tentative guide to the movement of prices of manufactures in general has its movements divided into approximately the same periods,[3] except that the gradual acceleration of prices which continued until 1958 began rather earlier than was the case with the cost-of-living index.

TABLE 4:2[4]

Peru: Share of Labour in Value Added in Six Manufacturing Industries, 1939-45

	Cotton Textiles	Woollen Textiles	Silk	Lace Making	Foot-wear	Beer	Number of Industries where, compared with previous year, the share of labour	
							(i) rose	(ii) fell
1939	30.3	33.5	26.0	27.6	43.5	10.7		
1940	32.8	34.7	38.6	20.2	48.8	10.0	4	2
1941	34.6	32.1	28.0	23.9	42.0	9.5	2	4
1943	14.8	21.6	20.7	18.8	41.0	9.7	1	5
1944	14.3	20.2	20.6	22.3	53.2	10.4	3	3
1945	16.4	27.4	18.4	23.8	52.0	11.7	4	2

Source: *R.P. Estadistica Industrial,* 1945, No. 4, 1946.

As with India, changes in income distribution in the modern manufacturing sector showed no very obviously regular relationship to price movements. Thus during the rapid wartime inflation, the share of labour first rose slightly at the beginning of the war, declined steadily to 1943 and rose thereafter, remaining throughout most of the war years lower than at the beginning of the war[5] (Tables 4:2, 4:3 and 4:4)—and so broadly confirming a wage-lag characterisation of inflation.

TABLE 4:3
Peru: Aggregate Share of Labour in Gross Value Added in Six Peruvian
Manufacturing Industries, 1940-49

Year	Percentages
1940	42.0
1941	40.2
1942	27.6
1943	23.8
1944	24.2
1945	25.1
1946	27.7
1947	30.8
1948	31.6
1949	43.5

Sources: *R.P. Estadistica Industrial,* 1945, 1949, No. 7, 1948, No. 6.

Unlike the case of India, however, the immediate post-war
period witnessed an *acceleration* of the price rise as compared
with the war period, but this did not prevent the direction of
income change corresponding to India's, i.e. a marked shift
in favour of labour in gross value added (Table 4:5).

The period of the 1950's is less easily characterised than
the two earlier periods. The share of labour in value added
first rose from 1949 up to 1952, then declined between 1952

TABLE 4:4[6]
Peru: Share of Labour in Gross Value Added in Registered Industry,
1942-46

Year	Percentages
1942	39.7
1943	35.0
1944	38.8
1945	41.8
1946	43.0

Source: Banco Central de Reserva del Peru, *Renta Nacional del Peru,*
1942-47, 1949.

and 1956 to a level lower than the 1949 percentage, thereafter climbing to reach a peak in 1959 higher than the figure
of any earlier year. Overall, labour's share was higher,
throughout, than at the beginning of this period (Table 4:6)–

TABLE 4:5[7]
Peru: Ratios of Wage Bill to Total Value of Production (*i*) and to
Expenditure on Raw Materials and Fuel (*ii*) in Six Peruvian
Manufacturing Industries. (1940 = 100)

Year	Percentages	
	(*i*)	(*ii*)
1944	66	73
1945	68	76
1946	75	84
1947	79	84
1948	86	98
1949	95	84

Source: *R.P. Estadistica Industrial,* 1945, 1946, 1948, 1949, 1950.

and 1949 was itself a year in which labour's share exceeded that of the five preceding years (Table 4:3).

TABLE 4:6[8]
Peru: Share of Labour in Gross Value Added in Registered Manufacturing
Industry, 1949-59

Year	Percentages
1949	27.1
1950	27.9
1951	28.4
1952	29.7
1953	29.4
1954	27.9
1955	27.0
1956	25.3
1957	28.2
1958	28.8
1959	30.4

Source: Banco Central de Reserva del Peru, *Renta Nacional del Peru,* issues for 1942-49, 1942-51, 1942-53, 1942-54, 1942-55, 1942-56, 1942-57, 1942-58, 1942-59.

Again, regular relationships of changes in income shares to price movements evade us. Thus, labour shares in the years 1949-52 continued to rise with the price increase, although high, decelerating, in contrast to the immediately preceding period, when expanding labour shares coincided with accelerating price increases. As prices continued to decelerate after 1952-53, albeit at a much lower rate of increase, labour shares now declined, and only began to rise again as the price increase accelerated after 1956. Thus, labour shares rose during periods of both price acceleration and deceleration and both rose and fell in different periods experiencing the same rate of price inflation. Moreover, labour shares also fell in the period of slowest price rise (1952-56).

The Peruvian Wartime Inflation 1939/40-1944/45

During the war, the two principal sources of demand pressure in the economy were the surplus on the current trade account and the budget deficits (Table 4:7). Of these, the budget deficits were the most important, although the payments surplus had already assumed importance by 1941. The changed trade position, as in India the result of the war,[9] was itself a part-determinant of the budget deficit insofar as a considerable proportion of government expenditure came under the food subsidy laws. These operated, together with government control of distribution and various other administrative measures, to limit the rise of food prices. Food imports were cut by five-sixths between 1940 and 1942,[10] while the increased industrial activity, associated with import substitution, raised the urban demand for food. The bulk of

TABLE 4:7[12]
Peru: Budget Deficits and Trade Balances, 1939-45 (Millions of Soles)

	Budget Deficit (−) or Surplus (+)	Balance of Payments on Current Account (Positive +, Negative −)
1939	− 44.8	+ 21.7
1940	− 18.2	− 3.8
1941	− 93.0	+ 30.1
1942	−122.8 (−4.2)	+102.8 (+3.5)
1943	− 72.9 (−2.3)	+ 23.6 (+0.7)
1944	−115.0 (−3.0)	− 2.6 (−0.07)
1945	−102.6 (−2.3)	− 3.6 (−0.08)

Sources: Budget deficits from R.P. *Balance of Cuenta General de la Republica,* 1946, 1947 and 1948, and R.P. *Anuario Estadistica,* 1946. For balance of payments figures, Banco Central de Reserva del Peru, *Belanza de Operaciones Internacionales de Peru,* 1938-52, 1954. For G.N.P. Banco Central de Peruana del Peru, *Renta Nacional del Peru,* 1942-44, 1951.

government expenditure was, however, devoted to defence,[11] very little being devoted to productive purposes.

Although the payments surplus contributed less to aggregate demand pressures than did the budget deficits, it nevertheless implied a more than proportionate stimulus to rising prices, insofar as it was partly the result of a decline in the physical volume of imports of those commodities which the domestic economy could least easily provide.[13] This decline in the volume of imports was particularly important after 1941. Declining food imports have already been mentioned. Town dwellers in particular suffered extremely badly from reductions in supplies of imported manufactures (Table 4:8).[14]

TABLE 4:8
Peru: Export and Import Quantum, 1938-46 (1955 = 100)

	Import Quantum	Export Quantum
1938	46	84
1939	41	76
1940	41	66
1941	41	75
1942	32	62
1943	36	57
1944	44	59
1945	44	66
1946	54	79

Source: E.B.L.A., Vol. 5, 1950, *Statistical Supplement,* pp. 42-43.

Investment, both private and public, although adding its pressures to the Peruvian productive system during the war, did not represent a major source of inflationary demand, owing to the physical difficulties of importing capital goods, well-illustrated by the marked post-war change in the proportion of national expenditure devoted to investment (Table 4:9) and by the decline in the proportion of total imports accounted for by machinery and vehicles after 1941 (Table 4:10). Indeed, private investment certainly represented a declining expansionary influence (compared with the pre-war period) at least until 1943 or 1944, when imports began to arrive in greater quantities.

Under these demand pressures, prices during the war rose substantially but not precipitously. The demand pressures were moderated by effective government[15] price and other controls, by the build-up of liquidity and by the positive response of the industrial sector to the demands of import

TABLE 4:9
Peru: Gross Investment as a Proportion of G.N.P., 1942-47

Year	Percentages
1942	6.8
1943	14.5
1944	13.8
1945	11.7
1946	20.5
1947	23.7

Source: *Renta Nacional 1942-49*, 1951, p. 39.

substitution and increased military expenditures (Table 4:11), although this response was limited by the difficulties of importing machinery.[16]

TABLE 4:10
Peru: Machinery and Vehicles as a Proportion of Total Imports by Value, 1940-47

Year	Percentages
1940	20.3
1941	20.8
1942	16.2
1943	14.2
1944	15.0
1945	19.1
1946	21.5
1947	23.2

Source: *Pan American Union*, 1950, p. 213.

On the other hand, up to 1943, the response of the agricultural sector to the diminution of food imports was extremely poor. From that year, vigorous government intervention to improve home food supplies brought about some improvement, but this was partly at the expense of cash crops, mainly for export (Table 4:12), and, as a result of poor communications, it did not prevent food shortages in certain areas.[17]

TABLE 4:11
Peru: Index of Physical Volume of Manufacturing Output, 1940-45
(1940 = 100)

Year	General Index	Cotton Goods	Woollens	Rayon	Foot-wear	Cement	Food-stuffs
1940	100	100	100	100	100	100	100
1941	109	120	103	90	109	122	104
1942	112	129	115	82	122	132	103
1943	121	134	125	91	129	140	114
1944	135	121	119	94	148	174	138
1945	140	127	122	75	172	195	140

Source: *Pan American Union*, 1950, p. 127, from physical output data
as retested in the manufacturing surveys of the Direccion de Industrias.

Further, the drastic reduction of imported supplies of
manufactures was accompanied by steeply-rising prices of such
manufactured imports as did come in, so that prices of
imports rose faster than internal prices. This was a direct
stimulus to a rising price level, and at the same time removed
any curb on rising prices from import competition.

TABLE 4:12
Peru: Indices of the Production of the Principal Agricultural Products,
1938-46 (average 1934-36 = 100)

	General Index	Ginned Cotton	Sugar	Wheat	Rice	Livestock slaughtered in Lima
1938	103.3	106.0	98.9	164.4	102.4	111.0
1939	106.8	101.1	102.6	178.1	105.1	114.2
1940	116.2	102.3	118.0	162.4	144.9	118.3
1941	112.6	88.1	115.4	160.0	185.1	111.4
1942	104.4	86.2	115.6	160.9	119.5	97.3
1943	90.3	70.1	95.9	144.0	138.5	79.0
1944	102.6	83.0	103.4	133.2	188.9	72.6
1945	105.0	87.0	104.3	137.2	193.3	69.9
1946	106.9	88.0	97.3	144.5	229.6	68.0

Source: *Pan American Union*, 1950, p. 236.

Using the data of Tables 4:13, 4:14, and 4:15 as evidence
of the relative movements during the war of prices and prime
costs (wage costs and raw material costs)[18] which have pro-

duced the changes in income distribution recorded in Tables 4:2 and 4:4, we may observe that they suggest the following picture. The shortlived increase in labour's share at the beginning of the war was the result of declining margins, due to both labour and raw material costs rising faster than final prices. The continuous decline of labour's share until 1943/44 was initially due to the fact that raw material costs accelerated relatively to labour costs, while final prices rose in response to rising raw material costs. Although rising final prices were not sufficient to prevent some slight reduction of margins, they exceeded the rise of labour costs sufficiently to reduce the share of labour in value added. After 1941, final

TABLE 4:13

Peru: Data Concerning Prime Cost Expenditures and Total Output Value in Six Peruvian Manufacturing Industries. Aggregate Figures 1939-45

Summary of Results

	(i) Number of industries in which Ratio of Wage Bill to Total Value of Production Rose (+) or Fell (−)	*(ii)* Number of industries in which Ratio of Expenditures on Raw Materials and Fuel to Total Value of Production Rose (+) or Fell (−)	*(iii)* Number of industries in which Ratio of Wage Bill to Expenditures on Raw Materials and Fuel Rose (+) or Fell (−)
1939-40	3+, 3−	4+, 1−, 1S	2+, 4−
1940-41	1+, 5−	5+, 1−	1+, 5−
1941-42	5−, 1S	3+, 3−	6−
1942-43	3+, 3−	3+, 3−	1+, 3−, 2S
1943-44	4+, 2−	1+, 5−	5+, 1S
1944-45	5+, 2−	2+, 4−	4+, 2−

(S signifies stability of ratio)

Source: R.P. *Estadistica Industrial,* 1945, No. 4, 1946.

prices rose very much faster than raw material costs, and rising labour costs lagged even further behind, so that margins improved and the share of labour declined even further.

From 1943/44 raw material costs and final prices rose at about the same rate, while labour costs rose faster than both, so that margins declined and the share of labour in value added again rose. Over the wartime period as a whole,

TABLE 4:14

Peru: Prime Cost Expenditures, Total Output Value and Gross Surplus in Six Peruvian Manufacturing Industries. Aggregate Figures, 1940-49

	(i) Gross Surplus as a Proportion of Total Value of Production (Percentages)	(ii) Ratio of Wage Bill to Total Value of Production (Index)	(iii) Ratio of Expenditure on Raw Materials and Fuel to Total Value of Production (Index)	(iv) Ratio of Wage Bill to Expenditure on Raw Materials and Fuel (Index)
1940	30.1	100	100	100
1941	29.9	92	108	85
1942	40.4	71	95	75
1943	43.7	63	90	70
1944	44.7	66	90	73
1945	44.2	68	89	76
1946	42.5	75	89	84
1947	39.0	79	94	84
1948	40.6	86	88	98
1949	27.0	95	113	84

Sources: R.P. *Estadistica Industrial*, 1945, 1949, No. 7, 1948, No. 6.

labour's share declined, as a result of rising profit margins and the lag of unit labour costs behind raw material costs.

TABLE 4:15[19]

Peru: Prime Cost Expenditures, Total Output Value and Gross Surplus in Registered Manufacturing Industry, 1942-46

	(i) Gross Surplus as a Proportion of Total Value of Production (Percentages)	(ii) Ratio of Wage Bill to Total Value of Production (Index)	(iii) Ratio of Expenditure on Raw Materials and Fuel to Total Value of Production (Index)	(iv) Ratio of Wage Bill to Expenditure on Raw Materials and Fuel (Index)
1942	23.0	100	100	100
1943	24.9	89	100	89
1944	22.1	94	102	92
1945	21.1	100	103	97
1946	19.6	98	106	92

Source: Banco Central de Reserva del Peru, *Renta Nacional del Peru*, 1942-47, 1949.

Wartime was the only period when a relatively clear tendency for labour's share to decrease was observable. As with India, a rising share for labour was the result of declining gross margins.

The rise of gross margins during the war years in Peru seems again to have resulted from almost exactly the same causes as in wartime India. Moreover, the basic mechanism at work seems also to have been the same, i.e. final prices rising independently of any push from rising costs. It is true that such a push does seem to have occurred at the very beginning of the war, in 1939/40 and, perhaps, in 1940/41, but the magnitude of the rise in the share of profits (recorded in Table 4:14) between 1941 and 1943, while prime costs were also rising, clearly indicates that final prices were rising independently of prime costs.[20]

As with India, the crux of the situation was the interruption of trade, owing to the disruption of shipping after 1941. Between 1941 and 1942 the volume of imports, mainly manufactures, declined for the first time since the war began. Similarly, the volume of exports, after a sharp rise between 1940 and 1941, declined continuously until 1943. Accordingly, the increased demands of domestic manufacturing industry for raw materials could be partly met by the enforced reduction in the volume exported. On the other hand, it was difficult to expand industrial capacity, owing to inability to obtain imported capital goods.[21] Again, as with India, the increased demand for manufactures, the sudden dearth of imported manufactures and the difficulty of expanding capacity caused prices of manufactures to rise irrespective of costs, while the modification of normal relative domestic supply availabilities as between agricultural and industrial commodities, owing to changed trade conditions, meant that raw material costs did not rise as fast as prices of manufactures.[22]

The slow rise of unit labour costs (relative to non-labour costs and final prices) underlying the decline in labour's share of prime costs, and partly underlying the rise in gross margins, was the result of government restrictions and a trade union leadership which supported the war effort, and which ensured that independent trade union activity to raise money wages was rather weak. Moreover, the government's own measures to ensure that money wages kept pace with rising living costs only gradually began to operate and take effect. As a result, money wages rose more slowly than final prices during the war. Despite the decline in productivity, the result was that unit labour costs rose more slowly than final prices, and also more slowly than raw material costs.

TABLE 4:16
Peru: Wholesale Prices, Export Prices, Import Prices and Terms of Trade, 1938-45

	Wholesale Price Index of Domestic Commodities Produced for Home Consumption	Import Price Index	Export Price Index	Terms of Trade (Import prices ÷ Export prices)
1939	100	100	100	100
1939	99	108	125	86
1940	104	143	157	91
1941	116	175	171	102
1942	132	185	168	110
1943	155	250	161	155
1944	174	215	197	109
1945	193	248	244	102

Sources: Wholesale price index of home-produced commodities from *Boletin*, 1958. Import and export price indices from *Operaciones Internationales*, 1954.

TABLE 4:17
Peru: Budget Deficits and Trade Balances, 1945/46-1950/51

	Budget Deficit (−) or Surplus (+)	Balance of Payments on Current Account (Positive +, Negative −)
	Millions of Soles	
1945	−143 (−3.2)	− 4 (−0.09)
1946	− 62 (−1.2)	−122 (−2.3)
1947	−126 (−1.9)	−124 (−1.8)
1948	− 54 (−0.6)	− 61 (−0.7)
1949	− 35 (−0.3)	+ 40 (+0.3)
1950	−	− 55 (−0.4)
1951	− 78 (−0.4)	−518 (−2.7)

Percentages of G.N.P. in brackets

Sources: *Renta Nacional del Peru, 1942-49*, and Banco Central de Reserva del Peru, *Renta Nacional del Peru, 1942-55*, 1956. Budget deficit is the balance of total fiscal revenues and expenditures, the latter including public investment.

The Immediate Post-war Inflation, 1945/46 to 1950/51

The immediate   post-war period was one in which the level of budget deficits declined somewhat compared with the later war years, and, after 1945, was largely offset by the import surplus (Table 4:17).[23] On the other hand, with the end of the war and the subsequent improved possibilities of obtaining capital goods, a considerable effort was made mainly by the private sector, to replace and expand capital equipment (Table 4:18).

The doubling of the investment co-efficient between 1945 and 1946, and the continuance of a high co-efficient into 1947, brought about a situation in which '. . . distributed profits and amortisation reserves were insufficient to finance investment on so large a scale, in the years in question.'[24]

The subsequent decline of the investment co-efficient to more moderate levels (at least till 1951) must háve substantially reduced expansionary pressures, particularly since only a limited proportion of private investment was financed by bank credit.[25]

TABLE 4:18
Peru: Gross Total Investment and Gross Private Investment as a
Proportion of Gross Product, 1945-51

	Gross Total Investment as a Percentage of Gross Product	Gross Private Investment as a Percentage of Gross Product
1945	13.3	—
1946	24.7	—
1947	18.7	18.0
1948	14.6	13.2
1949	17.0	15.0
1950	15.7	14.0
1951	23.3	20.0

Source: Banco Central de Reserva del Peru, *Renta Nacional del Peru, 1942-58*, 1960.

It thus appears that the aggregate excess demand, financed in large part by the increased liquidity inherited from the war years,[26] was an important inflationary influence immediately after the war, but not a sustained factor in the price rise.[27] However, the import controls of the period directed the rising volume of imports towards satisfying the needs of capital formation and current production rather than consumption demand, so that various sectoral demand pressures arose which contributed to the price rise between 1947 and 1949.[28]

Increased demand pressures in the economy[29] were partly absorbed by a healthy increase in per capita gross product, approximately 2.5 per cent per annum in this period,[30] an increase to which both the agricultural and industrial sectors contributed substantially.

The import controls which contributed to the maintenance of the increasing rate of production simultaneously restricted imports of manufactured consumer goods, which remained in short supply after the war.[31] Additionally, import prices

TABLE 4:19
Peru: Export and Import Quantum, 1946-51 (1955 = 100)

	Export Quantum	Import Quantum
1946	79	54
1947	58	60
1948	57	53
1949	58	61
1950	69	66
1951	70	94

Source: E.B.L.A., 1960, pp. 42-43.

TABLE 4:20
Peru: Indices of Wholesale Prices, Export Prices, Import Prices and the Terms of Trade, 1945-51 (1945 = 100)

	Wholesale Price Index of Domestically Produced Goods for Home Consumption	Import Price Index	Export Price Index	Terms of Trade (Import Prices ÷ Export Prices)
1945	100	100	100	100
1946	111	127	157	81
1947	157	162	178	91
1948	196	183	172	106
1949	238	376	338	111
1950	293	382	451	85
1951	451	466	580	80

Sources: *Boletin*, 1958. Import and export price indices from *Operaciones Internacionales*, 1954.

received an upward push immediately after the war ended as a result of decontrol of U.S. prices,[32] and subsequently as a result of the devaluations of the sol, which took place between 1947 and 1950.[33]

Resultant increases in living costs (25 per cent of external purchases were consumer goods and the elasticity of demand for imported consumer goods over the period 1948-55 was as high as 2—E.C.L.A., *Survey for 1958,* pp. 146 and 152) were followed by rising wage costs,[34] to which were added the effects on costs of increased indirect taxation. In addition to this, since 20 per cent of external purchases were raw materials (*ibid.,* p. 146), costs to industry were raised directly by rising import prices (Table 4:20). Post-war liquidity of the banking system and increased international reserves easily permitted the financing of industry's increased requirements of working capital.

TABLE 4:21

Peru: Index Numbers of Total Gross Product and Gross Product of Industry and Agriculture at 1955 Prices, 1945-51

	Total Gross Product	Gross Product of Agricultural and Animal Husbandry	Gross Product of Manufacturing
1945	100	100	100
1946	104	102	101
1947	106	103	109
1948	110	108	117
1949	118	116	128
1950	124	121	132
1951	134	128	124

Source: E.C.L.A., *Development of Peru,* 1959, p. 7.

We may again note that what we are concerned with is some kind of mark-up pricing system with a certain degree of flexibility of margins in normal times. This is suggested once more by the oligopolistic structure of the modern manufacturing sector,[35] and by the co-existence of excess capacity and rising prices within it, at certain periods. More direct evidence is provided by the limited degree of margin variability observable in the data of expenditures and receipts of registered industry.

The evidence on margin variability is much the same as in the case of India. It may be seen from Table 4:22 that from 1952 to 1959 margin variability was extremely small, the only year in which even a moderate change occurred being 1956/57, when an extremely bad harvest due to drought affected industry abruptly and severely. The greater degree of downward margin variation between 1949 and 1952 was the result of special circumstances. These special circumstances were the removal of all import restrictions in 1949, and the consequent inflow of competitive imports of manufactures which, occurring at the same time as a marked rise in costs of imported materials (the result of the declining international value of the sol), together with a lesser rise of unit wage costs,[36] enforced a substantial reduction in margins. This was, in other words, a period of once-and-for-all margin adjustment to the change from a protected to an unprotected domestic market.[37]

TABLE 4:22
Peru: Percentage Points Changes in Gross Margins, 1952/53-1958/59

1952-53	+ 0.7
1953-54	− 1.1
1954-55	+ 2.2
1955-56	+ 1.2
1956-57	− 3.9
1957-58	+ 0.6
1958-59	− 1.9

Sources: Banco Central de Reserva del Peru, *Renta Nacional del Peru*, issues for 1942-49, 1942-51, 1942-53, 1942-54, 1942-55, 1942-56, 1942-57, 1942-58, 1942-59.

The same point, i.e. the post-1949 freedom to import foreign manufactures, explains the somewhat greater degree of downward margin variation (in terms of the range of percentage points separating the highest from the lowest value of percentage gross margins during the periods we have taken as normal) to be found in Peru compared with India. Since the latter country's factory industry enjoyed a relatively protected domestic market after the war, it was, naturally, easier in India than in the case of Peru to adjust prices to take account of rising costs.

Similarly, the pre-1949 evidence of Tables 4:14 and 4:15 indicate that it was only with the trade disturbances of 1942 that any violent changes of margins took place, and indeed, unlike India, the immediate post-war years up to 1949 were not years in which a major displacement of conventional margins took place, even though there was undoubtedly severe pressure on them.

Again, as with India, co-existence of excess capacity with rising prices was characteristic of Peruvian factory industry throughout most of the post-war period, and perhaps in the later war years.[38] A continuous improvement in the product/capital ratio between 1945 and 1955 (from 0.33 to 0.41) is estimated by the U.N. to have occurred, attributable largely to improved capacity utilisation, yet, despite this improvement, it was possible to comment in 1959 ('Some Observations on the Industrial Development of Peru', *E.B.L.A.*, Vol. IV, No. 1, March 1959, p. 30) that there was 'plenty of room for utilising more intensively existing capital in manufacturing industry.'

The authors of the U.N. study (E.C.L.A., *Development of Peru*, 1959, p. 5) remark on this point that 'One of the problems which is most frequently held to limit the possibilities of a faster rate of growth is precisely that relating to the shortage of investment resources. . . It is therefore surprising that notwithstanding these difficulties a high proportion of idle capacity is registered.'

Excess capacity has been noted mainly in the industries catering for the home market, the export industries having a good record in this respect. Foreign competition and the establishment of new industries with capacity substantially in excess of current requirements has been the most important factor, together with imperfections in the capital market, lack of technical and skilled workers to permit additional shift working, and difficulties relating to night work. On the whole, supply problems have not been decisive in causing excess capacity,[39] owing to the favourable capacity to import in the 1950's, and the handling of trade controls in the immediate post-war years in such a way as to encourage those imports most conducive to economic activity.[40]

Thus, if relative margin inflexibility, an oligopolistic market structure and the co-existence of excess capacity (which is not principally the result of physical supply bottlenecks) with rising prices throughout much of the period denote some kind of mark-up pricing in the industrial sector, it remains to be considered why prices have been less than fully adjusted to rising prime costs in the immediate post-war years.

The immediate post-war inflationary period up to 1949 was one in which rising labour costs played the active role in reducing gross margins, and although raw material costs rose continuously, it appears from Table 4:14 that as often as not their rate of rise lagged behind that of final prices. In this respect, the general parallelism with India—of rising or falling gross margins consistent with rising or falling ratios of raw material costs relative to final prices—collapses, although it holds for other periods of price movement in Peru.

The more passive role of rising raw material costs in compressing margins in this period was the conjoint result of the excellent agricultural performance, together with the fact that, as previously remarked, the controls over imports were so utilised as to stimulate current production, i.e. they were

TABLE 4:23[41]

Peru: Ratio of Food Prices to the Cost-of-Living Index and the Clothing-Price Index, 1939-58

	(i) Ratio Index of Food Prices to the Cost-of-Living Index	(ii) Ratio Index of Food Prices to Clothing Prices
1939	100	100
1940	102	101
1941	107	106
1942	105	99
1943	108	98
1944	109	96
1945	108	94
1946	107	92
1947	115	103
1948	117	118
1949	118	119
1950	122	129
1951	124	128
1952	125	130
1953	130	141
1954	129	146
1955	130	149
1956	129	150
1957	129	153
1958	129	153

Sources: *Boletin*, 1958 and 1960.

oriented away from consumer goods so that domestic limitations in the supply of raw materials, components and spare parts etc., were alleviated. Rising labour costs, of course, meant rising labour income but since a significant and perhaps increasing proportion of such income was spent on imports and food,[42] this did not automatically provide sufficiently increased demand to offset rising costs.

The *primum mobile* of labour's increasing share of gross value added was thus the extremely fast rise of money wages. This was the result of the important simultaneous political and industrial changes (the post-war changeover to a democratic regime and to a trade union leadership anxious to exert maximum pressure to raise wages) which facilitated the reaction against the restraint and declining living standards of the wartime period.

The Inflation of the Nineteen Fifties, 1949/50 to 1958/59

The inflation of the 1950's was much more moderate than that of the immediate post-war period. One of the principal reasons for this changed situation was the increased flow of imports (Tables 4:19 and 4:25) resulting from the complete

TABLE 4:24
Peru: Budget Deficits and Trade Balances, 1950-58

	Budget Deficit (−) or Surplus (+)	Balance of Payments on Current Account (Positive +, Negative −)
	Millions of Soles	
1950	−	− 55 (−0.4)
1951	− 78 (−0.4)	−518 (−2.8)
1952	−197 (−0.9)	−733 (−3.5)
1953	− 85 (−0.4)	−1093 (−4.8)
1954	− 84 (−0.3)	−231 (−0.9)
1955	− 46 (−0.2)	−725 (−2.5)
1956	−482 (−1.5)	−1784 (−5.6)
1957	−281 (−0.8)	−2707 (−8.0)
1958	−702 (−1.9)	−2482 (−6.7)
	Percentages of G.N.P. in brackets	

Sources: *Renta Nacional, 1942-58; Renta Nacional, 1942-55;* and Banco Central de Reserva del Peru, *Renta Nacional, 1942-51* 1952.

abolition of trade controls in 1949, and financed by a rising volume of exports (Table 4:25), a favourable movement of the terms of trade (Table 4:26) and a large net inflow of foreign capital. The resulting import surplus far outweighed, throughout the whole period, the budgetary deficits, despite increased public investment, which rose as a proportion of both total investment and of G.N.P.[43]

The share of private investment in G.N.P., on the other hand, stayed relatively constant throughout the period. Generally speaking, this constant share of private investment in G.N.P. does not appear to have been financed by credit creation. Private saving was maintained at a high and fairly constant level throughout the period, and in some years even exceeded the sector's rate of investment (Table 4:27). Moreover, 'everything seems to suggest that the expansion of the money supply placed at the disposal of the private sector originated primarily in loans for the financing of current

TABLE 4:25
Peru: Export and Import Quantum, 1950-58

	Export Quantum	Import Quantum
1950	69	66
1951	70	94
1952	77	93
1953	86	99
1954	93	85
1955	100	100
1956	112	118
1957	114	130
1958	120	112

Source: *E.B.L.A.*, 1960, pp. 42-3.

operations, and only secondarily in investment by the sector in question.[44] Furthermore, this was a period when enterprises were increasing their gross savings, especially through depreciation funds.[45] Direct expansionary pressures appear to have been mainly those arising from a marked and increasing degree of dis-saving by households, financed through bank loans for the current operations of the entrepreneurial sector.[46]

The buoyancy given to the economy by rising export earnings, consumer dis-savings and a rising investment co-efficient was matched not only by a rising import surplus but also by an accelerated production response. Per capita gross product between 1950 and 1955 rose by 3.4 per cent per annum compared to 2.5 per cent in the preceding five years, despite the increased population growth after 1950.[47] Moreover, the

TABLE 4:26
Peru: Indices of Wholesale Prices, Export Prices, Import Prices and the Terms of Trade, 1950-58

	Wholesale Price Index of Domestic Commodities Produced for Home Consumption	Import Price Index	Export Price Index	Terms of Trade (Import Prices ÷ Export Prices)
1950	100	100	100	100
1951	98	112	145	77
1952	103	104	95	109
1953	108	112	115	97
1954	126	121	138	88
1955	136	130	137	95
1956	144	130	168	77
1957	157	130	147	88
1958	169	161	164	98

Source: E.C.L.A., *Survey for 1958*, p. 153.

TABLE 4:27
Peru: Gross Private Investment and Total Private Investment as a Proportion of G.N.P., 1950-58 (percentages)

	Gross Private Saving as a Percentage of Gross National Product	Gross Private Investment as a Percentage of Gross National Product
1950	21.8	18.2
1951	22.8	23.4
1952	22.2	21.9
1953	21.0	20.1
1954	23.2	19.9
1955	23.1	20.6
1956	23.4	22.5
1957	21.2	24.4
1958	21.4	22.0

Source: E.C.L.A., *Survey for 1958*, p. 155.

freeing of imports alleviated some of the sectoral bottlenecks of the previous period. It thus appears that 'the pressure of demand made itself felt to some extent in this period, but without, on the whole, determining any considerable price increases' (*ibid.*, p. 154).[48]

Such sectoral pressures did, however, continue to make themselves felt to some extent, and merged with wage increases and rising import costs to maintain the inflationary process as a constant feature of the period. In particular, agriculture lagged (Table 4:28), and, within agriculture, production for domestic consumption fared worse than cash crop production for export.[50] The resultant rise of the proportion of external purchases devoted to food[51] did not completely alleviate the pressure on food prices, so that money wages tended to rise faster than productivity.[52] The continuing rise of import prices added a further stimulus to raise money wages, and, of course, raised internal non-wage

TABLE 4:28[49]

Peru: Index Numbers of Total Gross Product and of Gross Product of Industry and Agriculture at 1955 Prices, 1950-58 (1950 = 100)

	Total Gross Product	Gross Product of Agriculture	Gross Product of Manufacturing
1950	100	100	100
1951	108	106	94
1952	112	108	114
1953	121	117	125
1954	127	121	137
1955	131	121	145
1956	135	118	149
1957	139	119	154
1958	136	117	154

Sources: E.C.L.A., *Development of Peru* (1959), p. 7, and E.C.L.A., *Survey for 1958*, p. 159.

costs directly. Since 1949 no par value had been established for the sol, so that external balance was maintained partly by devaluation in 1951, 1953, 1954 and 1958, at the cost of rises in the price of imports. On the other hand, in 1953 and 1954 international prices of some of Peru's imports, including raw materials and foodstuffs, declined, so that the effect of devaluation were largely offset and the price rise was very moderate.[53]

After 1948, the rise of unit labour costs slowed up relative to both final prices and raw material costs. However, up till 1952, raw material costs rose sufficiently fast to reduce profit margins to such an extent that the share of labour in value added rose. After 1952, final prices tended to rise slightly faster than raw material costs,[54] albeit in a fluctuating fashion, until 1955/56. Unit labour costs tended to lag behind the rise of final prices rather more than did raw material costs, so that between 1952 and 1956 the share of labour in gross value added declined, as a result of both the slight rise in gross profit margins and the relatively slow rise of labour costs compared to raw material costs. From 1956 onwards, profit margins again came under pressure, as both labour and raw material costs tended to rise slightly faster than final prices, and the share of labour in value added again rose. This was entirely the result of declining margins, as

TABLE 4:29

Peru: Prime Cost Expenditures, Total Output Value and Gross Surplus in Registered Manufacturing Industry, 1949-59

	(i) Gross Surplus as a Proportion of Total Value of Production (Percentages)	(ii) Ratio of Wage Bill to Total Value of Production (Index)	(iii) Ratio of Expenditures on Raw Materials and Fuel to Total Value of Production (Index)	(iv) Ratio of Wage Bill to Expenditures on Raw Materials and Fuel (Index)
1949	35.0	100	100	100
1950	31.9	94	107	88
1951	29.0	88	115	77
1952	26.2	85	127	67
1953	26.9	86	119	72
1954	25.8	77	124	62
1955	28.0	79	119	66
1956	29.2	76	117	65
1957	25.3	76	125	61
1958	25.9	81	122	66
1959	24.0	80	126	63

Sources: Banco Central de Reserva del Peru, *Renta Nacional del Peru*, issues for 1942-49, 1942-51, 1942-53, 1942-54, 1942-55, 1942-56, 1942-57, 1942-58, 1942-59.

labour costs rose slightly more slowly than raw material costs. Overall, in most years, the share of labour during the 1950's was higher than at the beginning of this period in 1949 and 1950.

Gross percentage margins thus reverted (after the exceptional post-war period) to the Indian pattern of moving parallel with the ratio of raw material costs to final prices. Why were rising raw material costs able to squeeze gross margins in the early 1950's, 1949-52, in the later 1950's, from 1956 to 1958, and unable to do so in the mid-1950's from 1952 to 1956?

We have already remarked that the years 1949 to 1952 represented a transitional period, in which Peruvian industry's gross margins suffered a downward adjustment as a result of increased import competition. All that need be said further on this point is that, although the inflow of imports also served to improve the supply of raw materials and semi-manufactured goods for industry, international demand pressures were in this period raising the prices of raw materials faster than those of manufactures. The result was that, given the greater competitiveness of foreign manufactures, the pressure of rising costs of domestic raw material prices[55] on gross margins could not be completely relieved by importing a higher proportion of raw materials.

The other period of declining gross margins co-existent with a rising ratio of raw material costs to final prices, i.e. that from 1956 onwards, was one in which, while agricultural production continued its decline which had already set in at an earlier date (Table 4:28), the capacity to import in 1957 and 1958,[56] for the first time since 1949, proved insufficient to cover an adequate volume of purchases of raw materials to cover internal needs. The result was that supply bottle-necks in the agricultural sector[57] could not be eased to the same degree as before, and industrial costs rose in the familiar fashion. Meanwhile, declining agricultural production limited the expansion of the market[58] necessary to absorb fully the increased costs in higher prices.[59]

The post-war rise of gross margins in the 'fifties is susceptible to fairly straightforward explanation. The rise of costs was gentle. Depreciation of the exchange value of the sol was largely offset by declining international prices, as far as imported raw materials were concerned. At the same time, freedom of imports moderated very considerably the rise in the domestic prices of food and raw material costs which might otherwise have been expected from stagnation of agricultural production.[60] As a result, home industry avoided the rise in costs and the diversion of urban expenditure from manufactures to take account of rising food prices which would otherwise have resulted. Accordingly, the increased income resulting from the rapid growth of the rest of the economy outside agriculture, provided a sufficiently easy market environment[61] to permit the gentle rise of costs to be passed on to prices in such a way as to raise gross margins somewhat. Although there were no barriers to imports, the major adjustment to the change from a protected market had already taken place in the previous period, 1949-52, and in the period after 1952 international prices of manufactures were rising steadily, thus 'giving room' for an increase in domestic prices of manufactures sufficient to raise margins.

After 1948 and up to 1956, the rate of rise of money wages, while continuing to be positive, lagged behind the rate of rise of both final prices and raw material costs—and from 1956 the situation was wholly or partly reversed. Changes in labour's share in value added were, thus, the result in the years 1949-56 of varying rates of increase in raw material costs and final prices, with rising labour costs playing rather a neutral role, so that the labour share rose up to 1949 and fell thereafter, although in both periods labour costs lagged. This lag was the result of the repressive policy pursued towards the trade unions by the new government ushered in by the 1948 coup d'état. The substitution of a more democratic regime in 1956 was the occasion for renewed labour activity with the result that rising labour costs again played a more active role in reducing the profit share of value added, principally by squeezing gross margins.

Conclusion: Proximate Determinants of the Income Redistribution in Organised Manufacturing Industry in Peru during Inflation

Inflation was continuous throughout the whole period. During the war the share of labour in gross value added declined. In the immediate post-war years up to 1952, the share of labour in gross value added increased remarkably. During the years 1952 to 1956, labour's share tended to decline slightly, recovering after 1956.

(i) The Wartime Inflation, 1939/40 to 1944/45

The decline in labour's share of gross manufacturing income in organised industry during the war was the result of an almost exactly similar situation to that in wartime India. As with India, both unit labour and raw material costs lagged behind final prices throughout most of the period. As with India, this was the result, with a slight difference of timing, of the disruption of foreign trade, together with the effect of increased wartime expenditures. As with India, the result was, on the one hand, to cut off imports of manufactures and to increase significantly domestic demands on the very small, modern industrial sector; and, on the other hand, to cut off foreign demand for Peru's raw materials. The strain on manufacturing capacity and the inability to increase it sufficiently quickly (owing to the inability to import capital goods) made prices of manufactures more than usually responsive to demand. They therefore rose faster than prices of materials for which foreign demand had been physically cut off. The tendency of prices of domestic manufactures to rise, irrespective of costs, was encouraged by the rise in prices of imported manufactures.

Although productivity declined significantly as a result of wartime supply disruptions and money wages rose under trade union pressure plus some governmental legislative-cum-administrative activity following the rising cost of living, unit labour costs nevertheless rose more slowly than final prices, and also more slowly than raw material costs. This was the result, not only of the slowness with which government measures to adjust money wages began to get under way, but also of the combination of government restrictions on independent trade union activity, plus the generally restrictive activities of the trade union leadership, which supported the war effort. Thus, the share of labour declined as the result of both increasing gross margins and a declining share of labour in total prime costs.

(ii) The Immediate Post-war Inflation, 1945/46 to 1948/49

The extremely rapid acceleration of the rise of money wages immediately after the war pushed up unit labour costs rather faster than the market could absorb at existing margins, so that there was a slight but significant decline in gross margins sufficient to raise labour's share of gross value added.

Raw material costs also rose fairly fast, albeit tending to lag slightly behind rising unit labour costs. The compensatory rise in the demand from rising incomes of wage-earners and agriculturalists associated with rising prime costs was limited by the fairly moderate lag of agricultural production behind the growth of national product. This limited the increase of the marketed surplus and, thus, demand for industrial output (which was rising fairly fast).

Labour's increasing share of value added was, however, most directly the result of the remarkably steep rise of money wages, which could be broadly regarded as the reaction to wartime conditions, a reaction in both industrial and political dimensions. On the one hand, the displacement of the former regime by a more democratic one was an important permissive influence, and on the other, the trade unions, freed from the bonds of wartime cooperation, and anxious to compensate for the wartime decline in living standards, exerted utmost pressure to raise wages.

(iii) The Interregnum, 1949/50 to 1951/52

The continuation of the rise of money wages, together with a marked decline of gross margins, caused labour's share to rise even further in these years. This was despite the fact that the rise of money wages had now become much more moderate than in the preceeding period, owing to restrictions imposed on trade unions by the new Government, following the coup d'état at the end of 1948. Declining margins were attributable to the fact that, with the freeing of imports in 1949, import competition forced Peruvian manufacturers to adjust their margins downwards. The continued rise of unit labour costs, of domestic raw material costs and of import costs contributed to the process of downward margin adjustment.

(iv) The Period of Comparative Stability, 1952/53 to 1955/56

1952 marked the end of the period of adjustment of Peruvian manufacturing industry to conditions of unrestricted entry of imported manufactures into the home market, and to conditions of international instability connected with the Korean war and its repercussions. Henceforth, changes in margins were much smaller.

Margins tended to rise until 1956, since increased demand

more than offset the moderate rise of costs. Of fundamental importance in bringing about this situation was the freeing of imports. This prevented prime costs from rising fast, and limited the diversion of expenditure towards agriculture (particularly by permitting increased food imports) which would otherwise have taken place as a result of lagging agricultural production.

Imports limited the rise of prime costs directly, by alleviating the bottlenecks in the domestic supply of materials, and indirectly, by limiting rises in the prices of food, thus restraining the pressures for increased money wages. The rise of money wages was at the same time hindered by a repressive government trade union policy. Furthermore, the (irregular) increase of productivity which further moderated the rise of unit labour costs was also partly due to the inflow of imports, permitting as it did the alleviation of various supply bottlenecks, and permitting, also, increased capacity utilisation through the favourable demand effects on the industrial sector of rising food imports. While increasing food imports ensured that lagging agriculture did not limit the market for manufactures, the extremely fast rate of growth of the economy as a whole provided a sufficiently rapidly expanding market to permit rising costs to be passed on to prices in such a way as to raise margins slightly.

(v) The Emergence of Instability, 1956/57 to 1957/58

After 1956, the share of labour once again showed a tendency to increase, associated with an increased rate of rise of money wages and declining gross margins. This was because, for the first time since 1949, the capacity to import proved insufficient to alleviate the effects of declining domestic agricultural production, so that the rate of rise of raw material costs speeded up, and the rate of growth of the economy slackened. These disequilibria were exactly coincident with a changeover to a more democratic regime in 1956 which, by giving greater freedom to the trade unions, permitted a simultaneous speeding-up of the rate of rise of money wages. An accelerated rise of prime costs was thus not matched by an equivalent expansion of the market, so that profit margins declined.

NOTES

1. The *cost-of-living index* is an urban working class index with a weight for food of 55 per cent. R.P. *Anuario Estadistica del Peru, 1950,* 1953. The *clothing-price index* is a constituent of the cost-of-living index.

2. The official cost-of-living index may underestimate the wartime rise in prices, owing to the existence of a blackmarket alongside governmental price controls (Pan American Union, 1950, p. 233). On the other hand, government price controls during the war were claimed to have been fairly effective *(ibid.,* p. 233), although this was disputed (Department of Overseas Trade, London, 1944, p. 14). Certainly, the government's control of food distribution during the war *(E.B.L.A.,* February 1962, p. 36), and of imports, should have facilitated price control. Whatever distortion was given to the official cost-of-living index by the existence of controlled prices must have been progressively reduced in the immediate post-war period, when many wartime measures were relaxed. (Pan American Union, 1950, p. 72). They were not completely dropped, and appear to have been actively utilised by the Government up till 1949 (Board of Trade, 1948, p. 17). After 1949, those remaining were largely eliminated by the first half of the 1950's (D.K. Jameson, *Overseas Economic Survey: Economic and Commercial Conditions in Peru,* London, July 1955, p. 51); not however, completely, see U.S. Bureau of Commerce, 1957, p. 8.

3. Partly occasioned, of course, by the fact that it is itself a constituent of the cost-of-living index.

4. Figures are from annual surveys based on questionnaires of a small number of establishments. It is not clear whether or not value added is net of depreciation. The wage bill includes salaries of salary earners.

5. And lower than its share just prior to it. See figures for the share of labour in value added over the years 1938 to 1945 in *Estadistica Industrial, 1945.*

6. Whereas the figures from the various issues of *Estadistica Industrial* come from the Direccion de Industrias of the Ministerio de Fomento y Obras Publicas, those of 'registered industry' from the Banco Central de Reserva del Peru are based on the work of the Servicio de Recursos Humanos del Ministerio del Trabajo. Registered industry may be taken to refer to the manufacturing sector. The wage bill figures of Table 4:4 cover remuneration of workers, salaried employees and a small proportion of working proprietors, family helpers and others. Gross value added includes wage bill as defined and depreciation, but excludes taxes on profits, indirect taxes and interest paid out.

Both the *Estadistica Industrial* statistics and the Registered Industry statistics of the Banco Central de Reserva del Peru suffer from rapidly changing coverage. Unless we have a major discontinuity in the coverage, it is unlikely that this will mean that the figures paint a distorted picture of the direction of income redistribution within manufacturing industry. Such a major discontinuity did not occur during the war years, but did occur between 1946 and 1947, when the number of establishments covered by the Registered Industry surveys rose from 345 to 2,816 and the total wage bill rose from 64,552 thousand soles to 245,834 thousand soles. For this reason, and because a rather odd jump between 1948 and 1949 occurred in the item 'investment charged to current account' (from 194,897 thousand soles to 618,071 thousand soles), which is not easily reconcilable with the parallel changes of other components of total value added, the Registered Industry data has not been used for the immediate post-war period.

Generally speaking, however, there is no specific reason to doubt the general reliability of the Registered Industry data from 1949 onwards (although it appears that the figures for unregistered industry are extremely dubious), which is based on the answers to questionnaires sent to the enterprises, and the treatment of the item 'investments charged to current account' (which is bracketed with, although not part of, depreciation in the *Renta Nacional* tables) appears to have remained unchanged after 1948/49. A difficulty, however, is that there appears to be no specific criterion distinguishing which establishments are eligible for registration. Broadly speaking, Registered Industry covers the more modern, relatively large-scale industry, (E.C.L.A., *Development of Peru*, 1959, pp. 52-53). U.N. estimates for 1955 (*ibid.*, pp. 52, 53 and 301) given below (the *Renta Nacional* figures for registered, unregistered and total manufacturing industry are inconsistent) show that a significant proportion of total manufacturing production and value added is accounted for by unregistered industry, although the productivity of the registered sector is very much greater than that of the unregistered sector.

Judging by the slow increase in the number of establishments covered after 1949, coverage did not change much in the 1950's.

TABLE 4:30
Peru: Some Data on Registered and Unregistered Industry, 1955

| | Thousand soles | |
	Registered Industry	Unregistered Industry
Gross Value of Production	10,037,000	6,000,000
Value Added	3,397,000	2,154,000
Persons Employed	121,510	400,000

Note: Value added is net of depreciation.

7.   See Note 4 above.

8.   Wage bill includes remuneration of the small proportion of working proprietors, family helpers, etc. employed in registered industry. Gross value added includes an item for 'investments charged to current account.' See also Note 4 above.

9.   The disruption of Peru's trade affected both imports and exports, but the decline in the volume of the former was greater than that of the latter (Table 4:8).

10. *E.B.L.A.*, February 1962, p. 56.

11. Nearly 40 per cent of total budgetary expenditures during and after the war were devoted to defence—a somewhat higher proportion than in pre-war years. Moreover, sizeable additional defence expenditures were carried as 'non-budgetary' expenditures, financed from the 300 million soles National Defence Loan from the Central Reserve Bank. Withdrawals from the account were as high as 87 million soles in 1943. 70-80 per cent of Central Bank credits to the government during the war were directed to defence purposes, about 10 per cent to food subsidies (Pan American Union, 1950).

12. Calculations of the *budget deficits* exclude receipts arising from credit operations. All expenditures, whether budgetary or extra-budgetary, covered by taxes, other regular Government revenue, or credit operations were included, but 'to order' accounts were excluded. 'To order' accounts comprise revenues derived from special taxes spent for special purposes. For some estimate of their importance, see Pan American Union (1950) pp. 167-170.

13. Pan American Union, 1950, pp. 171 and 229.

14. Department of Overseas Trade, *Peru: Review of Commercial Conditions*, 1944, pp. 13, 18, 22 and 25.

15. Pan American Union (1950), p. 223. But see Department of Overseas Trade (1944), p. 14, where the price controls were stated to have been effective. The government also controlled food distribution during the war, and imports, too, were controlled (*E.B.L.A.*, February 1962, p. 36).

16. Department of Overseas Trade, 1944, p. 18.

17. On the war-time agricultural response, see Pan American Union, 1950, pp. 14 and 19, and F.A.O. and I.B.R.D., *The Agricultural Development of Peru: Part I, General Report*, 1959, p. 2, Department of Overseas Trade, 1944, p. 19.

18. There is no general index of prices of manufactures in Peru, nor of prices of industrial raw materials. There is, however, a wholesale price index of textile raw materials and, taken in conjunction with the clothing price constituent of the cost-of-living index, we can obtain a very rough guide to the relative movements of prices and raw material costs in the largest manufacturing industry in Peru after food-processing (*ibid.*, p. 53). This is a very rough guide because the two indices are not strictly aligned as regards items covered and weighting. Moreover, the comparison ought to be ideally of the textile raw material prices with prices of yarns and fabrics, not of clothing. This is given in Table 4:31 below, in the form of a ratio of the indices of the wholesale price of textile raw materials over the clothing-price constituent of the cost-of-living index.

It may be observed that the picture given for the relative movements of final prices and raw material costs in textiles is roughly consistent

TABLE 4:31
Peru: Ratio of Wholesale-Price Index of Textile Raw Materials to
Clothing-Price Constituent of the Cost-of-Living Index, 1939-49

	Index
1939	100
1940	107
1941	114
1942	116
1943	114
1944	104
1945	93
1946	106
1947	94
1948	113
1949	154

Source: *Boletin, 1958.* The wholesale price index of textile raw
materials includes three types of cotton and seven types of wool,
including wool for export (Boletin, 1960). This index does not reflect
changes in import prices of raw materials since the cotton and woollen
clothing industry used principally home-produced raw materials
(E.C.L.A., *Development of Peru,* 1959, pp. 28, 67 and 88-89).

TABLE 4:32
Peru: Indices of Production, Wage Bill and Unit Labour Costs in the
Cotton Textile Industry, 1940-45

	(i) Wage Bill	(ii) Production	(iii) Unit Labour Costs (i) ÷ (ii)
1940	100	100	100
1941	124	120	103
1942	152	129	118
1943	167	134	125
1944	174	121	144
1945	226	127	178

Sources: Calculated from figures in Pan American Union (1950),
pp. 126-7. The employment figures have been abstracted from *Anuario
Estadistica, 1946* by the authors of the Pan American Union report.
The authors of *The Peruvian Economy* have calculated the index of
physical volume of output to cotton goods from physical output data
covering nine commodities, as reported in the manufacturing surveys of
the Direccion de Industrias. The items are weighted according to the
total value of output in 1940.

TABLE 4:33
Peru: Ratio of Index of Unit Labour Costs to Index of Clothing-Price
Constituent of the Cost-of-Living Index, 1940-45

	Index
1940	100
1941	95
1942	91
1943	85
1944	84
1945	91

with that given by the expenditure and receipts figures for all modern
manufacturing in the text (Tables 4:13 and 4:15). Similarly, we may
calculate an index of unit labour costs for cotton goods, and compare it
with the clothing-price index, again bearing in mind that the two
indices are not strictly aligned, since the clothing-price index covers
more than cotton goods. Moreover, it is not clear if 'cotton goods'
covers made-up textiles or simply yarn and fabrics. However, on the
assumption that 'value added' in the making-up process is small compared with that in the spinning and weaving processes, and/or that
labour costs rise at about the same rate in making-up as in spinning and
weaving, this will not cause our ratio to be very misleading. The results
are shown in Table 4:32 and 4:33. It may again be observed that the
picture suggested for the textile industry as regards the relative movements of labour costs and final prices during the war is broadly similar
to that suggested for all manufacturing industry by Tables 4:13 and
4:15.

19. Gross surplus is net profit plus depreciation, and is net of taxes on
profits, indirect taxes and interest payments.

20. And the very abrupt and considerable drop in some of the ratios of
expenditure on raw material costs and labour costs to total value of production, recorded in Note 22, for the same year, provide further
evidence that in 1941/42, final prices were rising independently of costs
or a cost-plus pricing system.

21. Department of Overseas Trade, 1944, p. 18.

22. The results summarised in the main text in Table 4:14 are given for
the six industries separately in Table 4:34 (see page 118).

23. Figures for the budget deficit (or surplus) for 1950 are not available
on a basis comparable to those for other years given in Table 4:17. However, figures given by the U.N. show the ordinary budget to have been
in surplus for that year, and also show the public sector to have accounted for a greater absorption of money supply in 1950 (−96.5 millions of
soles) than external factors (−41.1 millions of soles). (See Note 25.)

24. U.N., E.C.L.A., *Economic Survey for Latin America, 1958*, 1959, p. 153.

TABLE 4:34

Peru: Ratios of Wage Bill and Expenditure on Raw Materials to Total Value of Product for Six Industries, 1939-45

	Cotton Textiles			Woollen Textiles			Silk		
	(a)	(b)	(c)	(a)	(b)	(c)	(a)	(b)	(c)
1939	100	100	100	100	100	100	100	100	100
1940	103	109	93	110	96	114	123	111	104
1941	100	119	84	99	97	102	94	113	83
1942	66	94	70	78	85	93	81	112	74
1943	52	88	59	79	80	99	77	104	74
1944	51	86	59	80	72	111	78	103	109
1945	61	80	76	75	103	73	86	83	100

	Lace Making			Footwear			Beer		
	(a)	(b)	(c)	(a)	(b)	(c)	(a)	(b)	(c)
1939	100	100	100	100	100	100	100	100	100
1940	76	100	73	98	113	87	93	103	91
1941	82	103	79	79	119	66	88	100	88
1942	72	124	58	64	126	50	88	106	83
1943	87	102	53	65	132	50	83	116	73
1944	69	116	60	75	141	53	91	112	81
1945	79	109	73	82	133	61	101	114	89

Code:

Column *(a)* is the ratio of the index of wage bill to total value of product.

Column *(b)* is the ratio of the index of expenditure on raw materials and fuel to total value of product.

Column *(c)* is the ratio of the wage bill to total expenditure on raw materials and fuel.

Source: See Note 9.

The high propensity to import of Peruvian consumers, to which we refer below, is likely to have been a potent influence in raising prices of domestically-produced manufactures irrespective of internal costs, the more especially since the prices of these imports which did get in were rising faster than domestic prices (Table 4:16).

25. U.N. calculations show that for the period 1947-51 a maximum of 40 per cent of the increase in industrial assets was financed by bank credit. Moreover, the total of such financing, and thus the proportion, may have been significantly smaller, since the estimate was calculated as a residual, and 'their real total must have been much less because of the inevitable duplications involved in credits between enterprises, particularly those producing intermediate goods and those making finished goods.' U.N., E.C.L.A., *Analysis and Projections of Economic Development, vi, The Industrial Development of Peru*, Mexico, 1959, p. 150.

Since the commercial banks accounted for most of the bank credit advanced to industrial enterprises (*ibid.*, p. 251), the fact that 90 per cent of the commercial bank credits in this period were short-term discounts or advanced on current account (Pan American Union, 1950, p. 232), together with the fact that the banking system in Peru is notably weak in supplying medium and long-term finance (E.C.L.A., *Development of Peru*, 1959, p. 151) provide further confirmation that private industrial investment, at least, did not rely to any important extent on bank credit.

26. *Cf.* Pan American Union, 1950, p. 223, on wartime and post-war liquidity. Post-war liquidity appears to have been a factor in raising mainly investment expenditures. The Banco Central de Reserva (*Renta Nacional, 1942-49*, p. 54) actually records a change from net personal dissavings in 1944 and 1945 to positive personal savings in 1946 and 1947, although it is difficult to know how much reliability can be placed on these figures.

27. E.C.L.A., *Survey for 1958*, p. 154.

28. *Ibid.*, p. 154.

29. Rising export prices and incomes (Table 4:20) exerted a generally stimulating influence on the economy during the years immediately following the war (*Ibid.*, p. 145).

30. *Ibid.*, p. 145.

31. Board of Trade, Peru: *Review of Commercial Conditions*, 1948, p. 15.

32. Pan American Union, 1950, p. 223.

33. In addition to the official sol/dollar rate there was established in 1947 a free market rate which in effect devalued the sol and raised the price of imported goods. The rise in the free rate in 1949 and the exchange reform introducing a single rate in 1950 raised the price of imported goods even further (E.C.L.A., *Survey for 1958*, p. 154).

34. Our limited and tentative indices of productivity in manufacturing industry (Tables 5:7, 5:8) suggest that, while productivity was increasing up to 1949, money wages were increasing much faster (Table 5:1).

35. Examination, for example, of the date on registered establishments for the year 1948, as classified by the value of capital employed, shows that although the number of establishments in the top category of the five categories (i.e. the category in which the establishments using the most capital in value terms are to be found) was only 7.1 per cent of the total number of establishments, they accounted for 65 per cent of the total value added (from data in *Renta Nacional, 1942-49*).

36. Rising wage costs were also partly the result of the devaluation of the sol, which raised prices of imported consumer goods and, thus, the

cost of living.

37. This may also be observed in the sharp drop of gross margins between 1948 and 1949 observable in Table 4:15. This very sharp drop was due partly to the very heavy weight of cotton textiles in the aggregate figures for the six industries, since the market for cotton textiles was particularly vulnerable to foreign compeition.

38. A 'considerable improvement' in the product/capital ratio between 1945 and 1955 was recorded, due largely to improved capacity utilisation—E.C.L.A., *Development of Peru* (1959), p. 65. Since slowing-up of industrial growth associated with the transition to peacetime conditions did not occur till after 1945 (U.N., E.C.L.A., *Economic Survey of Latin America, 1951-52,* p. 173), there would appear to have been some slack in the Peruvian economy before the war ended.

39. Except insofar as supply problems have raised certain costs. However, physical supply problems of the type caused in India by balance of payments difficulties have been generally absent.

40. E.C.L.A., *Development of Peru,* 1959, pp. xxix-xxx and 65.

41. The food and clothing price indices are constituents of the cost-of-living index.

42. Relative food prices were rising somewhat in the period (Table 4:23).

43. *Renta Nacional, 1952-1958,* p. 53.

44. E.C.L.A., *Survey for 1958,* p. 155.

45. *Ibid.,* p. 135.

46. 'Appear', since the personal savings figures, originating from the calculations of the Banco Central de Reserva, and quoted by the U.N., were calculated as a residual and thus contained a considerable margin of error (E.C.L.A., *Survey for 1958,* p. 155).

47. E.C.L.A., *Development of Peru,* 1959, p. 8.

48. Referring to the period up to 1955, the 1958 E.C.L.A., *Survey* notes the small amount of compensatory movements of short-term capital as evidence that 'the sum of private savings and the net inflow of foreign capital largely offset the inflationary possibilities of excess demand.' (p. 146).

49. The figures for gross product of manufacturing industry were adjusted afterwards to bring them into line with the reissued figures for 1955 given in E.C.L.A., *Survey for 1958.*

50. U.N., E.C.L.A., *Survey for 1958,* p. 158.

51. Imported wheat in 1945-50 accounted for 65 per cent of Peru's

supplies and for 70 per cent by 1957. The corresponding percentages for butter are 22 per cent and 50 per cent, for meat 7 per cent and 10 per cent (U.N., E.C.L.A., *Survey for 1958*,p. 152).

52. It is of interest to note that the correlation of rates of price rise with import co-efficients given by data from various Latin American countries shows Peru to have a higher price rise than her import co-efficient would justify. (E.C.L.A., February 1962, p. 45).

53. Royal Institute of International Affairs, *Peru: A Background Note*, London, 1955, p. 13 *et seq.*; E.C.L.A., *Survey for 1953*, p. 104; U.N., E.C.L.A., *Economic Survey of Latin America*, 1954/1955, p. 192; E.C.L.A., *Survey for 1958*, pp. 146 and 157.

54. The ratio of the indices of the wholesale prices of textile raw materials to the clothing-price index is placed alongside the ratio of expenditure on raw materials to total value of production in registered manufacturing industry for the years 1949 to 1959, in Table 4:35. It can be observed that the year-to-year movements of the two ratios agree in all years except 1951-52. On the other hand, taking the war and immediate post-war periods as a whole, the greater year-to-year fluctuations of the wholesale raw material price/clothing price ratio compared with the expenditure/production-value ratio means that the broad periodisation of the two ratios no longer is in agreement. On the whole, the cotton goods cost price figures thus provide some slight confirmation of the expenditure/product value figures for all registered industry.

TABLE 4:35
Peru: Ratio of Wholesale Price Index of Raw Materials to Clothing Price Index, 1949-59 and Ratio of Expenditures on Raw Materials and Fuel to Value of Total Production of Registered Industry, 1949-59

	(i) Ratio of Wholesale Price Index of Raw Materials to Clothing-Price Index 1949-59	(ii) Ratio of Expenditures on Raw Materials and Fuel to Value of Total Production, 1949-59 (Registered Industry)
1949	100	100
1950	112	107
1951	138	115
1952	124	127
1953	121	119
1954	137	124
1955	134	119
1956	132	117
1957	141	125
1958	122	122
1959	131	126

Sources: For column (i), Boletin, 1958 and 1960; for column (ii), see Note 7.

55. Rising domestic prices of domestically-produced materials were themselves partly the result of the same international demand which raised prices of imported raw materials. Exports, about 50 per cent of which in 1950 were agricultural products—mainly coffee, cotton wool and sugar—increased very rapidly in this period, (E.C.L.A., *Survey for 1958*, p. 147). Peruvian agriculture is divided into a modern efficient export sector, the most important crops in which are cotton and sugar, and a very backward subsistence sector. The export sector is in the coastal region, agricultural production, which depends upon irrigation and the availability of fertilisers for which, since the supply is limited, there is competition between the sector of agriculture supplying the home market and that supplying the export market (*cf.* Pan American Union, 1950, p. 32; E.B.L.A., March 1959, p. 25; Ford, 1955, p. 70).

56. The weakening of the prices of, and the general demand for Peru's export commodities in 1957 and 1958 was unmatched by a correspondingly large increase in the net inflow of long-term foreign capital (E.C.L.A., *Survey for 1958*, pp. 147-150).

57. The drought in 1956-57 had particularly severe effects.

58. However, food prices rose scarcely faster than the cost-of-living index or clothing-prices in this period, so that the diversion of urban expenditure to agriculture as a result of rising food prices was not very great (Table 4:23).

59. Aggregate excess demand, which appears to have been characteristic of the economy in the later years of the 1950's, (*cf.* E.C.L.A., *Survey for 1958*, p. 73) could not, of course, have provided a cushion for rising raw material costs since, given the relative supply elasticities of the two sectors (agriculture and industry), the agricultural lag would have ensured that aggregate demand pressure would tend to directly affect production rather than prices in industry, and prices (and thus industrial costs) rather than production in agriculture.

60. The crucial importance of the capacity to import as a factor in permitting margins to increase is shown by the fact that the only year of the period we are considering in which margins declined, i.e. 1953/54, was also the only year in which the gross product or gross income exceeded available goods and services, since 'only in 1954 did the country need excess exports to cover a net outflow on the capital account, in addition to the small export surplus required to finance a deterioration in the terms of trade' (E.C.L.A., *Survey for 1958*, p. 150).

61. This was a period of rising capacity utilisation in manufacturing industry, E.C.L.A., *Development of Peru*, 1959, p. 65.

62. The periodisation of this section is dictated (roughly) by the changing direction of income redistribution, and differs slightly from that adopted in earlier sections.

CHAPTER 5

INFLATION AND THE BEHAVIOUR OF
MONEY WAGES IN PERU, 1939-58

During the war, the reduction of labour's share in value added
was partly a function of the lag of rising money wages behind
both final prices[1] and raw material costs, i.e. a result of both
rising gross margins and a declining share of labour in total
prime costs. In the immediate post-war inflation, on the other
hand, money wages rose extremely swiftly, so that they
exerted active pressure on gross margins, rising faster than
final prices,[2] while raw material costs tended to lag slightly
behind unit labour costs. The post-war rise of money wages
up to 1949 was, thus, the principal active factor in raising
labour's share in gross value added. Between 1949 and 1952
the rate of rise of money wages was rather slower than in the
immediately preceding years, and seems to have lagged
slightly behind final prices.[3] It was still sufficiently fast, however, in conjunction with the active pressure on gross margins
from rising raw material costs, to continue the shift towards
an increased share for labour in gross value added.

Between 1952 and 1956, although money wages rose faster
than final prices (Table 5:1 and 5:6), the overall rise of productivity in these years (Table 5:8) allowed rising unit labour
costs to lag behind final prices (Table 4:29). As a result of
this and the lag of raw material costs behind final prices, the
rate of rise of money wages relative to that of final prices did
not affect the direction of income redistribution (which
moved against labour while money wages rose faster than
prices) although they limited the extent of the shift away
from labour.[4]

After 1956, active pressure on gross margins from rising
raw material costs was accompanied by similar active pressure
from rising money wages, whose rate of rise speeded up compared with the previous period, and was considerably faster
than the price rise (Tables 5:1 and 5:6).

Thus, in all periods, except 1952-56,[5] the rise of money
wages partly determined the direction of income redistribution, was occasionally the active factor in squeezing margins,
sometimes supplemented in a passive way (i.e. money wages

lagged behind final prices) pressure on margins from more rapidly rising raw material costs, and during the war contributed to the rise of gross margins and the decline of labour's share by lagging behind the rise of final prices. What has determined the rate of rise of money wages?

(a) Money Wage Changes—The Labour Market

Again we have to explain the continuous rise of money wages, a rise sufficient to start real wages rising after 1944, so that the 1939 level was passed by 1946, and real wages increased by over 50 per cent in the next twelve years. Does scarcity of labour account for this rise in money wages?

Although there appears in the early 'fifties to have been some shortage of unskilled labour in the coastal agricultural region[6] (employing approximately 32 per cent of the agricultural labour force),[7] in the Amazon jungle region[8] and, at least in some periods, in the mines,[9] and although the emergence of a pronounced visible surplus of urban unskilled labour did not occur till some time in the 'fifties, there does not appear to have been any actual scarcity of unskilled urban labour at any time in our period.

As early as 1940, Dr. Manual Odria, then President, in announcing proposals 'to put an end to the constant migration of unskilled and more or less destitute workers to the larger cities', remarked that 'although unemployment does not exist in Peru on the same scale as in many other highly industrialised countries, it is considered that the employment market needs better organisation.'[10] (my italics). In 1941 the Government was following 'an active public works policy' in order to maintain employment, which it was feared might suffer owing to 'the effects of the war on the export trade to Europe.'[11]

In passing, we may note in this general context that the very occasional remarks[13] about labour shortages in the literature, not specifying agriculture or the mines, never refer specifically to urban unskilled labour shortage, and may well be concerned with the scarcity of skilled and of agricultural labour at a time when the adequacy of unskilled urban labour had not yet become a superfluity.[14]

By 1948, the 'to order' accounts, created mainly for the purpose of relieving unemployment, were as much as 30 per cent of total government expenditures. In 1947, the Ministry

TABLE 5:1[12]
Peru: Indices of Money Wages, Cost of Living and Real Wages, 1939-58

	Cost-of-Living Index	Money Wages	Real Wages
1939	100	100	100
1940	107	108	101
1941	116	110	95
1942	131	114	87
1943	144	131	91
1944	164	140	85
1945	183	167	91
1946	200	204	102
1947	258	276	107
1948	338	389	115
1949	389	511	131
1950	436	549	126
1951	480	599	125
1952	513	632	123
1953	550	665	121
1954	590	791	134
1955	618	846	137
1956	651	857	132
1957	699	1028	147
1958	755	1192	158

of Development and Public Works, which undertakes a large proportion of the projects covered by such accounts, spent 47 million soles (out of a total expenditure of 126 million soles) on projects concerned with the Santa River Development Corporation and public works to absorb unemployment. Expenditures under the 'make work' heading were on highway construction, flood control, irrigation and water supply projects, public welfare projects and miscellaneous public works.[15]

At the beginning of the 1950's, the position in Lima, together with Callao, the industrial centre of Peru (about 80 per cent of all those employed in manufacturing were in this area), could thus be summed up as being one in which there was 'neither a shortage of labour nor a great surplus,'[16] and this statement adequately summarises the position between 1939 and the early 1950's as a whole. 'As nearly as can be determined', remark Harbison and Burgess, 'the growth of the labour force in Lima has kept pace with the expansion of trade and industry.'[17] More generally, it was remarked in

1953 that '. . . insofar as industry is concerned no appreciable difficulty is experienced in meeting demands (for unskilled labour) other than for agriculture, due largely to emigration to the towns. . .'[18]

Throughout the 'fifties, the continued pressure on the land[19] began to transform the adequate urban labour supply into a growing and visible excess supply. By 1955, Indians migrating to Lima were running up against 'already over-crowded slums and a shortage of jobs',[20] and the same situation prevailed in the other large cities of Peru.[21]

As far as the supply of stable labour is concerned, even before urban unemployment had become serious, the Casa Grace study remarked not only that 'employers in Lima have a reasonably plentiful supply of labour', but also that it 'is at least fairly well committed to urban living'[22] and the subsequent surfeit of unskilled labour associated with the spread of slums attests further that, insofar as an adequate stable labour supply depends on disrupting the village nexus, this had been accomplished by the 'fifties, if not before.[23]

We may summarise by saying that the evidence testifies to a reasonably adequate supply of unskilled labour to urban industry from 1939 up to circa 1950, after which the adequacy developed into a surplus some time during the first half of the 'fifties. The supply of stable labour does not appear to have been a major problem at any time.

As with India, we must, in considering the possibility that labour scarcity has been directly responsible for the rise of money wages, decide whether or not the very adequacy of the urban unskilled labour supply we have noted above was the result of the rise of urban money wages.

In the 'fifties there can be little doubt that it was not simply the relative attractions of urban earnings compared with rural earnings which was responsible for the influx to the towns, but also the absolute deterioration in the employment opportunities offered by subsistence agriculture.

'The establishment and expansion of industry, commerce and other similar activities, mainly concentrated as they were in these urban centres had undoubtedly constituted an inducement to rural workers attracted by the hope of better wages. Probably, however, this internal population shift had not been entirely due to requirements deriving directly from the growth of the activities mentioned; the fact that the opportunities of productive employment in the rural areas were insufficient to absorb the local population increment, and even fortuitous phenomena such as the drought which recently scourged southern Peru, may have carried the urbanisation further than was justified by the economic growth of the centres in question.'[24]

The fact that the Government in 1940 was proposing measures designed to lessen the flow of destitute workers into the cities suggests that the lack of employment opportunities in agriculture has been an operative force throughout the whole period in pushing workers into the towns, as distinct from the pull of urban employers raising money wages to attract rural labour.

If, then, the relatively high urban earnings cannot alone explain the inflow to the towns,[25] we should further bear in mind that even if it could, it would not follow that this was the motive force behind the rise of urban earnings. This consideration is strengthened if we take account of the fact that, both historically and contemporaneously, employers have used means other than raising money wages in order to obtain the quantity and kind of labour they needed. For example, 'as labour requirements increase the company is planning to arrange for bus transportation for the additional workers required from Lima' (to the textile mill at Vitarto—8 miles away).[26]

Naturally, since unskilled urban labour has been adequate after 1939, it is difficult to acquire much evidence as to what urban employers might have done had there been a shortage of unskilled labour.[27] What is known, however, is what employers have done in the face of continuing scarcity of skilled labour, and the record makes no mention of raising money wages.

'Skilled workers must be trained on the job', report Harbison and Burgess (1954), p. 63.[28] Further, 'the most critical shortage is in trained technicians, engineers and persons with administrative skills. The educational resources to develop this kind of personnel, while growing. . . are still limited; and the large enterprises are still forced either to bring in such personnel from outside the country or to invest a considerable amount of money and energy.' (p. 63).[29]

Moreover, as with India, there is no evidence that the relative scarcity of skilled[30] compared with unskilled has brought about the kind of widening skill differentials to be expected if labour market conditions were decisive in bringing about the rise of money wages.[31] The non-widening of skill margins was largely the result of government policy favouring lower paid grades in periods of inflation.[32]

To conclude, our summary of the urban labour supply relative to demand and of the likely reactions of employers to labour shortage precludes almost certainly any general explanation of the rise of money wages during most of the 1950's in terms of labour scarcity, and suggests that labour scarcity is unlikely to have been the major force raising money wages prior to 1950.[33]

(b) Money Wage Changes—The Product Market

Turning to the role of industrial prosperity as a determinant in the money wage rise, we find that, again as with India, variations in the rate of change of gross surplus were more often than not followed by variations in the rate of change of money wages in the following year *in the same direction.*[34] Once more, this is what we should expect if the relationship between money wage changes and prosperity was not a purely economic one,[35] but one dependent, at least partly, on the operation of institutional factors the effectiveness of whose influence varied considerably in both the short and long term.

TABLE 5:2

Peru: Percentage Changes in the Cost-of-Living Index and Average Money Wages: Gross Surplus and Gross Margins in Six Manufacturing Industries Aggregated, 1940-49

	Average Money[36] Wages	Cost-of-Living Index	Gross Surplus
1940/41	+ 2.0	+ 8.4	+ 26.4
1941/42	+ 3.9	+12.9	+103.6
1942/43	+14.2	+ 9.9	+ 40.8
1943/44	+ 7.4	+13.9	+ 13.8
1944/45	+19.2	+11.6	+ 16.0
1945/46	+21.9	+ 9.3	+ 8.5
1946/47	+43.2	+29.0	+ 24.9
1947/48	+40.6	+31.0	+ 42.4
1948/49	+31.4	+15.1	− 16.0

Sources: R.P. *Estadistica Industrial, 1945,* No. 1, 1948, No. 6.

TABLE 5:3[37]
Peru: Percentage Changes in the Cost-of-Living Index and Average
Money Wages, Gross Surplus in Registered Manufacturing Industry,
1949-58

	Average Money Wages	Cost-of-Living Index	Gross Surplus
1949/50	+ 7.4	+12.1	+ 9.9
1950/51	+ 9.1	+10.1	+17.6
1951/52	+ 5.5	+ 6.9	− 6.8
1952/53	+ 5.2	+ 9.2	+19.1
1953/54	+18.9	+ 5.4	+26.5
1954/55	+ 7.0	+ 4.8	+ 9.6
1955/56	+ 1.3	+ 5.3	+24.0
1956/57	+20.0	+ 7.4	+16.5
1957/58	+16.0	+ 8.0	− 5.1
1958/59	+15.7	−	+14.0

(c) Money Wage Changes and Institutional Pressures

Consideration of Table 5:4 enables us to divide the rise of
money wages into an irregularly accelerating rise up to 1944
(characterising 1939/40 as an exceptional year); a tremend-
ously accelerated rate of rise thereafter until 1948/49, which
reached its peak acceleration in 1946/47; a much reduced
rate of rise between 1948/49 and 1955/56, although with the
average rate of rise remaining high in most years; and an
accelerated rate of rise in the later 'fifties.

With the exception of the marked acceleration of the rate
of rise of money wages between 1944 and 1946, which coincided with a deceleration in the cost-of-living index from the
peak year rise of 1943/44, these divisions may be seen to
correspond roughly to those of the movement of the cost-of-
living index.

Looking at the same phenomenon from a slightly different
angle, we may also observe from Table 5:4 that, in twelve
out of the seventeen years,[38] an acceleration or deceleration
of the rate of price rise in one year was followed by an
acceleration or deceleration of the rate of rise of money
wages in the succeeding year.

The general correspondence of the broad changes in money
wages with those of the cost-of-living index are due to a
combination of governmental and industrial pressures on
employers, and is itself evidence of this.

TABLE 5:4[39]
Peru: Annual Percentage Changes in Money Wages and the Cost-of-Living
Index, 1939-58

	Average Money Wages	Cost-of-Living Index
1939/40	+ 8.0	+ 7.0
1940/41	+ 1.9	+ 8.4
1941/42	+ 3.6	+12.9
1942/43	+14.9	+ 9.9
1943/44	+ 6.9	+13.9
1944/45	+19.3	+11.6
1945/46	+22.2	+ 9.3
1946/47	+35.3	+29.0
1947/48	+41.0	+31.0
1948/49	+31.4	+15.1
1949/50	+ 7.4	+12.1
1950/51	+ 9.1	+10.1
1951/52	+ 5.5	+ 6.9
1952/53	+ 5.2	+ 9.2
1953/54	+18.9	+ 5.4
1954/55	+ 7.0	+ 4.8
1955/56	+ 1.3	+ 5.3
1956/57	+20.0	+ 7.4
1957/58	+16.0	+ 8.0

For the period 1939 to 1950, more concrete evidence of
the role of institutional forces is to be found in the relationship between government wage decrees and regulations of one
sort or another and the rate of rise of money wages.

Concerning government action and the rate of rise of
money wages, without entering into details, it is necessary to
note that 'regulatory activities of the Government relating to
labour and social insurance are of great importance. Labour
legislation deals with every phase of the labour-management
relationship.'[40] These activities have included widespread
intervention in the processes of money-wage determination in
a fashion relating the movement of money wages to that of
the cost-of-living index.[41] The very scale of Government
intervention suggests that it will have had a major effect on
the rate of rise of money wages in general. In 1954, legislative
provision concerning wages covered the following industries,
persons and occupations: wage-earning women and young
persons; textile workers (cotton and woollen textiles);
workers in bakeries, salaried employees throughout the
Republic; workers in the printing trade; workers in the cloth-

ing industry; workers in knitted goods factories; workers in silk textile factories; workers in specific undertakings such as the Compagnie des Mines de Huaron, the International Petroleum Company and the Cerro de Pasco Corporation; Indian workers in the Sierra; homeworkers; dockworkers, and seamen; professional motor vehicle drivers in public and private service; and workers in the building industry.[42] Moreover, there is elaborate provision, legislative, administrative and judicial, to ensure that government regulations on wages are enforced.[43]

Consideration of Tables 5:5 and 5:1 together shows more concretely how increasing government intervention has affected the rate of rise of money wages. Table 5:5 lists the various government measures relating to wages and salaries for the period 1939-50 which, although not absolutely complete, is generally representative.[44]

From it, we may observe that the immediate post-war period marked a considerable increase in the scale of government intervention in the determination of the level of money wages, compared with the wartime period: that the earlier war years, i.e. 1939-42, although generally lacking the degree of direct government regulation of the level of money wages and salaries typical of the later years, nevertheless witnessed a considerable amount of government activity strengthening and developing the machinery for dealing with money wages; and that the years of the most marked Government wage regulation were 1944, 1945, 1947 and 1950, with 1946 and 1948 as the years of least government regulation in the post-war period.

Thus, the gradual acceleration of the rate of rise of money wages during the war corresponds to the gradual 'mobilisation' i.e. building up and strengthening, of the machinery for dealing with money wages; and the speeding up of the rate of rise of money wages during the post-war period corresponds to an intensification of Government activity affecting wage-levels in the post-war period. The years of most frequent and/ or widespread Government wage activity were years of acceleration of the general rate of rise of money wages in manufacturing industry,[45] with the post-war years of negligible Government intervention, 1946 and 1948 being years of deceleration of the rate of rise of money wages.

The general rate of rise of money wages appears, thus, to have been directly influenced by Government intervention.

TABLE 5:5
Peru: Chronological Table of Government Actions Affecting the
Money Wages of Labour, 1939-50

	Date	Governmental Action
1939	— September	Two laws enacted to regulate wages in industry and commerce during the war, with the Department of Supervision of Social Welfare set up to carry out its provisions.
1940	— 9 March	Tripartite Committee on Employment in Textile Industry set up to help eliminate causes of labour disputes.
	— 5 September	Act bringing Ships Officers within scope of Legislation for Protection of Salaried Employees.
1941		System of labour judges and labour appeal courts set up affecting wage-earners only.
(M)	—13 January	Decree concerning minimum wages in textile industry.
(M)	—19 February	Decree concerning minimum wages in textile industry.
	—16 April	Special labour court set up to hear appeals against decisions of magistrates in individual labour disputes.
1942	—11 January	Decree preventing reduction of wages and salaries.
	— 6 January	Court for Collective Disputes set up.
1943	— 7 October	Decree concerning minimum wages in woollen, silk and cotton industries in Provinces of Lima and Callao.
(M)	—24 October	Decree concerning minimum wages in textile industry of Lima and Callao.
1944 (M)	—20 July	Decree concerning minimum rates for salary earners (male and female) in Lima and Callao.
(M)	—14 October	Decree concerning minimum rates for male and female salary earners in certain provinces.
(M)**		Decree granting salary increases in private employment throughout the Republic.
(M)*	—27 November	Decree granting salary increases in provinces of Lima and Callao.
1945 (M)*	— 3 February	Decree concerning minimum rates for male and female salary earners in various provinces other than Lima and Callao.

	* — 2 March	Decree concerning wages in construction industry in Lima and Callao.
	(M)** —31 March	Decree concerning salary increases for private employees (in some provinces) in agriculture, stock breeding, fishing, extractive industries, transport and communications, banks and insurance companies, constructional industries, manufacturing undertakings employing five or more salaried employees and commercial undertakings employing more than ten salaried employees.
1946	* —14 July	Decree concerning minimum wages in construction industry in Lima, Callao and Balnearias.
1947		Tripartite Commission set up to report on minimum salary for non-manual workers.
	(M)* —14 August	Decrees concerning salary increases in private employment in Lima and Callao.
	* —10 September	Decree concerning minimum wages for stevedores in Callao.
	(M)* —16 October	Decree granting salary increases in private employment in Lima and Callao.
	* —30 December	Decree concerning minimum wages for construction industry in Lima, Callao and Balnearias.
1948 (M)	— 4 September	Decree granting salary increases to private employees in Lima and Callao.
	* —29 December	Decree fixing minimum wages for bank employees throughout country and prescribing wage increases.
1949 (M)*	— 3 September	Decree granting monthly bonus to private employees.
	(M)** —11 November	20 per cent increase decreed in wages and salaries in respect of first 400 gold soles of monthly earnings throughout Republic.
	(M)* —16 November	20 per cent increase in wages and salaries in respect of first 400 gold soles of monthly earnings throughout Republic decreed.
1950 (M)*	— 6 March	Decree prescribing salary increases for bank employees throughout country.
	(M)** —11 October	Salary earners and wage earners granted 25 per cent bonus in respect of first 400 soles of remuneration.
	(M)* —17 October	As above.
	(M)* —18 October	As above.

Code: *   Single asterisk denotes action directly affecting amounts of money wages or salaries paid (apart from preventing deductions).

      **   Double asterisk denotes the same as single asterisk, except that the action is particularly important.

     (M) Denotes that the action covers wholly or partly workers or employees in manufacturing, and relates to action characterised by an asterisk.

Sources: From information given in I.L.O., *Yearbook, 1939-40,* Geneva, 1940, p. 190; and 'Industrial Relations: Government, Employer, Worker Collaboration in Peru', *I.L.R.,* Vol. XLVII, No. 3, March 1943, p. 368; *Industrial and Labour Information;* Conditions of Work: Peruvian Ships Officers brought within the scope of Legislation for the Protection of Salaried Employees', *I.L.R.,* Vol. XLIII, No. 1, January 1941, p. 104; I.L.O., *Labour Courts in Latin America,* Geneva, 1949, p. 29; I.L.O., *Minimum Wages* (1954), pp. 150-153; 'Industrial Relations: The Introduction of Arbitration in Peru', *I.L.R.,* Vol. XLV, No. 6, June 1942, p. 7; and Torre, 1954, pp. 83-84. The principal source is I.L.O., *Minimum Wages,* 1954.

Note: The decrees of the 11 and 16 November 1949 relate to the same measure, as do those of 11 October, 17 October and 18 November 1950. It is not clear whether the same is the case with the decrees of 13 January and 14 February 1941, of the 14 August, 10 September and 16 October 1947, and of the 11 and 16 November 1949.

The possibility that the correlation of Government wage activity with the rate of rise of money wages is due to a reversal of the causal link we have postulated (i.e. that the general rate of rise of money wages has, in its variations, intensified Governmental activity in the attempt to prevent certain categories of workers falling behind the general level) must be discounted. Quite apart from the widespread nature of government intervention, which would in any case militate against such an interpretation, in the cases in which government has deliberately set out to narrow the differentials between the lower and the higher paid workers, it has done so in the context of raising money wages of all workers, both lower and higher paid.[46]

The variations in independent trade union activity showed much the same pattern over time as those of government wage activity, partly because the degree of trade union activity was very much dependent on government policy towards trade unions, and partly because trade union activity influenced, albeit not always in a simple fashion, the degree of government wage-fixing activity and intervention generally.

Alexander sums up the wartime period as being one in which, 'although the Prado regime kept in force the laws of its predecessors which provided for police surveillance of trade unions and political meetings, the government did allow a considerable development of the trade union movement.'[47] The limited nature of the wartime trade union activity was in part due to the then Communist leadership of the trade union movement (renewed in 1945) which was cooperating with the government, discouraging strikes and encouraging production during the war period, in accordance with its international anti-fascist policy.[48]

The end of the war saw simultaneously the end to this policy, a changeover to the much more liberal regime of President Bustamante and the beginnings of the post-war upsurge of industrial unrest.

'The general inflationary trend which has commenced during the war has continued. Strikes in all branches of trade have been a feature of Peru's post-war economy and these have been followed by increases in wages and salaries. . .'[49]

'During all this time [President Bustamante's election to his 1948 overthrow], prices were rising, wages were going up and strikes were frequent. The unions are becoming stronger and more compact.'[50]

That the coup d'état towards the end of 1948 established a more conservative regime which was always, although in varying degrees, hostile to trade unions and which controlled them fairly closely,[51] as far as possible, did not alter the basic pressures operating to raise money wages, either in the governmental or in the industrial field, although no doubt it altered their intensity and/or *modus operandi*. In fact, we have already seen that the first two years of the regime were marked by major government intervention to raise money wages and such government intervention to raise money wages in the post-1950 period.[52]

'President Odria at first adopted a very vigorous policy towards labour and trade union organisation, but in August 1952 he publicly stated his belief in the right of labour to strike in defence of its interests. There at once followed a series of strikes in which the workers were for the most part successful in obtaining their objectives. A railway strike in the autumn of 1952 threatened to paralyse the country, and since then there has been a tightening of controls on trade union activities.'[53]

It was only with the 1956 election in Peru, which brought

in a somewhat less authoritarian regime, that trade unions were able to operate more freely, albeit under many restrictions.

Even when trade unions have been working under severe restrictions, it has been possible for them to exert continuing pressures through governmental wage-fixing machinery. Thus, 'there are no legislative provisions stating expressly that workers shall have a say in the fixing of minimum wages, unless they are members of tripartite committees, consisting of employers, workers and government representatives set up by the government to study the exact position in the undertakings concerned and to make recommendations.

'It is very common, on the other hand, for workers to participate indirectly in the fixing of minimum wages through petitions or claims submitted to the authorities through their various organisations.

'It can be seen from the above that the strongest workers' organisations are likely to receive the greatest benefits under the system of wage fixing in Peru, and this indeed has been borne out by practice.'[54]

Possibly the best summary of the pressure on employers tending to encourage governmental wage-raising activity is that given by Burgess and Harbison in discussing the labour problems of Casa Grace.

'Perhaps the most perplexing problem for Casa Grace in its textile operations is its dealing with unions and government officials who are concerned with labour relations matters. Collective bargaining relations with unions affect labour costs in two ways: the unions exert continuous pressure for wage increases and other concessions and they tend to limit substantially certain very important managerial functions.

'Unions are now quite common in most of Lima's industries, and they are particularly strong among the textile workers and dock workers at the nearby Port of Callao. The government's objective is to prevent the politically ambitious from using the unions as a base for any attempt to undermine the Republic. Since the revolution of 1948, which brought the present government into power, unions outside the Lima area have been closely watched by the government in order to prevent infiltration of political elements who might capture them and organise a counter-revolution. No doubt for the same reasons, the government has attempted to discourage the formation of centrally-controlled national industrial unions, although in the Lima area it openly tolerates a federation of local textile unions, and would appear not only to tolerate but probably to encourage unionisation.

'The government is also in a position to pass civil judgment on disputes between labour and management. Any unsettled grievances between the management of a local plant and a local union is usually brought by the latter to the Ministry of Labour, where, by a process of mediation, or compulsory arbitration, settlements are finally reached. *In the opinion of neutral observers, the government appears to feel that unions should be allowed to make economic gains but not engage in political activities. In short, although the government has the power to control the unions, it respects and being aware of their potential power seeks to enlist their loyalty by supporting, if not sometimes anticipating their demands.'* (pp. 67-68, my italics).

As was the case in India, the forces raising money wages experienced varying degrees of success at different times, and a brief consideration of the reasons for this should throw some light on the operation of these forces.

The movement of real wages falls very naturally into a major and continuous decline from 1939-44; a major and continuous rise from 1945-49, relative stability in the first half of the 1950's, and a rise in the second half of the 1950's.

As with India, the relative success in obtaining real-wage gains in different periods bore no direct relation to the price rise. In the five years 1939-44, during which the average annual price rise was 10.4 per cent, real wages declined by 25 per cent. In the following five years, 1945-49, real wages rose by 63 per cent and the average annual rate of price rise was 19.2 per cent. Similarly, the five years from 1951 to 1955 saw real wages rise by only 5.2 per cent, whereas the following 3 years saw real wages rise by 12.1 per cent, although the average price rise was almost exactly the same in the two periods, i.e. about 7 per cent.

The questions we ask then are: Why were the institutional forces raising money wages unable to prevent a decline in real wages during the war, and yet were able to achieve a substantial gain in real wages in the subsequent period up to 1950, a period of very high rate of price rise, higher than during any other period?[55] Why were they able in the following period up to 1955 to achieve only a very small real-wage gain, although the average rate of price rise was much less than in the preceding period, and was in general decelerating? Why were they able to enforce, in the following three years, a rather more considerable real wage rise than in the preceding five years, although prices were accelerating again?

Our previous discussion has suggested some of the main developments affecting the relative success of efforts to raise real wages. The relatively small degree of governmental wage activity, combined with partially voluntary restriction of union activities during the war, explains the real-wage decline during the war. The post-war rise of real wages is explained, up to 1948, by the post-war upsurge of union activity, gaining impetus from the real wage decline of the previous period, favourable political conditions compared with those of the war years, and a substantially increased degree of government intervention in raising money wages, the trade union, political and governmental activities being interconnected. Major wage regulations by the new government in the following two years, 1949 and 1950 (perhaps intended to make more acceptable the new restrictions on trade unions) were responsible for the continuation of the immediate post-war successes.

The relative stagnation of real wages in the following period up to 1956 is directly attributable to the restrictions on trade unions in this period, together with the exhaustion of the post-war upsurge at a level of real wages substantially higher than in 1939.

Steadily rising real wages after 1956 were associated with a much higher average rate of rise of average money wages[56] than in the previous four years, and this resulted from the substantially greater degree of trade union activity permitted by the new government resulting from the 1956 general election.

Governmental and trade union pressures have thus acted in an interrelated fashion to raise money wages more or less in line with the rising cost of living, and the 'more or less' has depended upon the varying extent to which trade unions have been free to act or have, by their existence and activity, induced the government to act with more or less vigour in the wage-fixing field.

APPENDIX

Wage Relationships in Peru

Earnings/price relationship

The hypothesis that prices affect earnings was tested over the period 1939 to 1958 (twenty observations). The linear relationship showed evidence of auto-correlation, and when this was removed by taking first differences, the relationship was as follows.

$$\Delta E = 2.015 \quad \Delta p \quad - 13.235$$
$$ (0.462) (18.205)$$
$$R^2 = 0.536 \quad D.W. = 1.79$$

Where E is an index of money wages
P is a cost-of-living index.

The coefficient of price is significant at the 5 per cent level, and the relationship between earnings and prices is confirmed.

Earnings/profit relationship

The linear relationships between earnings and profits and earnings and profits lagged a period were estimated from data for the period 1940-1958 (nineteen observations). The relationships showed evidence of auto-correlation and, when this was removed by taking first differences, neither profits term was significant.

Conclusion

There is evidence that prices affect earnings, but no evidence that profits affect earnings.

TABLE 5:6

Peru: Indices of Average Money Earnings, Prices of Manufactures and
Ratio of Average Money Earnings to Clothing-Price Index, 1939-59

	Average Money Earnings	Clothing-Price Index	Ratio of Money Wages over Clothing-Price Index
1939	100	100	100
1940	108	108	100
1941	110	117	94
1942	114	140	81
1943	131	159	82
1944	140	185	76
1945	167	211	79
1946	204	231	88
1947	276	287	96
1948	389	337	115
1949	511	387	132
1950	549	411	134
1951	599	466	129
1952	632	492	128
1953	665	506	131
1954	791	522	152
1955	846	539	157
1956	857	561	153
1957	1028	589	175
1958	1192	634	188
1959	1379	670	206

Sources: Boletin, 1958 and 1960 for money earnings. Sources of
Tables 5:1 for clothing-price index.

Money wages lagged behind at least the clothing-price index—Table
5:6—(we have no general price index of manufactures), and the cost-of-
living index (Table 5:1). Figures for individual industries (Table 5:7)
indicate declining labour productivity during the war, so that the lag of
the rise of total wage bill behind that of total product value (Table 4:34)
must signify, insofar as these figures are representative of manufacturing
industry as a whole, a general lag of money wages behind final prices.

TABLE 5:7

Peru: Indices of Productivity for Four Manufacturing Industries, 1940-45

	Cotton	Wool	Rayon	Footwear
1940	100	100	100	100
1941	100	99	74	84
1942	95	100	74	90
1943	99	109	75	90
1944	90	90	85	74
1945	89	97	61	89

Source: Calculated from data on employment and production in Pan
American Union, 1950, pp. 126-7.

2. Again, money wages rose faster than the clothing-price index and the cost-of-living index, at least. Moreover, our limited figures for the period, in Table 5:8 (the productivity figures start at 1947, owing to the change in the coverage of the employment data from that date), show productivity to have been rising up to 1949, so that the money wage—induced rise of unit labour costs—must have been moderated. Accordingly, the faster rise of total wage bill than of total value of the product shown in Table 4:5 must have involved money wages in manufacturing industry generally rising faster than final prices.

TABLE 5:8

Peru: Indices of Production, Employment and Productivity, in Manufacturing Industry, 1947-59

	Production	Employment	Productivity
1947	100	100	100
1948	107	101	106
1949	118	101	117
1950	121	106	114
1951	132	117	113
1952	138	126	110
1953	153	141	109
1954	166	138	120
1955	176	136	129
1956	181	153	118
1957	197	171	115
1958	191	145	132
1959	206	154	134

Sources: From *Renta Nacional*, issues as sources for Table 4:6 for employment figures of registered industry. Production figures from Instituto Nacional de Planificación, *Estimaciones del Producto e Ingreso Real*, 1965. The manufacturing index is that of value added at 1960 market prices.

The production figures have a wider coverage than the employment figures, which almost certainly implies that the rate of rise of productivity is underestimated, or the rate of decline is exaggerated (since employment figures are for registered industry, whereas production figures are for all industry, in which production has almost certainly grown more slowly than in the modern sector alone). Clearly, the most that can be hoped for (and that without great confidence) is that the productivity index will indicate the direction of change of productivity over a period of years. That the index does in fact give a correct picture of the direction of productivity change is suggested by the fact that, when it is taken together with the evidence of money wages and price indices, the resulting picture of relative movements of unit labour costs and final prices is the same as that given by the evidence of total receipts and wage bill of registered industry (this point is discussed in this and the next note), at least so far as the direction of these relative movements is concerned.

3. Again, Tables 5:1 and 5:6 show that prices of clothing and the cost-of-living index rose faster than money wages. Moreover, since productivity was declining in these years (Table 5:8), the lag of total wage bill behind total product value shown in Table 4:29 must imply a slower rate of rise of money wages than final prices generally.

4. It could be argued that the slower rate of rise of money wages in this, compared with the previous period, contributed to the decline of labour's share.

5. From 1952 onwards, the share in total prime costs of the wage bill did not vary a great deal, so that there was no marked effect on the share of labour in gross value added resulting from this kind of change.

The point made in the text is simply that, had other things remained the same, the actually achieved rate of rise of money wages relative to the price rise would have raised labour's share in gross value added (and insofar as they did not, this does not seem to have been the direct result of the rise of money wages *in this period.* However, this increase in real wages must have helped ease the demand situation. In analysing a total situation some distinctions can be used only in an approximate fashion). Since other things did not remain the same, and the actually achieved rate of rise of money wages relative to final prices failed to raise labour's share, which instead declined, money wage changes may be said to have failed to influence the direction of income redistribution.

6. B. de la Torre, 1953, p. 81, and Pan Ameircan Union, 1950, p. 14.

7. Pan American Union, 1950, p. 1.

8. *Ibid.,* p. 7.

9. See Board of Trade, 1948, p. 16, referring to the immediate postwar period. However, the shortage may be of skilled labour alone. The context is ambiguous.

10. From the message transmitted by Dr. Prado at the opening of the Legislature, 28 July 1940, as reported in *I.L.R.,* November 1940, p. 249.

11. *I.L.R.,* February 1941, p. 206.

12. For cost-of-living index as for Table 4:1. For index of money wages, Pan American Union, 1950, pp. 126-127; *Anuario Estadistica del Peru,* 1950; *Estadistica Industrial,* issues for 1945, 1948 and 1949, and *Renta Nacional,* issues listed for Table 4:6, excepting that for 1942-49. Figures are of annual average earnings, and cover salary earners as well as manual workers. The money wage index of Table 5:1 is rather a hybrid, covering both wage and salary earners, and incorporating data from four different sources.

For the years 1940-59 the data were from the same sources as were used for the industrial income shares calculations of Section III, i.e. data from *Estadistica Industrial,* up to 1949, and from *Renta Nacional* from 1949 to 1959. In fact, the *Renta Nacional* figures pre-1949 were in sufficient agreement with the *Estadistica Industrial* figures (at least for annual percentage changes of average earnings) to justify this procedure (Table 5:9). For 1939-40, figures of wage bill (including salary earners) and employment for seven industries (cotton, wool, rayon, beer, footwear, foodstuffs and tobacco) given in Pan American Union, 1950, p. 126, were aggregated and averaged. From figures covering 'principal establishments' given in *Anuario Estadistica*, 1950, an alternative aggregate estimate for the 1939-40 percentage change was calculated. The two were averaged to obtain the movement of the index between 1939 and 1940. These latter figures from 'principal establishments' are not used elsewhere, as they are believed to be very unreliable.

TABLE 5:9

Peru: Average Percentage Changes in Average Earnings, 1942/43-1948/49
(percentage estimates from two sources)

	(i) Renta Nacional	*(ii)* Estadistica Industrial
1942/43	+11	+14
1943/44	+ 9	+ 6
1944/45	+22	+19
1945/46	+29	+22
1946/47	+29	+36
1947/48	+26	+41
1948/49	+29	+31

TABLE 5:10

Peru: Percentage Changes in Total Average Earnings of Manual Workers
and Average Earnings of Salaried Employees in Registered Industry,
1947-59

	Total Average Earnings	Average Earnings —Manual Workers	Average Earnings —Salaried Employees
1947/48	+26.2	+39.8	+13.1
1948/49	+28.9	+31.5	+15.4
1949/50	+ 7.4	+13.0	+ 3.0
1950/51	+ 9.1	+13.3	+ 3.9
1951/52	+ 5.5	+ 6.3	+ 1.9
1952/53	+ 5.2	+ 6.6	+ 3.7
1953/54	+18.9	+21.4	+11.5
1954/55	+ 7.0	+ 8.5	+ 3.2
1955/56	+ 1.3	+ 0.0	+ 6.9
1956/57	+20.0	+20.9	+ 9.9
1957/58	+16.0	+16.9	+12.3
1958/59	+15.7	+15.2	+16.1

Source: *Renta Nacional.*

The money wage index as given in Table 5:1 covers both wage and salary earners, since we are concerned with the share of wages and salaries jointly in value added. The discussion in the text, on the other hand, relates mainly to manual workers. Insofar as the textual discussion is related to the table, this presents no problem since, as can be seen in Table 5:10 below, the index of average earnings of manual workers changes in much the same way as that for manual workers and salary earners combined—in other words, changes in average earnings of manual workers dominate changes in manual plus non-manual average earnings statistically. Further, with wage rates of manual workers strongly cost-of-living oriented, and consequent tendencies for the wage/salary differential to be narrowed (observable in the figures of Table 5:10) owing to differential social pressures, earnings of salaried employees are likely to rise by a series of adjustments to the rise of unskilled rates, when the rise of skilled rates is not a direct function of the rising cost of living. Thus, our discussion of manual workers' average earnings also deals with total earnings in more than a simple statistical sense.

13. *Cf.* '. . . a large increase in wages (in part caused by shortage of labour). . .' and 'Shortage of labour especially of technicians may limit expansion of industry or retard the projected development of agriculture', Dept. of Overseas Trade, 1944, pp. 22 and 23; see also the Director General's *Report on the Fourth Conference of American States Members of the I.L.O.*, 1949, Report 1, Geneva 1951, which notes (p. 104) complaints of general manpower shortage in Peru, while on the previous page remarking upon a noticeable increase in unemployment, due partly to difficulties of obtaining necessary capital, machinery, other equipment and technical assistance.

14. The general state of full employment in the economy noted by the Pan American Union report, 1950, pp. 14 and 203, is consistent with underemployment in agriculture, and throughout the economy as a whole, on which it indeed remarks (pp. 62 and 197), and with an adequate supply of urban labour.

15. Pan American Union, 1950, pp. 169-170.

16. Burgess and Harbison, 1954, p. 69.

17. *Ibid.*

18. Peru, *Statistical and Economic Review*, 1953, p. 81.

19. Pan American Union, 1950, p. 62; and E.C.L.A., *Development of Peru*, 1959, pp. 4-5.

20. Royal Institute of International Affairs, 1955, p. 1.

21. B. de la Torre, Peru, *Statistical and Economic Review*, 1958, pp. 127 and 148.

22. Burgess and Harbison, 1954, p. 63.

23. On the subject of labour turnover in general, the literature is

remarkably silent. It does not appear to have been such a major urban phenomenon as was the case in Turkey.

24. E.C.L.A., *Development of Peru*, 1959, pp. 4-5.

25. Besides economic compulsion, other compulsions have been at work. 'There is also an involuntary movement to Lima from the provinces of large numbers of conscripts for their prescribed period of military service. Under Peruvian law all males completing high school are exempt from conscription, so that the majority of these in the army are of Indian stock, from the highlands where there are few schools. Having been exposed to life in the Lima area these conscripts tend to remain in the urban centre after their term of military service is completed. Thus the . . . military system. . . . functions as an important channel for new labour into the Lima market', Harbison and Burgess, 1954, p. 66.

26. *Ibid.*, p. 66.

27. The literature is again silent on this point.

28. *Ibid.*, pp. 62-3. Casa Grace, employing about 2000-2500 of the 120,000 Lima factory workers, most of whom are in textile factories, is 'an important but certainly not dominating influence (in the Lima/Callao area) tending to conform to economic and social patterns rather than to set them. In Lima, therefore, the labour and manpower problems of Casa Grace are not very different from those faced by other large foreign or domestically-owned enterprises.'

29. *Ibid.*, p. 63. See also B. de la Torre, Peru, *Statistical and Economic Review*, 1953, p. 81. It is of interest to note that the major historical changes in the Peruvian labour market have been closely linked to administrative or compulsory methods of obtaining labour. The Spanish conquest saw the enslavement of the Indian population to work the silver mines. The resulting disastrous effects on agriculture brought about the introduction in the sixteenth century of African slaves for work on commercial crops, particularly sugar-cane; and the abolition of slavery brought about the importation of cheap Chinese labour from the middle of the nineteenth century. The subsequent importation of Japanese labour was a continuation of the same process. *Cf.* Pan American Union, 1950, pp. 34 and 67.

30. See also B. de la Torre, Peru, *Statistical and Economic Review*, 1958, p. 8.

31. It should be borne in mind that the supply of unskilled labour was in growing excess of the demand throughout the post-war years.

32. For statements of government wage policy favouring the lower paid see 'Conditions of Work: Wage and Salary Increases in Peru', *I.L.R.*, Vol. LII, No. 1, July 1945, pp. 80-81; *Methods of Remuneration of Salaried Employees,* Third Item on the Agenda, Fifth Conference of American States Members of the I.L.O., Rio de Janeiro, April 1952, Geneva, 1952, pp. 59-61.

33. Some limited data on the skilled/unskilled differentials are given in Tables 5:11, 5:12, 5:13 and 5:14 below. These figures cover only four industries, and show no clear tendency for either a widening or a narrowing of skill margins between 1941 and 1950.

However, at the risk of placing too heavy an interpretative strain on this very limited data we may, with the help of Table 5:14 speculate a little on some of the characteristics of wage determination in Peru suggested by these figures.

The general picture is easily summarised. Eliminating the two two-year periods, 1942-44 and 1947-49 (which, in their results, cancel one another out), money-wage rates of unskilled workers rose faster than those of skilled workers in three out of five years.

It is worth noting that only in 1945/46 and 1944/45 do all industries taken separately not correspond to the pattern shown in Table 5:14. In other words, the method we have used appears to give us a fairly representative picture.

TABLE 5:11
Peru: Mechanical Engineering. Ratio of Wage Rates of Unskilled Labourers to Wage Rates of Fitters and Tuners, Iron Workers, Pattern Workers

	(i) Fitters and Turners	(ii) Iron Workers	(iii) Pattern Workers
1941	100	100	100
1942	86	91	91
1943	—	—	—
1944	111	74	119
1945	113	89	73
1946	100	79	78
1947	110	88	98
1948	—	—	—
1949	81	70	—
1950	136	103	129

Sources: Figures in I.L.O., *Yearbook of Labour Statistics, 1942*, Montreal, 1943; I.L.O., *Yearbook of Labour Statistics, 1943-44*, Montreal, 1945; I.L.O., *Yearbook of Labour Statistics, 1945-46*, Geneva, 1947; I.L.O., *Yearbook of Labour Statistics, 1947-48*, Geneva, 1949; I.L.O., *Yearbook of Labour Statistics, 1949-50*, Geneva, 1951; I.L.O., *Yearbook of Statistics, 1951-52*, Geneva, 1952.

Notes: (1) Figures relate to October of the year in question.
(2) Adult male wage-earners.
(3) The figures are for Lima, except in 1950, when they refer to the whole country. This is likely to mean that the 1950 index figure underestimates the change over 1949, since Lima rates are likely to be higher than in other parts of the Republic.

TABLE 5:12
Peru: Printing and Publishing etc. Ratio of Wage Rates of Unskilled
Labourers to Wage Rates of Hand Compositors, Machine Compositors,
Machine Minders, Book Binders

	(i) Hand Compositors	(ii) Machine Compositors	(iii) Machine Minders	(iv) Book Binders
1941	100	100	100	100
1942	100	86	83	88
1943	—	—	—	—
1944	111	99	109	109
1945	93	62	67	61
1946	105	60	78	78
1947	113	67	91	76
1948	—	—	—	—
1949	81	53	67	69
1950	106	74	84	79

Source: As for Table 5:11.

TABLE 5:13
Peru: Electric Light and Power. Ratio of Wage Rates of Unskilled
Labourers to Wage Rates of Electrical Fitters

	Electrical Fitters
1941	100
1942	82
1943	—
1944	98
1945	102
1946	112
1947	113
1948	—
1949	97
1950	104

Source: As for Table 5:11.

Taken over the period as a whole, i.e. comparing 1950 with the 1941
levels, the money wage rates of unskilled ended up at a higher level
than those of skilled in two out of four industries, i.e. in mechanical

TABLE 5:14

Peru: Building. Ratio of Wage Rates of Unskilled Labourers to Wage Rates of Plumbers, Bricklayers and Masons, Structural Iron Workers, Concrete Workers, Carpenters and Joiners and Capstan Fitters

	(i) Plumbers	(ii) Bricklayers and Masons	(iii) Structural Iron Workers	(iv) Concrete Workers	(v) Carpenters and Joiners	(vi) Painters	(vii) Capstan Fitters
1941	100	100	100	100	100	100	100
1942	113	66	56	94	88	104	89
1943	–	–	–	–	–	–	–
1944	–	78	85	109	108	128	85
1945	–	80	89	109	112	–	71
1946	100	73	70	70	102	113	67
1947	104	72	75	70	96	109	75
1948	–	–	–	–	–	–	–
1949	–	–	–	–	–	–	–
1950	97	80	76	80	106	106	56

Sources and Notes: As for Table 5.11.

TABLE 5:15

Peru: Summary Analysis of Comparative Rates of Rise of Skilled and Unskilled Money-Wage Rates, 1941-50

Relative Movement

(+ signifies wage rates of unskilled rising faster than rates of skilled;

— signifies rates of unskilled rising slower than rates of skilled;

S signifies equality of rates of rise unskilled and skilled)

1941-42	—
1942-44	+
1944-45	+
1945-46	S
1947-49	—
1949-50	+

Sources: Tables 5:11, 5:12, 5:13, 5:14.

Note: The results above were produced by finding out whether or not in a given year or period of years a majority of the skilled occupations within the industry have their wage rates rising faster than those of the unskilled workers within the industry, and in turn finding out whether or not a majority of industries have the same phenomenon. If so, we record a plus (+), and so on. These are the only industries for which we can obtain such a comparison.

engineering and in electric light and power. This suggests that the external forces able to raise unskilled money wages faster than skilled were, to an extent reversed, at least as regards their effect on narrowing differentials. This does not affect the argument that in most years institutional factors were the principal determinant of the money wage rise, since some re-establishment of differentials by the employers and/ or the skilled workers is to be expected, and may be regarded as a secondary consequence of the institutional forces at work raising money wages of unskilled workers in the first place.

Incidentally, Table 5:15 provides additional evidence of the role of government in money wage determination, since the only years or periods of years in which skilled money wage rates rose faster than unskilled were either those in which government intervention was just beginning (1941-42) or was unusually negligible, i.e. 1945-46 and 1947-48 (in the 1947-49 period).

Further, a rough correlation can be seen to exist between the accelration of the rise of the cost-of-living index and the relatively faster rate of rise of money wages of unskilled workers, and the deceleration of the rise of the cost-of-living index and the relatively slower rate of rise of money wages of unskilled workers, if Table 5:1 and 5:15 are compared. The exceptional years in this respect are 1941-42 and 1949-50, which are explained by the relative government inaction in 1942 and the considerable scale of government action in 1949. All this is what we should expect if institutional forces were raising money wages in response to a rising cost of living.

34. In 4 out of 7 cases from 1940 to 1949 and in 6 out of 8 cases from 1949 to 1959 (Tables 5:3 and 5:4).

35. *Cf.* L.A. Dicks-Mireaux, *Cost of Demand Inflation?* Woolwich Economic Papers, No. 6, London, 1965, p. 13, on the 'semi-political' effects of variations in industrial prosperity on the rise of money wages.

36. *Average money wages* includes earnings of salaried workers.

37. Sources: as for Tables 5:1 and 4:6. Notes as for 36 above.

38. The exceptional years were again mainly grouped in the immediate post-war period, i.e. at that period the result of money wages accelerating irrespective of a decelerating cost-of-living index (see Table 5:4).

39. Sources and Notes: as for Table 5:1.

40. U.S. Foreign Commerce Bureau, *Investment in Peru: Basic Information*, 1957, p. 9; *cf.* B. de la Torre, 1953, p. 81 *et seq.*

41. See, on governmental activities relating wage changes to changes in the cost of living, I.L.O., *Minimum Wages in Latin America*, 1954, pp. 148-9; *I.L.R.* July 1954, pp. 80-81; I.L.O. Fifth Conference, 1952, p. 59; S.E. Harris (ed.) *Economic Problems of Latin America*, 1944, p.2.

42. I.L.O., *Minimum Wages*, 1954, p. 149.

43. *Ibid.*, pp. 150-152.

44. The bulk of the information of Table 5:5 comes from I.L.O., *Minimum Wages*, 1954, the list of decrees and orders which, relating to money wages and salaries, are stated to be 'among the most significant' since 1941. The remaining information comes almost exclusively from I.L.O. sources. In the case of direct government intervention affecting the amounts of salaries and wages paid, all alternative sources suggest the list is fairly complete. We are thus fairly safe in assuming it to be representative from 1941 onwards.

45. With one exception, 1950, and this exception is explained by the very high rate of rise of money wages and the very great degree of government intervention in 1949.

46. *Cf.* I.L.O., *Minimum Wages*, 1954, pp. 152-3; I.L.O., *Fifth Conference*, 1952, pp. 59-61; and B. de la Torre, 1953, pp. 82-83.

47. R.J. Alexander, p. 230.

48. *Ibid.*

49. Board of Trade, 1948, p. 17.

50. A.H. McDonald, p. 366.

51. *Cf.* I.L.O. *Fourth Conference of American States Members of the I.L.O. 1949, Record of Proceedings*, pp. 210-211; I.L.O., *Fifth Conference*, p. 128; Harbison and Burgess, p. 67; Royal Institute of International Affairs, 1955, p. 3; Ford, pp. 1 and 9.

52. The government issued decrees on money wages also in 1951, 1952 and 1953 (I.L.O., *Minimum Wages*, 1954, p. 153).

53. Royal Institute of International Affairs, 1955, p. 3.

54. I.L.O., *Minimum Wages*, 1954, p. 150.

55. 'Periods' in this context are those of the movement of real wages, not of prices.

56. The association of rising real wages with an accelerated price rise both in the immediate post-war inflation and after 1956, besides being the result of the mobilisation of institutional forces affecting money wages arising from the price rise itself, was also the result of a feedback effect which resulted from the influence of rising money wages in sustaining the price rises. In this connection, we may recall that, in both periods, rising money wages were an active factor in exerting pressure on gross margins in manufacturing—this quite apart from demand effects of the money wage rise (real wages appear to have risen faster than productivity in both these periods—see Tables 5:1 and 5:8).

CHAPTER 6

INFLATION IN TURKEY
Inflation and Income Redistribution, 1939-58

Lacking a nation-wide cost-of-living index, we have averaged those for Istanbul and Ankara, the two main industrial centres, to obtain a cost-of-living index which relates to families whose income falls between working class and civil servant levels.[1] This shows (Table 6:1) the nineteen years of the period to have been predominantly inflationary.

Price movements divide themselves fairly naturally into three main periods:

1. 1939/40-1942/43, the wartime inflation, of very steeply accelerating price rise, decelerating very slightly in 1942/43 —the period of steepest price increases between 1939 and 1948—with near stability in the last years of the war.

2. 1945/46-1950/51, the immediate post-war period, which was a period of comparatively mild and irregular price movements—both up and down.

3. 1951/52-1957/58, the inflation of the 1950's—a period of continuous and latterly substantial price rise.

Prices of manufactures[2] may be observed to have moved in a very similar fashion to the cost-of-living index, the major inflationary periods being the same for both sets of prices.

TABLE 6:1[3]
Turkey: Percentage Changes in the Cost-of-Living Index and a Price
Index of Manufactured Articles, 1939-58

	Annual Percentage Changes	
	(a) Cost-of-Living Index	(b) Price Index of Manufactured Articles
1939/40	+ 9.8	+13.9
1940/41	+19.6	+21.7
1941/42	+66.4	+54.3
1942/43	+41.3	+35.7
1943/44	+ 3.2	+22.9
1944/45	+ 3.1	+ 4.4
1945/46	− 0.3	− 6.9
1946/47	− 1.5	− 0.9
1947/48	+ 2.4	+ 4.6
1948/49	+ 5.4	+ 9.6
1949/50	− 4.1	− 4.5
1950/51	− 0.3	+ 9.0
1951/52	+ 5.8	+ 1.2
1952/53	+ 4.1	− 2.4
1953/54	+10.2	+ 5.1
1954/55	+12.4	+ 7.7
1955/56	+11.4	+11.9
1956/57	+12.0	+ 8.8
1957/58	+16.3	+23.2

Source: R.O.T., *Monthly Bulletin of Statistics*, No. 65, July, 1959.

TABLE 6:2[6]
Turkey: Share of Labour in Gross Value Added in Manufacturing
Industry, 1938-45. Various Estimates.

	Percentages		
	(i)	(ii)	(iii)
1938	21.5	12.1	−
1939	19.2	11.9	30.2
1940	19.2	−	−
1941	20.1	−	30.2
1942	−	−	−
1943	−	−	−
1944	−	16.9	31.4
1945	−	−	35.6

The direct evidence of Table 6:2, and some direct evidence
taken from outside manufacturing industry for the vital year

1941/42,[4] indicates that in the period of rapid price acceleration,[5] 1939/40 to 1941/42, the share of labour rose
marginally.

Tables 6:3 and 6:4, besides providing confirmation of one
another, show the increased share of labour to have been the
result of declining profit margins, which were in turn the
result of raw material costs rising faster than final prices. The
lag of unit labour costs behind raw material costs was not
sufficient to counteract completely the effect of declining
profit margins.

TABLE 6:3[7]
Turkey: Final Prices, Raw Material Costs and Unit Labour Costs in
Manufacturing Industry, 1939-48

	Prices of Manu- factured Articles	Wholesale Prices of Raw Materials	Indices Unit Labour Costs	Ratio of Unit Labour Costs to Final Prices	Ratio of Raw Material Costs to Final Prices	Ratio of Unit Labour Costs to Raw Material Costs
1939	100	100	100	100	100	100
1940	114	129	112	98	113	87
1941	139	173	127	91	124	73
1942	214	281	182	85	131	65
1943	290	347	227	78	120	65
1944	357	354	256	72	99	72
1945	373	345	308	83	93	89
1946	347	368	321	93	106	87
1947	344	440	—	—	128	—
1948	359	445	—	—	124	—
1949	394	352	—	—	115	—
1950	376	415	569	151	110	137
1951	410	521	614	149	127	118
1952	414	452	666	161	109	147
1953	406	442	797	196	109	180
1954	425	494	785	185	116	159
1955	459	596	819	178	130	137
1956	511	687	1036	203	134	151
1957	557	842	1160	208	151	138
1958	668	1037	—	—	151	—

TABLE 6:4[8]
Turkey: Prime Cost Expenditures, Total Output Value and Gross Surplus
in Larger Industrial Establishments, 1938-41.

	Gross Surplus as a Proportion of Total Value of Production (Percentages)	Ratio of Wage Bill to Total Value of Production (Index)	Ratio of Expenditure on Raw Materials and Fuel to Total Value of Production (Index)	Ratio of Wage Bill to Expenditure on Raw Materials and Fuel (Index)
1938	41.5	100	100	100
1939	44.7	93	95	98
1940	43.6	91	98	93
1941	38.8	86	109	79

Source: *Small Statistical Abstract*, 1949.

The direction of income redistribution during the inflation of the 1950's[9] was not clear. What is clear is that no marked change either way took place. If we base ourselves on the smoothed figures of Table 6:5, the position could be summarised by saying that a decline in labour's share at the beginning of the inflation was gradually reversed[10] throughout the remaining years.[11] Table 6:6 shows this rising share of labour to have been primarily the result of declining margins. This in turn has been the result, between 1953 and 1955, of raw material costs rising faster than final prices.

It may be observed that the share of labour in gross value added moved inversely with the ratio of labour costs to final prices up to 1955, owing to the counteracting influence of changing raw material costs. Thus, from 1951 to 1953, the lag of rising raw material costs[13] raised the share of profits, despite the faster rise of labour costs than final prices; and between 1953 and 1955 the share of labour in gross value added rose as raw material costs squeezed margins, despite the lag of labour costs behind final prices. The stability of shares was partly the result of counteracting movements of the ratio of unit labour costs to raw material costs, which at first limited the decline of labour's share by rising, and then limited the rise of its share by falling very slightly.

TABLE 6:5[12]
Turkey: Share of Labour in Gross Value Added in Manufacturing
Industry, 1950-59

	Actual Figures	Percentages Three-year Moving Average
1950	35.5	
1951	+37.4	34.8
1952	−31.6	−34.0
1953	+33.1	−32.8
1954	+33.9	−34.0
1955	+35.1	+34.5
1956	−34.7	34.5
1957	−33.8	+35.2
1958	+37.2	+36.2

Source: R.O.T. *Annnaire Statistique, 1959*, Ankara, 1961.

TABLE 6:6[14]
Turkey: Data Concerning Prime Cost Expenditures, Total Output Value
and Gross Surplus in Manufacturing Industry, 1950-59

	Gross Surplus as a Proportion of Total Value of Production (Percentages)		Ratio of Wage Bill to Total Value of Production (Index)		Ratio of Expenditure on Raw Materials and Fuel to Total Value of Production (Index)		Ratio of Wage Bill to Expenditure on Raw Materials and Fuel (Index)	
	(a)	(b)	(a)	(b)	(a)	(b)	(a)	(b)
1950	22.2		100	99	100		100	
1951	20.2	22.9	98	99	103	98	96	100
1952	26.2	24.0	99	100	94	97	105	104
1953	25.7	25.4	104	102	94	95	111	107
1954	24.3	24.0	102	101	96	97	106	105
1955	22.0	22.7	98	101	101	99	98	102
1956	21.9	22.5	102	99	100	100	102	100
1957	23.5	22.3	98	105	98	103	100	102
1958	21.4	21.9	116	106	112	104	103	101
1959	20.7		103		102		101	

Source: *Annnaire Statistique, 1959*, Ankara, 1961.

Note: Column (a) gives actual figures and column (b) gives 3-year moving averages.

It thus appears to be the case that Turkey exhibits a greater degree of regularity in the observed relationship between price behaviour and income redistribution than did India and Peru, in the sense that the two periods of substantial inflation at the beginning of the war and in the 1950's had the same income redistribution effect, *viz* nil; and the period of price deceleration and decline, i.e. from 1942/43 through to the later 1940's, appears tentatively to have been one of increased labour share.

The Wartime Inflation, 1939/40-1944/45[15]

Although Turkey was not a belligerent in the war, she nevertheless engaged in large-scale mobilisation.[16] Simultaneously, home production had to meet a new range of demands arising from the needs of import substitution. Military mobilisation involved a substantial increase in government military expenditure (between 50 per cent and 60 per cent) of the budget was allocated to defence[17] which was not covered by taxation[18] or long-term borrowing,[19] but by resorting to the Central Bank. This was supplemented by the export surplus which originated in the difficulties of obtaining imports, the volume of which declined much more than the volume of exports (Table 6:7). The budget deficit, however, constituted the principal and primary source[20] of expansionary pressure in the wartime economy (Table 6:8). The export surplus, although less important than the budget deficit, was nevertheless always of significance, particularly in the later war years. Private investment, although it declined, partly because of the disincentive effects of the Varlik, but primarily as a result of the difficulties of importing equipment and constructional materials,[21] constituted a declining expansionary influence.

Broadly speaking, the price rise of the war years, including the period of price deceleration of the later war years, can be explained in terms of the poor aggregate supply response of the economy to the demands imposed upon it, together with the reduction in the supply of imports of both final and intermediate goods. The large-scale mobilisation of resources for the enlarged army, particularly of manpower, resulted in a slowing down of the growth of industrial production in the larger establishments to about 5 per cent per annum,[22] and an overall decline in agricultural production of about 30 per

TABLE 6:7
Turkey: Export and Import Quantum, 1939-45 (1938 + 100)

	Import Quantum	Export Quantum
1939	82	91
1940	36	70
1941	29	64
1942	48	67
1943	48	63
1944	40	49
1945	40	52

Source: Ministry of Economy and Commerce, *Conjoncture*, Nos. 10-12, October-December, Ankara, 1955.

cent[23] during the war years. In the same broad terms, the deceleration of the price rise in the later war years[24] can be explained partly in terms of the reduction of demand pressures on the economy (in part connected with the increase in taxation),[25] and partly in terms of the increased supply response domestically, at least as regards industrial production (Table 6:9). The increase in industrial production of the later war years resulted from an increased inflow of equipment and materials from 1943, the result initially of German assistance and subsequently of the inclusion of Turkey in the Lend-Lease Scheme.[26] No doubt too, the experience acquired by the Government in the exercise of its various controls over the economy, which were greatly augmented at the beginning of the war, would have been a factor in mitigating the price rise later in the war. Apart from deliberate efforts to increase industrial production,[28] the government also attempted to control prices directly. Although the effects of government price control are not clear, it does appear to have operated to limit the rise of industrial prices insofar as this was possible on the basis of the cost-plus pricing system which was adopted.[29] Import prices were not, on the other hand, a major influence on internal prices, the former rising more slowly over the war period than the latter (Table 6:10). The independence of the internal price rise from changes in import prices was in part a result of the dramatic decline in the volume of imports since the war began.

During the wartime inflation[31] the improvement in labour's share of gross value added was partly, if not mainly,

TABLE 6:8[27]
Turkey: Budget Deficits and Trade Balances, 1939-45 (Millions of
Turkish Lira)

	Budget Deficit (−) or Surplus (+)	Balance of Trade (Positive +, Negative −)
1939	125.3	9.1
1940	229.3	42.5
1941	197.5	48.3
1942	18.7	17.3
1943	145.4	54.1
1944	82.5	67.6
1945	65.6	92.8

Sources: *Budget deficits* from data compiled by Hershlag (1958' p. 201).
Trade balance data from *Monthly Bulletin*(July 1959).

TABLE 6:9
Turkey: Index Numbers of Industrial and Agricultural Production,
1939-45

	Industrial Production	Agricultural Production
1939	100	100
1940	108.2	90.5
1941	107.3	98.0
1942	94.2	86.0
1943	109.5	81.9
1944	116.2	70.4
1945	115.4	89.5

Sources: *Industrial production* from Hershlag, pp. 235-6. *Agricultural
production* from V. Eldem, 1947-48, *op. cit.*, p. 80. The industrial production index is based on official data concerning the changes in production in state and the larger private enterprises, but has been modified
by Hershlag in the light of unofficial enquiries and estimates.

the result of pressure on gross margins from rising raw
material costs.[32]

As before, our argument will proceed on the basis of the
view that changes in gross margins take place within a pricing
system operating on the basis of a conventional margin with a
degree of flexibility, and, as before, this view is based on the
oligopolistic market structure of the modern manufacturing
sector in Turkey, on the limited degree of margin variability

TABLE 6:10[30]
Turkey: Wholesale Prices, Export Prices, Import Prices and the Terms of
Trade, 1939-45

	Home Products	Imported Commodities	Exported Commodities	Terms of Trade (Imports ÷ Exports)
1939	101	105	104	101
1940	123	130	121	107
1941	167	156	169	92
1942	326	229	276	83
1943	699	410	355	116
1944	487	500	359	139
1945	482	441	345	128

Source: *Monthly Bulletin,* May 1959.

actually observed, and on the co-existence of excess capacity
with rising prices.

We have seen declining wartime gross margins and a consequent declining share of gross profit in value added to be due
to the rise of raw material costs faster than final prices
between 1939 and 1942. The reasons why rising prime costs
were not fully passed on to final prices were principally the
difference in the supply response of agriculture compared
with industry, coupled with the cost-plus pricing policy.
Although, as in India and Peru, exports and imports were
disrupted at the beginning of the war, any relaxation of
demand pressures on agriculture due to the consequent
export decline[33] were more than offset by the dramatic and
continuous decline[34] of agricultural production between
1939 and 1944. This was mainly the result of mobilisation
'since agriculture, not being mechanised, depended heavily
on manpower.'[35] Poor harvests,[36] lack of credits and
equipment, and the disincentive effects of the Varlik tax[37]
also contributed to the decline of agricultural production.
Furthermore, competitive buying of Turkey's exports by the
belligerents[38] put such great pressure on agricultural prices
that, during the inflationary years 1940-42, the terms of
trade[39] moved in Turkey's favour, the reverse of what was
happening during the years of high wartime inflation in India
and Peru.

The increased domestic and foreign demand for Turkey's
agricultural products, coupled with the decline in their

production, had its familiar impact. Raw material costs to urban industry rose steeply, the problem being aggravated by the reduction in supplies of imported raw materials[40] and intermediate goods, particularly before 1943.[41] Although agricultural money incomes and demand for industrial products also rose, the decline in agricultural production meant that over the whole period, total rural money demand did not expand sufficiently to permit existing margins to be maintained in the face of rising prime costs, which rose to a greater extent.[42] Although the primary expansion of demand from public deficits, coupled with the reduction in supplies of imported manufactures, quickly brought about a much fuller utilisation of existing capacity,[43] the governmental control over prices of manufacture[44] prevented a consequential disruption of the normal mark-up pricing mechanism[45] in favour of a policy of maximum exploitation of the initial favourable demand conditions, as in India and Peru. On the other hand, the increased capacity utilisation helped offset pressure of rising prime costs on gross margins.

The Inflation of the Nineteen-Fifties. 1950/51-1957/58

The irregular price movements of the immediate post-war period[46] give way to a continuous price rise in the 1950's. Until 1954 the inflation was moderate—thereafter it gained accelerating momentum. The change in the pace of the price rise after 1953 is to be explained in broad aggregate terms, partly by increased demand pressures, and partly by the change to a poorer supply response of the economy and the reduced import surplus after that date.

Between 1951 and 1953, budget deficits absorbed a roughly constant share of the G.N.P., and were more than offset by the large import surplus (Table 6:11) of these years, associated with the liberalisation of trade in 1951, which led to a sharp rise in imports until the reimposition of controls in 1953 (Table 6:13).

In addition to the budget deficit, which partly financed an increasing appropriation of national resources for public investment[48] (Table 6:12), private investment and investment of the State Economic Enterprises also absorbed a somewhat higher annual average share of G.N.P. in these three years than in 1950. The increased investment of the State Economic Enterprises seems in this period to have been financed largely from internal savings,[49] and unlikely there-

TABLE 6:11[47]
Turkey: Budget Deficits and Trade Balances, 1950/51-1957/58 (Percencentages of G.N.P. in brackets)

	Budget Deficit (−) or Surplus (+)	Balance of Payments on Current Account
	Million Turkish Lira	
1950/51	−156 (−1.5)	−184 (−1.8)
1951/52	−202 (−1.7)	−320 (−2.7)
1952/53	−251 (−1.8)	−398 (−2.9)
1953/54	−262 (−1.5)	−503 (−2.9)
1954/55	−361 (−2.2)	−446 (−2.7)
1955/56	−700 (−3.3)	−313 (−1.5)
1956/57	−511 (2.1)	−214 (0.8)
1957/58	−354 (−1.2)	−354 (−1.2)
1958/59	−588 (−1.6)	−179 (−0.5)

Sources: *Budget deficits* from R.O.T., State Planning Organisation, *First Five Year Plan, Development Plan 1963-67*, Ankara, 1963, p. 15. *Balance of payments* from N. Geyda, *Turkish Economic Review*, Vol. 1, No. 4, May 1960, p. 3.

fore to have contributed substantially to increasing pressures of excess demand.

The extent to which private investment has been credit-financed is a moot point. On the whole, increasing private

TABLE 6:12[50]
Turkey: Gross Investment as a Proportion of G.N.P., 1950-58 (Percentages of Total Gross Investment in Brackets)

	Total Gross Investment as a Proportion of G.N.P.	Private Sector Investment as a Proportion of G.N.P.	Investment of State Economic Enterprises as a Proportion of G.N.P.	Public Sector Investment as Proportion of G.N.P.
1950	9.6 (100.0)	5.5 (57.0)	1.4 (15.0)	2.7 (28.0)
1951	10.3 (100.0)	6.3 (61.0)	1.3 (13.0)	2.7 (26.0)
1952	12.8 (100.0)	7.9 (62.0)	2.1 (16.0)	2.8 (22.0)
1953	12.4 (100.0)	6.9 (56.0)	2.1 (17.0)	2.4 (27.0)
1954	14.7 (100.0)	8.7 (59.0)	2.4 (16.0)	3.6 (25.0)
1955	14.3 (100.0)	6.3 (44.0)	3.9 (27.0)	4.1 (29.0)
1956	13.4 (100.0)	6.7 (50.0)	2.7 (20.0)	4.0 (30.0)
1957	13.2 (100.0)	5.7 (43.0)	2.9 (22.0)	4.6 (35.0)
1958	14.0 (100.0)	5.0 (36.0)	3.4 (24.0)	5.6 (40.0)

investments appear to have been financed mainly from the internal savings of the private sector, with the exception of investment in agriculture and housing.[51] In the case of industry, an increasing tendency for its capital needs to be met from retained profits was observed in the 1950's, when profits were at a high level.[52]

TABLE 6:13
Turkey: Export and Import Quantum, 1945-58, (1938 = 100)

	Import Quantum	Export Quantum
1945	40	52
1946	50	78
1947	103	89
1948	110	93
1949	125	120
1950	146	115
1951	176	116
1952	243	140
1953	240	170
1954	237	161
1955	218	121

Source: *Monthly Bulletin*, September, 1959.

This tendency is partly the result of the fact that credit facilities for the private sector of industry from the banking system were extremely limited throughout the 'fifties.[53] The other main area of private sector investment (besides residential dwellings and agriculture), namely, trade, accounted for a steadily declining proportion of private sector investment between 1949 and 1952,[54] and while housing construction appears to have been financed to a considerable extent from bank credits,[55] this, too, constituted a steadily declining proportion of total investment.[56]

On the other hand, agricultural investment, in which private investment is of considerable importance, increased steadily as a proportion of G.N.P., and as a proportion of total investment, in every year between 1948 and 1952, and 'the investments were either public, or, if private, were largely financed by the government's liberal credit policy. Agricultural medium and long-term credits in 1952 far exceeded private investment in agriculture for that year. In fact, there is evidence that private investment in agriculture actually declined in 1953, despite rising agricultural incomes and credit.'[57] The limited increase in voluntary savings from rising agricultural incomes has been partly the result of a tendency towards conspicuous consumption by the richer farmers (and, indeed, by profit receivers generally) and increased self-consumption by the peasantry, financed by credit extended by the Agricultural Bank and rising price supports for agricultural products.[58] The expansionary effects of the activities of Toprak and the Agricultural Bank have also contributed to the expansion of industrial investment indirectly.[59]

TABLE 6:14
Turkey: Value and Composition of Imports, 1948-58 (1,000 Turkish Lira)

| | Investment Goods | | | | | | |
| | (i) Construction Materials | | (ii) Machinery and Equipment | | Consumption Goods | | Raw Materials | |
		% of total		% of total		% of total		% of total
1948	84,007	10.9	218,234	28.3	190,965	24.8	227,246	3.60
1949	94,167	11.6	249,572	30.7	165,775	20.4	302,757	37.3
1950	94,660	11.8	273,402	43.2	164,719	20.6	267,078	33.4
1951	118,937	10.6	364,840	32.4	279,170	24.8	362,894	32.2
1952	186,700	12.0	599,321	38.5	343,268	22.1	427,296	27.4
1953	238,203	16.0	537,437	36.0	295,183	19.8	420,314	28.2
1954	209,652	15.6	500,368	37.4	262,330	19.6	367,046	27.4
1955	251,860	18.1	504,453	36.2	204,236	14.6	432,835	31.1
1956	155,226	13.6	508,173	44.6	126,889	11.1	350,137	30.7
1957	133,570	12.0	350,458	31.5	136,492	12.3	491,431	44.2
1958	75,533	8.6	306,166	34.7	107,871	12.2	392,704	44.5

Source: *Monthly Bulletin*, September, 1959.

It thus appears that the expansionary pressures in the economy arose primarily from budget deficits, an expansion of investment by the State Economic Enterprises and the private sector, partly financed directly and indirectly by credit expansion, and an increased propensity to consume in the agricultural sector, also financed largely by credit, largely governmental.

These aggregate demand pressures, as already remarked,

were partly absorbed by the import surplus. It is significant, however, as an indication of the important role of imports in ameliorating *sectoral* bottlenecks,[60] that the period of trade liberalisation actually witnessed only a very slight rise in the proportion of consumer goods in total imports (Table 6:14), while on average the proportion of investment goods in total imports rose by rather more.[61] This small rise in the proportion of consumer goods in total imports, following the liberalisation of trade, also serves as a significant pointer to the importance of the extraordinary expansion of domestic production as an absorbent of expanding monetary demand.

The expansion of home production in the 1950's was very remarkable indeed. Throughout the 1950's, industrial production increased at an annual average rate of 7.5-8 per cent per annum,[62] with agricultural output growing at around 4-5 per cent.[63] The crucial factor was the performance of agriculture. The agricultural stagnation of the war and immediate post-war years was radically altered in the 1950's, thanks to a combination of several factors, *viz* the extent of uncultivated but cultivable land which could be quickly drawn into production, rapid mechanisation of agriculture made possible partly by generous American aid, the liberal credit policy of the new (1950) Government, the rapid development of transport services and the favourable weather conditions, all of which made possible a considerable expansion of output, particularly between 1950 and 1953.[64] The progress was such that, even when in 1954, 1955 and 1956 grain production had fallen below the record 1952 and 1953 levels, owing to poor or indifferent harvests, the average volume of production in those years still exceeded the average 1948-50 level by 50 per cent.[65] Agricultural advance in turn provided the main expanding markets for industry, contributing an increasing flow of raw materials, as evidenced by the declining proportion of raw materials in total imports. Moreover, by permitting a greatly increased volume of exports (Table 6:13) and reducing the proportion of raw materials imported, agricultural expansion increased the capacity to import capital goods, spare parts and semi-processed goods necessary to sustain an increasing volume of industrial production.

The overall excellent production performance, however, conceals a marked slowing-up of the growth of production after 1953, even though a by-no-means negligible increase in production was achieved between 1953 and 1958 (Table 6:15). The change in the tempo of development and the transition to a much faster price rise was marked by the bad harvest of 1954. At the same time as the rate of growth of production ślowed down, pressures of aggregate demand on the economy were increased after 1953, while increasing indebtedness brought about the abolition of the trade liberalisation policy, and brought increasingly severe restrictions on imports thereafter.

Thus, while in 1954 the import surplus continued to outweigh the budget deficit, it did so by a much smaller margin than previously (Table 6:11) and was accompanied by an increase in the share of investment by the State Economic Enterprises and by the private sector in G.N.P. (Table 6:12).

In the years 1954-58, the average proportion of G.N.P. absorbed by budget deficits rose, compared with the years 1951-53; and the reverse was the case with the import surplus, which declined steadily[66] from 1954, and accounted for a smaller average annual proportion of G.N.P. than in 1951-53. Moreover, the import surplus in every year after 1954 fell short of the budget deficit, again a reversal of the 1951-53 situation.

TABLE 6:15
Turkey: Index Numbers of Total Gross Product, Gross Product of Manufacturing Industry and Agricultural Gross Product, at 1948 Market Prices, 1948-58 (1948 = 100)

	Gross National Product	Gross Product of Agriculture	Gross Product of Manufacturing Industry
1948	100.0	100.0	100.0
1949	89.2	78.4	99.3
1950	103.3	97.1	106.6
1951	119.1	117.1	116.5
1952	129.4	124.7	125.1
1953	143.7	136.6	137.9
1954	130.6	109.8	139.5
1955	140.6	119.7	145.9
1956	150.1	130.1	153.7
1957	159.6	133.5	163.9
1958	176.6	155.7	176.7

Sources: *Monthly Bulletin,* September, 1959; and October, 1960.

Nor was there an offsetting decline in demand pressures from investments of the State Economic Enterprises and private sector. Although the proportion of G.N.P. jointly accounted for by the investment of these two sectors declined steadily after 1954 (Table 6:12), the average proportion still remained above the high levels of 1951-53.[67] The reduced rate of growth of total output, which in 1954 and 1955 was still below the level achieved in 1953 (Table 6:15), indicates that these high investment levels were unlikely to have been financed by higher levels of voluntary savings than in the earlier period,[68] and although industry was able to call upon reserves accumulated earlier from high levels of profits, these represented to a degree an influence dampening demand pressures in the earlier rather than the later part of the '50s.

TABLE 6:16
Turkey: Wholesale Prices, Export Prices, Import Prices and the Terms of Trade, 1948-58 (1948 = 100)

	Wholesale Price Index of Home Products	Import Price Index	Export Price Index	Terms of Trade (Imports Exports)
1948	100	100	100	100
1949	107	112	102	110
1950	91	104	96	107
1951	94	120	116	103
1952	101	128	102	124
1953	110	126	102	123
1954	120	130	113	115
1955	126	151	134	112
1956	145	163	158	102
1957	175	175	177	98
1958	205	288	195	147

Source: *Monthly Bulletin,* September, 1959. All indices are constituents of the general wholesale price index prepared by the Chamber of Commerce of Istanbul and covering 52 items.

The Turkish inflation of the 1950's was complicated by the fact that after 1953 the agricultural lag which then emerged created sectoral supply problems and balance of payments difficulties which particularly caused rising raw material (and, indirectly, labour) costs to emerge as an independent influence raising prices at times.[69] Rising costs were almost entirely the result of internal conditions—it was only in 1950/

51, 1954/55 and 1957/58 that import prices rose faster than domestic prices (Table 6:16).[70] As earlier remarked, the analysis which follows of the independent role of the upward thrust of costs on prices (independent of generalised excess demand pressures) is based on the oligopolistic market structure of the modern manufacturing sector in Turkey,[71] on the limited degree of margin variability actually observed, and on the co-existence of excess capacity with rising prices.

The evidence of Table 6:6 shows, as before, very small year-to-year variations of gross margins between 1952 and 1959,[72] the biggest change between one year and another being 2.3 percentage points. It will be noted, however, that there was an exceptionally large rise of the gross margin between 1951 and 1952, and that the range between the lowest and the highest gross margin was as great as 6 percentage points. These two facts do not, however, indicate a greater degree of margin flexibility than say, in the case of Peru. The large jump in margins between 1951 and 1952 was the result of a decline in raw material costs, with final prices comparatively steady,[73] i.e. rising only very slightly, and the greater range of margins over the period as a whole after 1951 was simply a result of the gradual re-establishment of the margin displaced by the 1952 fall in raw material costs, i.e. was a function of the size of the rise of gross margins between 1951 and 1952.

TABLE 6:17[74]
Turkey: Utilisation of Capacity in Certain Industries

Capacity and Production—annual average in thousands of tons			
Product and Period	Capacity	Production	Utilisation %
Pig iron 1953	100	56(2)	56
1954	100	83(2)	83
Food, preserved 1950/53	7-8	5(3)	60-70
Worsted textiles 1953	6.5	3.9	60
Woollen yarn 1953	22	13	55
Woollen textiles 1953	24	13	52
Soap 1950/53	90-100	45	45-50
Worsted yarn 1953	15	5	33

Source: Estimates by the U.N., from unpublished data, provided by the Industrial Development Bank of Turkey. Reproduced from U.N., *Manufacturing Industry in Turkey*, pp. 81-2.

Excess capacity in a number of manufacturing industries was a feature of the inflation of the 1950's, among which iron and steel, coarse and printed cotton, textiles, cotton ginning, rubber industries, silos and sugar factories may be specified.

In a more general way, Hershlag has calculated (pp. 270-272) that a marked rise took place in the industrial capital/output ratio between 1933-1939 and 1954/55, which he attributes partly to a decline in the degree of capacity utilisation.[75]

The evidence is not clear on the extent to which excess capacity was the result of market as opposed to supply factors. However, it is perhaps worth noting that both the year of Hershlag's calculation, and the evidence of Table 6:17 relate to excess capacity in the period before balance of payments difficulties had caused shortfalls in the supply of imported materials, fuel and semi-processed goods (although not, of course, the supply of consumer goods, which were restricted somewhat before 1956). The U.N. study *(Manufacturing Industry in Turkey, 1958, pp. 81-2)* reports, as reasons for excess capacity, failure of demand to expand as anticipated (iron and steel), too rapid an expansion of capacity due to unco-ordinated investment decisions (textiles), shifts of demand (e.g. from coarse to fine textiles) and lack of imported raw materials in the later '50s (wool and rubber).

Having glanced at some of the indications of an oligopolistic pricing system, we are now in a position to conclude our analysis of the relative movements of prices and costs in the Turkish inflation of the 1950's.

We have seen that on the basis of smoothed figures, labour's declining share of gross value added was the result of the lag of raw material costs behind final prices (with unit labour costs rising faster than final prices) leading to rising gross margins. The reversal of this trend after 1953, i.e. a rising share of labour in gross value added, was again due to a reversal in the direction of change of gross margins, and again the active role in the downward movement was raw material costs, which rose faster than final prices after 1953, labour costs lagging behind the rise of final prices until 1956, and consequently playing a passive role until then.

This summary suffices to emphasise the crucial role of raw material cost changes in altering gross margins and, thus, labour's share. Consideration of the figures of Tables 6:15

and 6:16, however, shows that for the earliest period of the inflation we must take account of the actual rather than the smoothed figures to obtain a clear idea of the course of events.

The actual figures, then, suggest that the very sharp rise in gross margins near the beginning of the inflation in 1952, caused by the slight decline in raw material costs, suffered a steady erosion throughout the rest of the period. They further indicate that this erosion at first (1952-53) was the active result of rising unit labour costs, with raw material costs lagging; that in the next stage (1953-55) it was the active result of rising raw material costs, with labour costs lagging; and that in the final stage, gross margins were eroded by the active pressure of both rising labour and rising raw material costs. The crucial aspect of the situation identified by the *actual* figures is that the early part of the inflation did not witness a continuous rise of gross margins, but rather an initial short, sharp rise which at first suffered only the slightest erosion. The crucial aspect of the situation identified by the *smoothed* figures (apart from the value of those figures in periodising events post-1953) is the fact that gross margins on average in the earlier years, 1951 to 1953, were higher than at the beginning of the inflation and higher than in the later years of the inflation, so that, despite the fact that gross margins moved upwards in only one year, this was nevertheless in a sense a period of redistribution away from labour. From whichever aspect the matter is viewed, however, the

---

TABLE 6:18
Turkey: Percentage Points Changes in Gross Margins, 1950/51-1958/59
(actual figures)

1950/51	−2.0
1951/52	+6.0
1952/53	−0.5
1953/54	−1.4
1954/55	−2.3
1955/56	−0.1
1956/57	+1.6
1957/58	−2.1
1958/59	−0.7

Source: R.O.T., *Annuaire Statistique*, 1959, Ankara, 1961.

overall lag of raw material costs behind final prices between 1951 and 1954 must be explained if we are to explain either the higher average gross margins of this period compared with the beginning of the inflation (or compared with the later years of the inflation), or if we are to explain the slowness of margins to revert to former levels after the sharp rise in 1952 (Table 6:18).

The lag of raw material costs behind final prices during the early years of the inflation is simply attributable to the extraordinarily good supply response of the agricultural sector, for reasons already mentioned. The remarkable increase in agricultural output in this period was not sufficient to prevent raw material costs and food prices from rising throughout the period (except in 1952 for the former),[76] under the pressure of home and export demand. However, since unit labour costs were rising faster than raw material costs, and since demand was sufficiently good to permit final prices to be adjusted nearly fully to rising prime costs (so that the abnormally high margins of 1952 were more or less maintained until 1955), raw material costs lagged behind final prices. Thus, behind the fact of lagging raw material costs lay the relatively faster rise of unit labour costs, the cost-plus pricing system and the favourable market situation for manufacturing industry—all combining to push up final prices faster than raw material costs. (With the cost-plus pricing system we have already dealt.) The relatively faster rise of unit labour costs over raw material costs, and the favourable demand situation for manufactures, were both wholly or partly the result of the rapid advance of agricultural output.

The favourable demand situation was a result of the fact that the direct rise in costs transmitted from agriculture (raw material costs) was more than matched by the increase in monetary demand from agriculture. This situation was the result of four factors: the fact that there was a rapid rise of agricultural output during this period, in contrast to the wartime inflation; the fact that this took place on a base of *initially* high rural living standards in terms of food;[77] the fact that the mass of the peasantry gained from the increase of production; and the fact that the peasantry were at this period subjected to a number of factors tending to broaden their horizons and increase the range of their material wants. The result of all this was to increase the marketed surplus from agriculture and to direct the proceeds towards the purchase of a wide range of manufactured consumer goods.

The factors extending the range of the peasants' material wants are well described by Alec Alexander. 'A large degree of self-sufficiency at a level close to subsistence has traditionally characterised the village economy, but marked increases in production and exchange occurred during the 1950's. The gradual spread of education, improved transportation, more frequent commercial contacts with urban centres, military duty in an army undergoing intense modernisation, and the long-term effects of the earlier reforms, have all contributed to important changes in village life. The disruption of traditional cultural patterns has been coupled by an increased awareness of the new opportunities for material betterment and of the practical value of new ideas and techniques.'[78]

TABLE 6:19[82]
Turkey: Indices of Expenditure on Selected Consumer Items, 1955
(1950 = 100)

Consumer items	Index	
	1950	1955
Cereals and pulses	100	159
Vegetables and fruit	100	165
Sugar	100	169
Beverages	100	219
Meat	100	259
Textiles	100	262
Pharmaceutical Products	100	209
Printed matter	100	229
Services	100	215

Source: From Union of Chambers of Commerce and Industry and Commodity Exchanges of Turkey, *Problems of Industrialisation and Investment in Turkey*, Ankara, 1957, in Turkish, quoted in U.N., *Manufacturing Industry in Turkey*, 1958, p. 22.

Since, as noted above, the expansion of production and wants took place on the basis of already high living standards in terms of food, the result was that, 'the bulk of this surplus has gone into consumption, everything from more cigarettes and sugar to better clothing. . .'[79] (Table 6:19). The ability to increase consumption expenditures in this case was closely connected with the easy credit afforded to the peasants by the

agricultural bank, much of which, apart from being utilised
for consumption purposes, had the probably even more
important indirect effect of reducing the dependence of the
peasant on money-lenders.[80] The reluctance of the peasant to
utilise his increased disposable surplus for investment purposes meant that peasant affluence resulted in 'the boom in
the domestic consumption goods industries [which] was
largely based on the expansion of markets among the
Turkish farmers.'[81]

In addition to the favourable demand situation for manufactures in the early 1950's, we also observed the relatively
faster rise of unit labour costs than raw material costs to be a
reason for the lag of raw material costs behind final prices.
This, too, was partly a result of conditions in the agricultural
sector, which resulted in food prices and, thus, the cost of
living index rising faster than prices of raw materials between
1951 and 1954. Given that money-wage changes were cost-of-
living oriented, this was an influence in raising money wages
and, thus, unit labour costs faster than raw material costs.

All this changed in the late 1950's. Agricultural production
declined in 1954, and thereafter rose much more slowly than
hitherto, so that raw material costs began to rise faster, and,
albeit irregularly, exerted the familiar pressure on gross margins. The decline in gross margins became really significant in
1955, when the effects of the bad harvest of 1954 were fully
felt, and the only partial signs of any recovery in margins were
in 1956 and 1957 (Table 6:18), when extreme foreign
exchange difficulties led to even more severe import restrictions which almost completely eliminated imported
manufactured consumer goods.[83]

CONCLUSION

**Proximate Determinants of Income Redistribution in
Organised Manufacturing Industry in Turkey during
Inflation**

The share of labour in gross value added rose slightly during
the wartime inflation. During the inflation of 1950/51 to
1957/58, labour's share did not change decisively in either
direction. In the earliest years of the 1950's inflation, labour's
share was, on average, below its pre-inflation level; in the
later years it tended to rise above it. It was, thus, the years of
very mild price rise which witnessed a decline in labour's

share, and the years when the price rise got properly under way which saw labour's share move decisively, although not continuously, upwards.

(i) The Wartime Inflation, 1939/40 to 1944/45

The very slight shift towards labour during the wartime inflation was the result of declining gross margins, as raw material costs rose faster than final prices. Money wages rose also, but lagged behind both rising final prices and raw material costs, so that the declining share of labour in total prime costs partly, though not completely, offset the effect of declining gross margins in raising labour's share.

The encroachment of rising raw material costs on gross margins was the result of the disastrous and nearly continuous decline of agricultural production, together with governmental price control along cost-plus lines. The former more than counteracted the effects of the reduction in exports (mainly agricultural commodities) in increasing domestic supplies from agriculture, and the latter counteracted the effects which the increased capacity utilisation of industry (due to the primary expansion of demand and the dramatic decline in the volume of imported manufactures) might have had in disrupting the mark-up pricing mechanism.[84] The decline of agricultural output had the effect of raising agricultural prices and, thus, industrial costs rather faster than money demand from agriculture for manufactures, so that a very slight pressure on margins was exerted.

The lag of the rise of money wages behind prices, which ensured that the share of labour in gross value added changed only imperceptibly during the most inflationary years of the war, was due to the absence of either a trade union movement or pre-existing governmental machinery for the regular review of money wages. Nor was there any strong political voice in this period either representing organised labour or appealing to it. The net result of this was that institutional pressures raising money wages in line with the cost of living were extremely weak, so that money wages lagged behind all other prices.

(ii) The Inflation of the Nineteen Fifties, 1950/51 to 1957/58

Abstracting fluctuations from year to year and using our smoothed figures, we may say that the inflation from 1951 to 1958 resulted in a shift in relative shares in favour of labour.

This shift, although definite, was very slight, and the period as a whole might well be described as one of relative stability of income shares. The determinants of this situation are more clearly seen if we note that the first three years of the inflation witnessed a reduced share for labour, and the remaining years a rise in labour's share. [85]

The changes in labour's share in these two sub-periods (pre-1954 and post-1953) were principally the result of changing pressures on margins. In the earlier years gross margins were higher than at the beginning of the inflation, and from 1954 onwards they were lower.

During the first sub-period of the inflation, the higher gross margins were the result of raw material costs lagging behind final prices. Lagging raw material costs more than offset the rise of unit labour costs which, in fact, was greater than that of final prices. The favourable demand situation permitted labour costs to push up final prices faster than the rise of raw material costs; this was a consequence of the marked increase in agricultural output, which led to an expansion of rural demand for manufacturesd consumer goods and at the same time moderated the rise of raw material costs.

With the falling off in the rate of increase of agricultural production after 1953 these conditions began to be reversed, so that, while the pressure of demand raised raw material costs faster than before, rural demand for urban products did not rise to a similar extent, and it became less possible to pass prime cost increases on to prices without affecting sales, so that margins were squeezed. Thus, despite the almost complete stability of labour costs between 1953 and 1955 due to a less sympathetic official attitude towards trade unions, there nevertheless took place in these years a slight reduction in profit shares. After 1955 the renewed rise of money wages, as the cost of living accelerated, accentuated the pressure of prime costs on margins, despite the relief afforded after 1956 by the near-elimination of all imports of manufactured consumer goods.

It is worth remarking that, in a sense, the inflation of the 1950's only really established itself in 1954. In the 1951-53 period, prices of manufactures rose very gently and prices of raw materials in one year declined. The significant point about this is that, if we choose to date the inflationary period proper as starting from 1953/54, there is no doubt that this inflationary period was one of a rising share of labour in gross value added in manufacturing industry.

NOTES

1.   There are a number of cost-of-living indices relating to Istanbul and Ankara, which are given below, Table 6:20, from *Monthly Bulletin*, No. 68, October 1959, the average of which is used in the text, in fact, the average of the four which cover the whole period.

In averaging the Istanbul and Ankara cost-of-living indices we are

TABLE 6:20
Turkey: Various Cost-of-Living Indices, Istanbul and Ankara, 1938-58

	Ankara ((i)—(iii))			Istanbul ((iv)—(vi))			Average
	(i)	(ii)	(iii)	(iv)	(v)	(vi)	(vii)
1938	100	100	—	100	100	100	100
1939	102	103	—	101	—	101	102
1940	112	112	—	112	—	112	112
1941	133	131	—	133	—	138	134
1942	221	221	—	212	—	233	223
1943	322	303	—	289	—	347	315
1944	330	327	—	304	—	339	325
1945	333	345	—	306	—	354	335
1946	321	360	—	302	299	343	332
1947	326	336	—	302	299	344	327
1948	330	354	—	310	310	346	335
1949	355	376	—	341	408	379	363
1950	340	365	—	325	392	261	348
1941	336	374	—	323	390	355	347
1952	353	391	—	346	413	376	367
1953	370	403	—	366	430	389	382
1954	403	434	—	419	491	426	421
1955	454	515	515	458	519	463	473
1956	505	552	529	523	559	529	527
1957	567	635	600	563	598	593	590
1958	655	259	723	667	702	666	686

Source: *Monthly Bulletin* May, 1959.

Notes: (1)   From Conjoncture Office of the Ministry of Commerce, base 1938 = 100;

(2)   70-commodity index from Central Statistical Office, base 1938 = 100;

(3)   134 commodity index from Central Statistical Office, base 1955 = 100, arithmetically transposed to 1955 value of index (2) with consequent upward adjustments for remaining years;

(4)   From Istanbul Chamber of Commerce, before 1939;

(5)   From Istanbul Chamber of Commerce, after 1939;

(6)   From Conjoncture Office of the Ministry of Commerce;

(7)   Average of the four indices covering the whole period 1938-58.

following Eldem's example (in V. Eldem, 'Changements survenus depuis la guerre dane le niveau de vie des fonctionnaires et des salariés de l'Etat', *Revue de la Faculté des Sciences Economiques de l'Université d'Istanbul*, thirteenth year, Nos. 1-4, October 1951—July 1952, p. 157). This procedure seems to be justified by the degree of correspondence shown by the movements of these various indices, which are based on the budgets of families whose average monthly income is above that of the working class but below that of civil servants. R.O.T., Central Statistical Office, *National Income of Turkey (and Family Expenses in Country and Towns) Estimates (1927-45), Forecasts (1948-52)*, Ankara, 1949, by Sefik Bilkur, Director General, Central Statistical Office, pp. 46-47. Family budget enquiries on which these indices are based were conducted in 1938 and 1954 *Monthly Bulletin*, September 1959, and the weights for food varied between 40 per cent and 50 per cent (Bilkur, *op. cit.*, pp. 48-50, *Monthly Bulletin* (September 1958). Almost certainly, a working class cost-of-living index would have shown a higher rate of rise, owing to the greater preponderance of food in the working class budget. This is partially confirmed by an independently estimated cost-of-living index relating to Shell Company employees (Table 6:21), which shows a considerably higher rate of increase and uses a relatively heavy weighting for food, i.e. 48 per cent, and by the report of the American Economic Attaché in Ankara, Mr. E.B. Lawson, who calculated that with 1938 = 100, the cost-of-living index was 600 in 1943 in Istanbul and Ankara, a level well above that of any of the official or semi-official estimates (U.S. Department of Commerce, *Foreign Commerce Weekly*, Volume 39, No. 25, 19 June 1948, p. 28).

TABLE 6:21
Turkey: Cost-of-Living Index for Shell Company Employees in Turkey, 1939-47

August	1939	101.35
"	1940	141.75
"	1941	185.79
"	1942	295.23
"	1943	321.08
"	1944	420.74
"	1945	410.23
"	1946	428.32
"	1947	526.64

Source: Cited in Lingeman, 1947, p. 162.

2. The break in the rise of prices of manufactures in 1952/53 contrasts with the continuous rise of the cost-of-living index throughout the 1950's. However, this appears to have been a statistical quirk arising from the heavy weighting of textiles in our index of prices of manufactures, and the implicit price index of manufactures (whether at factor cost or market prices), calculated from the national income figures

(*Monthly Bulletin,* September 1959), shows prices of manufactures rising continuously throughout the 1950's. The national income figures on which calculation of the implicit price index is based do not cover the period 1939-48.

3. The cost-of-living index is an average of 4 indices, 2 covering Istanbul and 2 Ankara. The index of prices of manufactured goods is a crude arithmetic average of these manufactured groups from the Istanbul cost-of-living indices for which specific information is given. As such, it is extremely limited, both as regards its geographical coverage and the range of commodities covered. The weight of food in the cost-of-living index is between 40 per cent and 50 per cent.

Lacking a general index of prices of manufactured articles, a crude substitute was obtained by taking all the group price indices covering manufactured articles given in the *Monthly Bulletin of Statistics* relating to Istanbul, in order to be aligned with the only index of raw material prices available which related only to Istanbul: the Business Research Department's national index includes semi-manufactured goods. The justification for using such an index is that there are grounds

TABLE 6:22

Turkey: Various Price Indices of Manufactured Articles Relating to Istanbul, 1938-58

	Heating and Lighting		Clothing	Clothing and Furniture	Textiles	Unweighted Arithmetic Average
	(i)	(ii)	(iii)	(iv)	(v)	(vi)
1938	100	100	100	100	100	100
1939	98	95	105	101	105	101
1940	109	106	124	115	120	115
1941	117	125	176	145	136	140
1942	158	194	293	244	190	216
1943	213	251	373	333	288	293
1944	234	274	445	408	439	360
1945	249	305	493	416	418	376
1946	241	306	429	391	381	350
1947	240	306	435	378	376	347
1948	250	330	425	378	432	363
1949	331	366	422	378	493	398
1950	309	314	411	375	491	380
1951	297	381	436	415	642	414
1952	323	309	437	414	611	419
1953	328	326	441	407	542	409
1954	340	398	461	425	528	430
1955	361	407	518	479	550	463
1956	390	482	574	552	591	518
1957	440	507	679	610	583	564
1958	484	561	831	762	838	695

for believing that it does not, in the uses to which it is put, give a mis-leading picture of the variables on which it is focusing attention. There are two such uses in this chapter—the periodisation of price changes of manufactured articles, and the relative movements of prime costs and final prices. On the former, it can be seen that the broad trends of movement of the constituent items in Table 6:22 are sufficiently close to the average and to one another to give assurance that the periodisa-tion is roughly correct, with the exception noted in note 2 above. On the latter, as will be seen later, (some) direct evidence of changes in relative shares in value added, and on expenditures on wages and raw materials compared with the total receipts, is broadly consistent with the picture of the direction of change (albeit not the extent of change) given by these relative price/prime cost movements, using this index of manufactured prices.

The first four indices are sub-groups of the two Istanbul cost-of-living indices, (i) and (iii) coming from the one compiled by the Conjoncture Office of the Ministry of Commerce, and (ii) and (iv) from the Istanbul Chamber of Commerce indices. Indices (i) and (iii) cover 4 and 7 items respectively. Index (v) is of wholesale prices, and comes from the Istanbul Chamber of Commerce indices.

The index of the industrial wage bill was constructed from partial series given by Eldem, summarised in Table 6:23 below.

TABLE 6:23
Turkey: Estimates of the Total Industrial Wage Bill, 1939-46

| | | | | Indices | |
	(i)	(ii)	(iii)	(iv) (a)	(v) (b)
1939	100	100	100	100	100
1940	121	—	—	127	—
1941	138	135	135	154	136
1942	—	—	—	195	172
1943	—	—	243	289	255
1944	—	296	293	343	303
1945	—	355	—	—	—
1946	—	—	—	427	377

(a)   Non-adjusted index.   (b)   Adjusted index.

Sources: Indices (i) and (iii) calculated from figures in Eldem (1946/7); indices (ii) and (iv) from figures in Eldem (1948/9).

Notes: (1)   Index (i) excludes the state-owned tobacco and alcohol monopolies but includes, as do the others, mining and electricity and gas, i.e. it covers large-scale industry covered by the Law on the Encouragement of Industry (revoked in 1941).

(2)   Index (iii) covers industry under the Labour Law, i.e. all establishments the nature of which would necessitate the employment of 10 workers or more, and some of the

establishments which would require 5-9 workers (U.N., *Manufacturing Industry in Turkey*, 1958, p. 102) and includes the value of wages in kind.

(3) Index *(ii)*, using 'diverse sources', appears to have been based mainly on Labour Law figures, and includes state establishments, electricity and gas, state monopolies, private industry, other establishments under the Labour Law and military factories.

(4) Index *(iv)* is based on Eldem's own aggregate estimate of the wage bill in non-artisan industry, and includes the value of wages and salaries in kind, while excluding electricity and gas. The figures for 1942 to 1944, inclusive, are stated to be provisional or approximate.

(5) All indices include salaries as well as wages.

The series broadly correspond, apart from a rather faster rise of index *(iv)* in the earlier years. This was adjusted downwards (the movement of this index unadjusted, after 1941, was sufficiently similar to the movement of the other indices to justify this) and the indices were averaged to obtain the wage-bill index and, thus, together with the production index, the index of unit labour costs.

TABLE 6:24
Turkey: Index of Unit Labour Costs, 1939-46

	(1) Wage Bill	*(2)* Production	*(1) ÷ (2)* Unit Labour Costs
1939	100	100	100
1940	121	108	112
1941	136	107	127
1942	172	94	182
1943	249	110	227
1944	298	116	256
1945	355	115	308˙
1946	377	117	321

The 1939-46 and 1950-58 unit labour cost indices were linked together at 1950 by finding the levels of the indices of money wages, employment and production in that year over 1939. Employment figures were obtained from U.N., *Manufacturing Industry* (1958), p. 16; and Eldem (1946/7), p. 77; the former relating the 1938 figure to the 1950 figure and the latter the 1939 figure to the 1938 figure; both referred to the larger establishments. The 1950 value of the industrial production index (1939 = 100) was obtained from Hershlag (1958), appendix 6, chart 5), and was a continuation of that used for the wartime period, as such not being strictly aligned with the 1950-58 production index used to obtain the unit labour cost index, which covered manufacturing only.

The level of the money wage index in 1950 above 1939 was obtained in such a way as to make it as consistent as possible with the

1939-46 wage bill estimates on which the unit labour cost calculations were based. To only two of the wage bill estimates of Table 6:22 did there exist corresponding employment figures, i.e. for wage bill series *(i)* and *(iii)* (the employment figures for wage bill estimate *(ii)* included working owners). The wage bill and employment indices of *(i)* and *(iii)* were averaged, and the index of money wages obtained (Table 6:23). Since the wage-bill index so obtained did not differ greatly from that used for the unit labour cost index, the money-wage index may be regarded as roughly consistent with the unit labour cost index up to 1944. It should be noted that, since the employment figures corresponding to wage-bill index *(i)* are for total man-days worked, we have in Table 6:25 a mongrel index of average daily and average annual earnings. However, as may be seen from Table 6:26 below, the annual index, at least of wages of employees in state industrial enterprises, does not differ substantially from that of the daily index. From figures given by Eldem (1951/52, *op. cit.*, p. 159) for 1938/1948/53 and for 1938-46 'Le Revenu National de la Turquie.' *Revue de la Faculté de Sciences Economiques de l'Université d'Istanbul,* 1947/48, p. 112, giving average daily wages for employees in state industrial establishments, it was possible to construct an index, base 1939 = 100, which was found to correspond roughly to the money wage for the 1939-44 index of Table 6:25, and for the period 1950-53 to correspond roughly to the money-wage index for all manufacturing calculated from the annual business survey figures (Tables 6:26 and 6:27).

TABLE 6:25
Turkey: Wage Bill, Employment and Money Wages, 1939-44 (Indices)

	Wage Bill	*Employment*	*Money Wages*
1939	100	100	100
1940	121	112	108
1941	137	115	119
1942	—	—	—
1943	243	134	181
1944	293	137	214

Accordingly, taking the index of money wages of Table 6:25 (i.e. that corresponding to our unit labour cost index) as our bench-mark figures, a continuous series (excepting values for 1942 and 1947) for 1939 to 1950 was obtained by adjusting the post-1944 daily state industrial index values upwards (by multiplying them by the ratio of their 1944 index number divided into that of the index of money wages *(iii)*.

We thus have index numbers for production, employment and money wages in 1950 over 1939, which enable us to link together the unit labour cost indices of 1939-46 and 1950-58.

The calculations above gave us an index of money wages between 1939 and 1950 for all industry except for the years 1942 and 1947. An index number for 1942 was interpolated by averaging the 1942 index values for annual and daily state industrial employees given in Table 6:26. The wage bill and employment figures from the business survey data finally permitted a continuous series to be constructed from 1939-58.

4. Tables 6:2 and 6:3 leave open the question of whether or not the share of wages rose in the vital price acceleration year of 1941/42. However, evidence relating to railways, state airlines, municipal gas services and metropolitan bus services all show 1941/42 as a year of increasing labour shares—only in the case of Istanbul's urban railways did labour's share decline. Generally speaking, the share of wages in value added in these activities changed in a similar direction to that in manufacturing. Thus, between 1941 and 1942 the share of the total wage bill in value added (calculated as the wage bill plus the difference between receipts and total expenses) changed from 76 per cent to 100 per cent in Istanbul and Kadikoy gas services combined; from 72 per cent to 79 per cent in Yemikoy gas services; from 60 per cent to 91 per cent in Izmir gas, from 71 per cent to 94 per cent in railways 'exploités par l'Etat'; from 49 per cent to 84 per cent in Ankara autobus service; and from 49 per cent to 59 per cent in Izmir autobus service. The State airlines saw the net current loss rise further, while the wage bill rose. On the other hand, Istanbul's metropolitan railways witnessed a decline in the share of wages in total value added from 121 per cent in 1941 to 52 per cent in 1942. This was the only case, however, in the figures examined of such a decline between 1941 and 1942 (R.O.T., Central Office of Statistics, *Annuaire Statistique, 1942-43,* Volume 14).

5. The discussion is conducted in the framework of the wartime inflation. Actually, a gentle rise of the cost-of-living index took place in 1938/39, judging from our average index (note 1). For Istanbul, at any rate, this was the first rise since the rise in 1935/36, itself the only increase during the 1930's (*Monthly Bulletin,* July 1959, Bilkur, 1949, *op. cit.,* p. 53). However, as may be observed from the figures of Table 6:2, conclusions concerning income redistribution throughout the war-time inflation are not materially affected by taking 1938 as our base date.

6. Estimates for column *(i)* from data given in R.O.T., *Small Statistical Abstract of Turkey, 1949,* Ankara, 1951; estimates for columns *(ii)* and *(iii)* from data given in V. Eldem, 1947/48, *op. cit.,* pp. 90-2, 107 and 145. Estimate *(i)* is based on figures from establishments covered by the Law for the Encouragement of Industry (large-scale industry, including, as well as manufacturing industry, gas, electricity, mining and quarrying, but excluding state monopoly enterprises producing alcohol and tobacco). Estimate *(ii)* is based on Eldem's estimates of wage bill and value added for all industry, excluding handicrafts. Estimate *(iii)* covers state establishments, monopolies, private industry, other establishments covered by the Labour Law (i.e. other than the above-mentioned, plus gas, electricity and building) and military factories. Estimates *(i)* and *(ii)* include an estimate for the value of wages in kind. Estimate *(iii)* does not. All cover salaried employees as well as wage earners. Estimates *(i)* and *(iii)* are percentages of *gross* value added. In estimate *(ii),* Eldem's figures of amortisation and interest payments for all industry were attributed entirely to the non-artisan sector to obtain the figures for value added.

7. For *prices of manufactures* see note 3, *Monthly Bulletin*, July 1959. *Raw material costs* were taken from the index of wholesale prices of raw materials compiled by the Chamber of Commerce of Istanbul (*Monthly Bulletin*, No. 67, September 1959). They relate mainly to home-produced materials, and are made up from observations of 9 items of animal origin and 8 items of vegetable origin (*Annuaire Statistique*, 1952). Turkish industry is largely based on home- produced raw materials. The value of imported raw materials (probably including semi-processed intermediate goods) used by industrial establishments coming within the scope of the Law for the Encouragement of Industry was 19.3 per cent of the total value of all raw materials used in 1938 (E.R. Lingeman, Board of Trade, *Overseas Economic Surveys: Turkey*, 1947, p. 84). This proportion appears to have declined. Thus, between 1938 and 1953-55, calculated at constant prices, imports of major producer goods (defined as consisting of hides, wool for pulp, cellulose and wood pulp, rubber, cocoa in powder form, wool yarns, cotton yarns, dyes and varnishes, paper for printing, cigarette paper and iron and steel other than for construction) used mainly in manufacturing, rose by 20-25 per cent, whereas the increase in manufacturing production was much greater. U.N., *Manufacturing Industry in Turkey*, 1958, p. 26). *Unit Labour Costs* for 1939-46, were obtained by dividing Hershlag's index of industrial production by an estimated index of the industrial wage bill. Hershlag's index was taken in preference to Eldem's two estimates (Eldem, 'Les Progrès de l'Industrialisation en Turquie', *Revue de la Faculté des Sciences Economiques de l'Université d'Istanbul*, Eighth Year, 1946-47, p. 77), since it is more up-to-date, incorporating modifications to Eldem's estimate (Hershlag, 1958, *op. cit.*, pp. 235-6). Moreover, as Eldem admits (1946-7), the undoubted decline in productivity in some sectors of industry may well mean some exaggeration of the growth of output during the war in his index, which is largely based on figures of the number of man-days worked in large-scale industry. Hershlag's index shows a significantly smaller increase in industrial output than do Eldem's two indices for the war period.

Although the index of unit labour costs thus obtained for this period of necessity referred to all industry, not just manufacturing industry, manufacturing accounted for 89 per cent of total industrial income in 1938—the remainder being accounted for by mining and quarrying and gas and electricity (R.O.T. Central Statistical Office, *National Income of Turkey, 1938, 1948-54*, Ankara, 1955).

For the period 1950 to 1958, the index of unit labour costs was obtained by dividing an index of the total wage bill (taken from the annual survey of the activities of manufacturing started in 1950, *Annuaire Statistique*, 1959) by an index of manufacturing production (O.E.E.C., Statistical Bulletins, *Industrial Statistics, 1900-1959*, Paris, 1960). The surveys from which the wage bill was taken cover establishments using more than 10 horse power and employing more than 10 workers. These annual surveys are estimated to cover enterprises accounting for approximately 75 per cent or more of total manufacturing, whether considered in terms of employment or value added. The O.E.E.C. production index is based on value added weights of 1938 (for these and other details, see O.E.E.C., Statistical Bulletins, Definitions and Methods, Part 1, *Industrial Production*, 1st edition, Paris, 1953).

TABLE 6:26
Indices of Money Wages

	(i) Annual Average— State Industrial Establishments	(ii) Annual Average— State Industrial Establishments	(iii) All Industry Average Money Wages
1939	100	100	100
1940	103	105	108
1941	116	115	119
1942	135	139	—
1943	178	161	181
1944	203	192	214
1945	224	219	—
1946	—	227	—
1947	—	—	—
1948	—	355	—
1949	—	376	—
1950	—	397	—

Sources: (i)   Eldem, 1946-7, p. 91;
          (ii) Eldem, 1947-8, p. 112; and 1951-2, p. 159.
          (iii) Table

Notes: (1)   The 1939, 1948-50 figures of (ii) are not strictly com-
               parable with those in (ii) for 1939-46, since the latter,
               as well as industrial establishments, also cover
               'collectivites publiques', whereas the former do not.
               'Collectivites publiques' include the state monopolies,
               Defence Ministry repair workshops, railways and State
               airways, electricity, gas, water and public slaughter
               houses. Figures are before tax.
         (2)   Index (i) covers salary earners as well as manual workers,
               as of course does index (iii). Index (ii) covers manual
               workers only.

The comparability of the indices of raw material costs and unit
labour costs with the price index can only be approximate at best.
Although both the index of prices of manufactures and that of raw
materials relate to Istanbul (which ensures their geographical alignment, if not their representativeness for the whole country) the former
has been constructed in a highly arbitrary fashion, and the latter is
constructed from only 17 items. The reduction in imported supplies
during the war, and the way in which the wholesale price index of
imported articles rose faster than our index of prices of manufactures,
indicates that the latter largely covered home products, as did the
index of wholesale prices of raw materials. Even more doubtful is the
index of unit labour costs. Alignment weaknesses are also built into the
attempt to link up the wartime index with the unit labour cost index
for the 1950's. Thus the 1938/39 employment change related to
workers only, whereas the 1938-50 change referred to workers *plus*

salary earners, as did the wartime wage-bill indices. Similarly, the
linking of money wages between the wartime period and 1950 relied on
figures relating to manual workers only, whereas the wartime average
earnings indices relate to both manual workers and salary earners.

The main problem here, however, is the index of industrial production. We have seen that there were two alternatives for the war
period, and the same applies to the 1950's (*Monthly Bulletin*, September 1959, and R.O.T., Ministry of Finance, *Budget Speech, 1957*,
Istanbul, 1957-58, p. 74). For the war period the most up-to-date
estimate was taken, and for the 1950's the estimate was taken which
yielded a ratio index of unit labour costs to final prices corresponding
most closely to the ratio of wage bill to total receipts obtained from the

TABLE 6:27
Turkey: Average Earnings in State Industry and All Manufacturing
Industry, 1950-53 (Indices)

	(i) State Industry and Collective Publiques	(ii) All Manufacturing Industry
1950	100	100
1951	110	109
1952	120	112
1953	136	137

Sources: (i) Eldem, 1951-2, p. 159;
         (ii) *Annuaire Statistique, 1959*.

business survey figures. This partly helped take care of the subsidiary
problem that the index of industrial production related to both artisan
and modern sectors (at least in principle), whereas the wage bill and/or
money wage and employment indices related to the modern sector.
Even given this element of juggling, the approximate correspondence in
the 1950's of the ratios of unit labour costs to final prices and of raw
material costs to final prices to the ratios of wage bill to total receipts
and expenditure on raw materials to total receipts (Tables 6:3, 6:4
and 6:6) is encouraging, and the compatibility of year-to-year changes
in relative shares given in Tables 6:4 and 6:6 with the movements of the
price/cost ratios all suggest that, despite their inadequacies, these ratios
are not too unreliable a guide to the broad direction of the relative
movement of prices and costs. It should, however, be noted that the
domestic nature of the index of raw material wholesale prices, while the
index of manufactured prices reflects changes in some imported prices,
means that we cannot expect the price/cost ratios to confirm exactly to
the picture shown by the various direct industrial statistics, as they do
not. On the other hand, the small proportion of imported raw materials
used in manufacturing industry implies that they ought to show a
broad agreement, as they do.

8.   Gross surplus = value of production less total wage bill (defined to

include salaries paid to non-manual employees) and the value of raw materials. These figures correspond to those of column *(i)*, Table 6:2.

9. If the price-cost ratios of Table 6:3 are smoothed by taking a three year moving average of the figures, the directional trends shown are almost exactly the same as those shown by the smoothed receipts/expenditure ratios of Table 6:4.

10. The actual figures of Table 6:4 show this reversal to have been irregular and the initial decline to have been very brief.

11. The previous period, 1945/46-1950/51, during which price increases were only sporadic, was one in which, as the price/cost ratios of Table 6:3 indicate, there took place a rise in labour's share due to declining gross margins, itself the result of active pressure from rising unit labour costs and sporadically rising raw material costs. Relaxation of import controls in 1946, and the controlled but still significant flow of imports thereafter, served to limit the extent to which it was possible to pass rising prime costs on to prices while maintaining existing margins. *Cf.* U.N., *Manufacturing Industry in Turkey*, 1958, p. 50; Z.Y. Hershlag, 1958, pp. 194 and 246; and I.B.R.D., 1951, p. 105.

12. The figures cover about 75 per cent of manufacturing industry, whether measured in terms of employment or value added. They relate to establishments using more than 10 horse-power and employing more than 10 workers.

13. It should be noted that the decline of raw material costs from 1951-53, observable from Table 6:3, may be misleading, since the heavy weighting of this index by textile materials and its limitation geographically to Istanbul make it unrepresentative, and textile final and raw material prices were subject to special factors in 1952. Calculations of implicit price indices of agricultural products from the national income figures (*Monthly Bulletin*, September 1959) show agricultural prices to have risen continuously after 1949/50. However, the price/cost *ratios* are less misleading, since the special problems of textiles and their overweighting affect *both* the raw material and the final price indices. Moreover, the rates of price rise for both agricultural and industrial products shown by the implicit indices seem implausibly high in the light of the movement of the various group indices based on actual price observations, which in fact suggest that raw material prices were rising in every year of the 1950's (after 1949/50) except one, i.e. 1952.

14. Total value of production is total value of sales and receipts.

15. The dating here refers to prices of manufactures.

16. Hershlag, 1958, gives the remarkable figure of one million persons as having been mobilised for military service (p. 179).

17. *Ibid.*, p. 193. Government investment expenditures, although much

reduced compared with the pre-war period, also continued in manufacturing and road and rail transport, and added to expansionary pressures. U.N., Department of Economic and Social Affairs, *The Development of Manufacturing Industry in Egypt, Israel and Turkey,* New York, 1958, pp. 8 and 9.

18. Income tax was introduced only in 1950. Although to finance the defence expenditure a severe capital levy (the Varlik) was imposed together with a 10 per cent tax on agricultural produce, this was not until 1942. Moreover, both these taxes seem to have been to a degree self-defeating, in that they had disincentive effects on production, partly owing to their nature and partly, at least in the case of the Varlik, owing to the harsh and arbitrary methods of implementation.

19. The market for government securities and the money market in general was extremely feeble (*cf.* I.B.R.D., 1951, pp. 211-2, 213, 217 and 219).

20. Speculation, with associated hoarding of goods, acted as a secondary inflationary influence. Department of Overseas Trade, Turkey, *Review of Economic Conditions,* 1945, p. 26).

21. U.N., *Manufacturing Industry in Turkey,* 1958, p. 8; Hershlag, 1958, p. 180.

22. This compares with an annual average growth rate of industrial production of about 12 per cent between 1930 and 1939, U.N., *Manufacturing Industry in Turkey,* p. 17.

23. Agriculture appears to have been particularly severely hit by the effects of manpower mobilisation (*ibid.,* p. 15). Adverse weather conditions, together with the shortage of credit, also contributed to the difficulties of agriculture (Hershlag, 1958, p. 180).

24. In effect, we are here referring to 1942/43 and 1943/44, since the small price rise of 1944/45 was partly the result of the ending of wartime conditions, and we are here considering the period of the war economy only.

25. Hershlag, p. 193.

26. *Ibid.,* p. 235. The improved supply of imported complementary goods for industry is not reflected in the aggregate quantum import index which, however, is no guide to the disinflationary effect of import policy, since the government closely controlled imports during the war (as it did most other aspects of the economy) and pursued a deliberate policy of importing essential items. (*Ibid.,* pp. 177, 179 and 245; U.N., *Manufacturing Industry in Turkey,* 1958, p. 7.)

27. Budget deficit figures are inclusive of the operation of the various State Economic Enterprises and such government enterprises as Etibank and Toprak which were not, however, of great importance during the war. The official balance of trade figures record only visible imports and

exports. It is likely that the weakness of Turkey's merchant marine to some extent affected the positive balance shown, though not completely (*cf.* Hershlag, pp. 155 and 245).

28. *Cf.* Department of Overseas Trade, 1945, p. 28.

29. *Ibid.,* p. 50; Hershlag, p. 235. On the other hand, Lingeman, Commercial Counsellor to H.M. Embassy at Ankara, (1947, *op. cit.,* p. 28) states that price control proved ineffective, but this may well reflect the influence of cost increases on industrial product prices and the less controlled movement of agricultural prices. Grain prices in fact received support from Toprak, the Office of Soil Products, (I.B.R.D., p. 79).

30. *Monthly Bulletin,* May 1959. Istanbul Chamber of Commerce figures. The three price indices are constituents of the general wholesale price index.

31. As in the latter half of the 1950's.

32. In fact, as we have seen, during the war rising labour costs played an entirely passive role, actually lagging behind final prices, while the decline in the share of profits was accomplished alone by the rise in the ratio of raw material costs to final prices.

33. In 1938, 91 per cent of Turkey's exports were agricultural products, i.e. mainly cereals, fruits and vegetables, tobacco, cotton and mohair wool, U.N., *Manufacturing Industry in Turkey,* 1958, p. 25.

34. Except for 1941.

35. *Ibid.,* p. 37.

36. Department of Overseas Trade, 1945, p. 25.

37. Hershlag, p. 180.

38. Thornburg, Spry and Soule, p. 161; Department of Overseas Trade, 1945, p. 27.

39. The terms of trade were, in effect, the ratio between exports of agricultural commodity and imports of manufacturers.

40. Imported raw materials (accounted for slightly under 25 per cent of the total value of raw materials (including intermediate goods) used in the establishments under the Law on the Encouragement of Industry (i.e. large-scale industrial establishments) in 1938, (Lingeman, 1947, *op. cit.,* p. 84.)

41. Hershlag, p. 235.

42. This was so because, while industrial raw material costs per unit of output were rising at a rate roughly determined by the rate of rise of

agricultural prices, agricultural money demand for industrial products
was rising at the same rate as agricultural prices (industrial raw material
costs), less the reduction in supplies marketed. (See Department of
Overseas Trade, 1945, p. 28; U.N., *Economic Conditions, 1951-52*,
p. 39.)

43. Department of Overseas Trade, 1945, p. 28; U.N., *Economic
Conditions, 1951-52*, p. 39.

44. 'In Turkey most industrial prices were controlled during the war and
rose less than agricultural prices, which shot up because mobilisation
resulted in reduced production,' (U.N., *Manufacturing Industry in
Turkey*, 1958, p. 50.)

45. During the war, 'Turkey continued to benefit from emergency conditions of production, with almost no foreign competition and little
interference by world market prices with her own prices, which were
influenced by the local fairly high costs of production.' (Hershlag,
p. 235).

46. Immediately after the war an improved supply of imports, together with a rapid improvement of agricultural production, facilitated
by demobilisation and E.C.A. aid for agricultural mechanisation, served
to absorb the expanding pressures of increasing private investment and
a probable rise in the proportion of rural income spent on consumption.
A rather poor industrial performance and rising prime costs did not
affect prices of manufactures markedly as competition from foreign
imported manufactures acted as a partial check during most of the
period.

47. *Budget deficits* relate to both general and annexed budgets, but do
not include State Economic Enterprises. Transfers of interest and
capital are included in the current transactions of the *balance of payments*. The balance of payments fiscal year is a twelve-month period
between July and the following June.

48. The greatest share of budget expenditure was absorbed by
economic development (32 per cent), followed by defence (24 per
cent), and education (13 per cent), (O.E.E.C. *Economic Conditions in
Member and Associated Countries of the O.E.C.: Turkey*, Paris 1958,
p. 17). The influx of Bulgarian refugees (250,000 in 1950 and 1951),
who had to be provided with food, clothing and housing, also added to
budgetary expenditures (U.N. Department of Economic Affairs, *Review
of Economic Conditions in the Middle East, 1951-52, Supplement to
World Economic Report*, 1953, p. 71).

49. While the total internal floating debt of the State Economic
Enterprises increased steadily between 1950 and 1953, this was
almost entirely accounted for up to 1952 by the Central Bank holding
an increased volume of Treasury guaranteed bonds on behalf of Toprak,
the Office of Soil Products, the enterprise concerned with agricultural
price supports. In 1952/53, however, the increase in the Central Bank's
holdings of Toprak's bonds was not large enough to account for the
increase in the floating debt of the State Economic Enterprises, and

this may well have been due to investments (from data in *Monthly Bulletin of Statistics*, No. 67, September 1959, p. 65).

50. Proportion of gross investment in G.N.P. from *First Five Year Plan*, 1963, p. 15. Division of gross investment by type of investor from Okyar, 1962, quoted in Gultan Kazgan, 1965, p. 153.

51. Budget deficits were, of course, a contributory factor in the expansion of incomes permitting the private sector to finance investment from savings rather than from credits directly.

52. The high level of profits in manufacturing has also been an inducement to households to invest in this sector. U.N. *Manufacturing Industry in Turkey*, 1958, p. 75; U.N., Department of Economic and Social Affairs, *Economic Developments in the Middle East, 1945-54, Supplement to World Economic Report, 1953-54*, 1955, p. 216.

53. '. . . there was until recently no institution providing long-term credit to private industry. Although its statute assigned this function also to the Sumerbank, the latter has not been able to perform it. Moreover obstacles to the formation of joint stock companies, added to the initial absence of a capital market, restricted the possibility of raising capital through sale of stocks and bonds. A limited supply of short-term (mostly 90-day) credits was available from commercial banks, at rates varying between 9 and 12 per cent. The Industrial Development Bank founded in 1950 with the exclusive aim of financing private investment has improved the situation with regard to medium-term and long-term credit. . . However, the bank cannot meet all needs for long-term credit and private enterprise therefore still encounters difficulties in this field.' (U.N., *Manifacturing Industry in Turkey*, 1958, p. 75.)

54. G. Kazgan, p. 155.

55. U.N., *Economic Development, 1945-54*, p. 231.

56. Financing of investments in residential dwellings was also partly accomplished by personal funds seeking a hedge against inflation and seeking profitable outlets in an economy with a very limited capital market. The inflation hedge motive for investment in housing became particularly important in the later '50s. (G. Kazgan, pp. 154-55; I.B.R.D., p. 209.)

57. A.P. Alexander, p. 491. See also U.N., *Economic Developments, 1945-54*, p. 224.

58. A.P. Alexander, pp. 482, 491 and 492. Price supports contributed to excess demand insofar as Central Bank credit financed the difference between the prices paid to the producers and those received from exporters.

59. Agricultural and commercial profits have been an increasing source of finance for investment in manufacturing industry (*ibid.*, p. 496).

60. The supply of tractors is a good example.

61. i.e. comparing the average of 1951 and 1952, with that of the three previous years. The decline in the proportion of raw materials in total imports was due to the same upsurge in home production, especially agricultural production, which limited the increase in imported consumer goods.

62. O.E.C.D., 1963, p. 10.

63. U.N., Economic Commission for Europe, *Economic Survey of Europe in 1961, Part II. Some Factors in Economic Growth during the 1950s,* 1964, p. 28. The growth of agricultural output was half as fast again as that of population, O.E.C.D., 1963, p. 9.

64. U.N., *Manufacturing Industry in Turkey,* 1958, pp. 8, 15, 19; Meyer, p. 74.

65. U.N., *Manufacturing Industry in Turkey,* 1958, p. 16.

66. Except for 1957-1958.

67. Moreover, private sector investment became increasingly directed towards less productive activities or less immediately productive activities, in particular, residential construction and speculation, and away from manufacturing industry after 1954. Speculative activities relating to imports have also directed funds away from manufacturing (G. Kazgan, pp. 155 and 160-62).

68. Financing from outside resources, mainly the Central Bank and the commercial banks, of total expenditures of all State Economic Enterprises, excluding Toprak, rose from 611 million Turkish lira in 1955 to 836 million Turkish lira in 1956 and 964 million in 1957. The corresponding figures for the volume of internal finance were 2340 million Turkish lira, 2443 million Turkish lira and 3516 million Turkish lira, O.E.E.C., 1958, p. 20. The average annual level of floating debt of the State Economic Enterprises, including Toprak, was nearly 50 per cent higher in the period 1954-58 than in the period 1951-53. *Monthly Bulletin,* September 1959, p. 15.

69. On 'the double character of the inflationary spiral in Turkey, the demand and cost inflation,' see Hershlag, pp. 197-98. On the influence of rising raw material costs in raising the price level of final output, see U.N., Department of Economic and Social Affairs, *Economic Developments in the Middle East, 1955-56, Supplement to World Economic Survey,* 1956, 1957, p. 97; and U.N., *Economic Developments, 1945-54,* p. 231.

70. *Cf.* U.N., *Economic Conditions, 1951-52,* p. 72.

71. Establishments employing 200 or more persons accounted for 85 per cent of the total value of equipment in 1954, 73 per cent of value added and 36 per cent of total employment. This concentration is partly the result of the fact that the state enterprises tend to be very large (average number of persons engaged per unit in 1950 being 738

as compared with 63 in the private sector in establishments with 10 or more persons), both because state activity tends to be more heavily concentrated in branches of industry of large optimum size such as iron and steel, and paper, and because, in specific sectors where there were both state and private establishments, the former tended to be larger. The state accounted for 45 per cent of all employment in medium and large-scale industry in 1950. (U.N., *Manufacturing Industry in Turkey*, 1958, pp. 38, 43 and 54). Publicly-owned enterprises have operated on the basis of some kind of cost-plus pricing policy (Hershlag, p. 242) and have tended to generalise this policy throughout the manufacturing sector through their role as price leaders. The role of price leaders played by government-owned establishments is partly the result of the fact that prices of state enterprises are sometimes set so high as to permit generous profit margins for private entrepreneurs operating in the same field, so that there is little, if any, incentive for private enterprise, which often has lower costs, to take independent price initiatives. (See Hershlag, p. 197, for a post-war example of this, and U.N., *Manufacturing Industry in Turkey*, 1958, p. 50, for the wartime.) Moreover, the government has actively intervened during the 1950's to control prices in some relation to costs so that 'Until the introduction of the stabilisation programme (in 1955), most prices were thus either controlled directly or indirectly through the compulsory application of a "cost plus" formula, profit margins being determined by government decree,' (O.E.E.C., 1958, p. 5.)

72. Of course, downward inflexibility of prices of manufactures means that margins will be much more variable when costs are declining. We are here concerned only with circumstances in which prime costs are rising, which is generally the case during inflation. The essence of the situation in 1951/52 was that the inflationary process witnessed a 'pause', during which the decline of world demand after the stock-piling of 1951 led to a decline in raw material prices, while prices of manufactures rose only slightly. The large decline of gross margins in state industry between 1940 and 1941 was connected with the fact that this year was the first in which the wartime supply difficulties had actually brought about a decline in industrial production.

73. The Business Research Department's national wholesale price index of industrial raw materials and semi-products fell from 446 to 424 between 1951 and 1952, while the overall wholesale price index, of which the former is a constituent, rose from 482 to 486. The Istanbul Chamber of Commerce wholesale price index of raw materials fell from 642 to 611 between 1951 and 1952, while its wholesale price index of home products rose from 467 to 500 (1938 = 100 for both indices), *Monthly Bulletin*, September 1959. As regards the rise of the prices of manufactures, our synthetic index of Table 6:16 seems to have given an exaggerated impression of the rate of rise.

74. *Utilisation* is defined as production as a percentage of capacity. For pig iron the production figures refer to the quantity used within the producing establishment or sold. Production was approximately equal to capacity, amounting to 99,000 tons, in 1953, but a large part

was neither used internally nor sold, and accumulated as stocks. For food, the production figures refer to millions of cans, 1950-53 average.

75. See also F.A.O., *Mediterranean Development Project*, Rome, 1959, p. 29. '... virtually throughout the region, capacity in non-durable consumption goods industries has increased more rapidly than output, and the same holds good for many other industries as well.' The 'region' referred to covers Iraq, Syria, Lebanon, Tunisia, Morocco, Spain, Greece, Yugoslavia, Israel and Turkey. On the emergence in Turkey of excess capacity in manufacturing in the later 1950's, following on the investment boom of the first half of the '50s, see O.E.E.C., 1958, p. 7.

76. In this respect the index of raw material costs in Table 6:3 is somewhat misleading, showing as it does a continuous decline in raw material costs between 1951 and 1953. However, this covered Istanbul only. The Business Research Department's national overall index of 'Industrial Raw Materials and Semi-Products' declined in only one year. Both indices show food prices rising continuously after 1950 (*Monthly Bulletin*, July 1959). (Actually, the Business Research Department's index of 'Industrial Raw Materials and Semi-Products', shows a decline in 1953, but this appears to have been a clerical error, since those of its constituent elements which decline in the period do so only in 1952. *Monthly Bulletin*, July 1959, p. 34.)

77. In 1948 the per capita consumption of calories per day was 2,480 in Turkey and only 1,620 in India. The difference in cotton textile consumption was much less (U.N., *Manufacturing Industry in Turkey*, 1958, pp. 2-3; Meyer, pp. 69-70).

78. A.P. Alexander, pp. 488-9.

79. Meyer, p. 77.

80. *Ibid.*, p. 77; A.P. Alexander, p. 491.

81. *Ibid.*, p. 491.

82. The figures are estimates, and cover items the total value of which in 1950 amounted to approximately 70 per cent of aggregate personal consumption. Services do not include communications, amusements and travel.

83. G. Kazgan, pp. 158-160. The very small decline in gross margins in 1959 was the lagged result of the good harvest in 1958. (*Cf.* O.E.E.C., *Turkey*, 1958, p. 7.)

84. As happened in India and Peru.

85. Compared with the beginning of the inflation.

CHAPTER 7

MONEY WAGES AND INFLATION IN TURKEY, 1939-58

Income Redistribution and the Behaviour of Money Wages During Inflation

During the war, labour's share in gross value added was relitively stable, rising very slightly. The rise of labour's share was the result of active pressure on gross margins from rising raw material costs. The rise in money wages ensured that this was sufficient to reduce the share of gross profit. However, since the rise of money wages lagged behind that of raw material costs and final prices,[1] the declining proportion of labour costs in total prime costs all but counteracted the effect of declining gross margins.

During the 1950's,[2] money wages rose faster than final prices, although between 1953 and 1955 the rise of productivity caused unit labour costs to lag behind final prices (see chapter 6, Table 6:3). The rise of money wages was the initial active force tending to erode the large profit margins of 1952 (albeit not very successfully) and, subsequently, was sufficiently fast to ensure that the active pressure from raw material costs on margins would raise labour's share. Between 1955 and 1957, although the productivity increase caused unit labour costs to lag behind final prices, and although raw material costs also lagged behind final prices, the rise of· money wages was sufficiently fast to ensure that the resulting decline in labour's share was very small. After 1957, the rise of money wages became an active factor in compressing margins and increasing labour's share of gross value added.

Thus, in both the wartime and the 1950's inflation, the rise of money wages partly determined the direction of income redistribution. The role of rising money wages was principally a passive one, entirely so during the war, when active pressure on gross margins came from rising raw material costs, and mainly so during the inflation of the 1950's, in the sense that rising money wages then *supplemented* pressure on gross margins from rising raw material costs.[3] Accordingly, we turn again to explaining the rise of money wages.

Money Wage Changes—the Labour Market

We again find that money wages rose continuously throughout the period (Table 7:1). The rise of money wages started to raise real wages in 1944 and achieved the 1939 level of real wages in 1948. The next decade witnessed money wages rising sufficiently to increase real wages by about 55 per cent, despite the fact that the cost of living more than doubled. Again we turn first to the possible role of labour scarcity as a causal factor in the rise of money wages.

Prior to the war, urban unskilled labour[4] does not appear to have been plentiful, although since observers have not always distinguished between the supply of temporary and the supply of permanent labour, the position is not clear. Parker and Smith, for example, commenting on 'the difficulty of getting labour, especially skilled labour', remark that 'the mass of the people still work on the land and look on industry as a source of obtaining the means of buying a small holding rather than as a permanent career. Hence it has been necessary to attract labour and try to keep it in industry'.[5]

On the Turkish labour market were imposed the demands of war, including, as we have said, the mobilisation of large numbers of men for the army and the expanded needs of industry which 'resulted in a scarcity of productive labour'.[6]

There is reason to believe that, as appears to have been the case in India and Peru, the strain on manpower was felt more in connection with skilled labour and labour for the mines and agriculture than in connection with unskilled urban labour. The 1945 Department of Overseas Trade Review commented that 'the needs of the army resulted in a scarcity of agricultural workers' (p. 25). Although a *general* manpower scarcity is attested whenever the topic of labour supply is raised, nowhere is a lack of unskilled urban industrial labour referred to. This type of labour, after all, constituted only a very small proportion of the total economically active population.[7] The measures, described in the 1947 Board of Trade Review, to overcome labour supply problems during the war (p. 28), while establishing a maximum working day of 9 hours, authorised the working of 2 hours overtime daily in only certain special categories of labour, a clear indication that the crux of the problem lay in the supply of skilled workers. Further, Karpat (1959), p. 91, records that the 3 August, 1941 Amendments to the National Defence Law of 19 January, 1940 (stating that workers and

TABLE 7:1
Turkey: Indices of Money Wages, Cost of Living and Real Wages, 1939-58

	Cost-of-Living Index	Money Wages	Real Wages
1939	100	100	100
1940	110	108	98
1941	131	119	91
1942	219	138	63
1943	310	181	58
1944	319	214	67
1945	328	244	74
1946	325	253	78
1947	321	—	—
1948	328	396	121
1949	356	419	118
1950	341	443	130
1951	340	483	142
1952	360	536	149
1953	375	607	162
1954	413	669	162
1955	464	740	159
1956	517	917	177
1957	579	1046	181
1958	673	1258	187

Sources: Cost-of-Living index as for Table 6:1. For money-wage index see Chapter 6, note 7.

qualified personnel be provided to industrial and mining enterprises and that workers and technicians could not leave their work without an acceptable reason), empowering the use of security force by district and provincial governors against those who fled their workplace or failed to perform their work obligations, was aimed principally at peasants living in the mining areas. Such personnel difficulties do not appear at least to have been so acute in the towns. This is not, of course, to say that they were entirely absent, even for unskilled labour.

TABLE 7:2
Turkey: Total Employment Applications and Placings, 1946-50 (Public
Employment Office

	Applications	Placings	Placings as a Proportion of Applications (Percentages)
1946	2,110	1,742	82.5
1947	3,516	3,208	91.3
1948	3,625	2,336	64.4
1949	4,007	1,863	46.5
1950	4,514	1,701	37.7

Source: Calculated from figures in *Monthly Bulletin*, September 1959, p. 8.

The post-war period from its inception was one of a plentiful supply of unskilled urban labour, developing, round about 1950, into one of visible excess. The 'excessive demand for work' was considered to be a reason for the small proportion of workers in the higher age-ranges in industry, revealed by an enquiry undertaken by the employment service in 1946[8] and Karpat (1959, p. 367) considered lack of employment to be one of the reasons for the 'leftist' success in trade unions and among intellectuals immediately after the war. Moreover, while the shift of labour from agriculture appears to have become a more important source of urban labour than the internal urban population growth only after 1950,[9] nevertheless, pressure on the land was severe in the earliest post-war years[10] as well as subsequently.[11]

The I.L.O. mission reported in 1950 that 'it is. . . generally recognised that with the exception of skilled workers. . . the available manpower is greatly in excess of industrial requirements. This fact is admitted only by the employment agencies, which have great difficulty in finding employment for workers, but also by the undertakings visited, since these, despite the great instability of labour, invariably find themselves with far more candidates than jobs,' *Labour Problems*, 1950, p. 167.[12]

In the late 1940's and early 1950's the pressure on the land began to result in a visible urban surplus, not simply adequacy, of unskilled labour. The U.N. 1952/53 *Summary of Recent Economic Developments in the Middle East*, reported (p. 101) a large influx of unskilled labour from the villages into the towns. Meyer, referring to the land shortage,

says, 'relief has come through growing migration into the
cities. From 1950 to 1955 alone, Turkey's urban percentage
rose by 3.3 per cent—including a movement of about
800,000 people off the land. Life in the growing slums of
Ankara and İstanbul seemingly offered increasing appeal to
Turkish peasants' (*op. cit.*, p. 77).[13] To the continuous
pressure of the growing population on marginal land has been
added the displacement resulting from mechanisation, displacement which was manifest as early as 1950.[14] '. . . Mechanisation may have to some extent displaced labour in the
newly cultivated areas, where large landowners have taken
possession of village communal grazing lands for tractor
farming. Of the new area brought under cultivation, 62 per
cent is estimated to have been grazing, or forest land, and its
appropriation for commercial farming not only displaces
herdsmen but probably also undermines the position of
peasant farmers who use the communal grazing land as an
adjunct to farming on their small holdings.'[15]

Additionally, unemployment due to declines in effective
demand has been known in the1950's, for example in the
textile industry in 1950[16] and 1951,[17] not to mention
technological unemployment in modern industry.[18]

Although since the end of the war employers in urban
areas have experienced no difficulty in obtaining unskilled
labour *per se*, the large-scale movements of migratory (often
seasonal) labour from agriculture into the towns have
suggested to a number of observers that the urban labour
force, including its industrial constituent, is predominantly
composed of temporary, uncommitted labourers.[19] If this is
so, it is rather surprising, in view of the marked acceleration
of urbanisation since 1950 and the extensive efforts by state
establishments to reduce high turnover rates.[20] Indeed, other
observers have, by contrast, expressed the view that a considerable proportion of the labour force is now committed
permanently to urban industry.[21]

The difference between those two views may be ascribed to
the fact that part of the high turnover may be the result of
factors internal to urban industry causing movement between firms by fully-urbanised workers. Another explanation
of these contrasting views may lie in the fact that apparently
rather few of the migrants, at least in the 1950's, sought
industrial employment (this may, of course, be due to the
difficulty of obtaining it) which suggests that the temporary
nature of the urban labour force is not the same thing, or is

to a decreasing extent the same thing as, a temporary *industrial*[22] labour force; therefore, insofar as high labour turnover in industrial establishments is a product of rural/urban movements, it may be on the decline. Thus, 'service occupations are overcrowded since the city offers migrants the prospects of setting up as small traders and craftsmen, street sellers, peddlers and porters; such speculative dealings are more attractive than industrial employment.'[23] The possible hiatus between the seasonal swing of labour movement and the stability of the industrial labour force is clear.

To summarise, urban, unskilled, temporary labour was plentiful throughout the whole period, with the possible, though doubtful, exception of the war period. Round about 1950, a visible urban surplus began to appear, which has grown throughout the '50s. Stable labour appears to have been rather less plentiful, but even for stable labour the supply seems to have been both significant proportionately, and growing. Thus, at first sight, scarcity of labour does not appear to have been a major factor in the uninterrupted war and post-war rise of money earnings.

But what of the possibility that the excess labour supply post-war is itself the lagged result of the rise of money wages? If this were so then, at least for the war period, scarcity of labour as an explanation of the rise of money wages would appear more plausible. However, in Turkey, as in India and Peru, the migration of rural labour to the towns is the product rather of deficiency of rural employment opportunities than of the relatively higher earnings in the towns. Discussing the flow of rural labour to Istanbul, the I.L.O., 1960, *Movement of Labour* Report remarks that '... there is insufficient land to support the agricultural population... According to a recent I.L.O. survey... 36 per cent of the civilian labour force in the villages surveyed were forced to take employment outside the village for part of the year, while a further 24 per cent were reported as being interested in outside employment if opportunities were available.' (pp. 171-172).

Employers have also used methods other than raising wages to obtain labour. Such methods have been various, made by both private and public authorities. They include provision of housing and schools 'for apprentices and young workers,'[24] and official labour placement organisation (which also provides cheap housing for transit labour)[25] which appears to be able to 'match fairly well the present requirements of many employers'[26] for skilled workers, advertising in leading newspapers or contacting the relevant trades and craft organisations (which are an important source for the employer), the offering of small advances when recruiting village labour, and the provision of transportation between village and work place.[27] Even when labour was obtained by a classical (or neo-classical) process of bidding for labour the result was not necessarily to raise money wages. Referring to the period before 1946, Karpat (p. 887) says that 'in the southern parts of the country labour was sold at auctions by entrepreneurs who would father the unemployed men in the villages and offer them to the highest bidder in the cities, keeping for themselves the difference between the wages they paid to the peasants and the amount received from the employer.' Further, any rise of money wages via a bidding-up process must have been restricted to some extent by the fact that managers of state enterprises did not have the power to set wage rates, at least in 1950, on the basis of local labour market conditions.[28]

During the war, the period when the urban labour supply appears to have been least adequate, the principal[29] method of recruiting industrial labour was straightforward direction by the state.

'The state, faced with the need for additional materials to meet the needs of the army and civilian population, tried to increase production. . . Since there was an acute shortage of manpower in mines and industry, chiefly because of low wages and a lack of a class of industrial workers willing to work in such enterprises, the state imposed compulsory work obligations on certain people under the Milli Korunna Kanunu, National Defence Law passed in 1940.'[30]

All this does not preclude efforts to obtain labour by means of raising money wages. 'The most intensively cultivated part of Anatolia is the West. . . Here the demand for labour. . . is so great that there is often considerable labour shortage, and high rates of cash wages are paid.'[31] Other writers[32] have referred to the difficulty of obtaining labour as being the principal support of urban wages and noted that wage rates varied from place to place according to local supply and demand conditions in the labour market, although they have in mind the pre-war period and not the period with which we are concerned.[33]

Just as employers have found means other than raising money wages to obtain labour, the literature does not record that they have raised money wages to ensure stability of the labour force. Turkish private employers tend in any case to take a short-term view of matters[34] and, of course, the adverse effect on working class bargaining power of labour instability[35] will have offset the disadvantages in terms of productivity.[36]

Moreover, as we have remarked, nearly all efforts to reduce labour turnover have been made on the part of the state enterprises and the inducements reported have been entirely non-monetary, including social services and payments in kind, such as food and clothing, housing, medical care and recreational facilities,[37] good labour relations,[38] retention of workers during slack seasons,[39] and schools and canteens.[40] Housing has been perhaps the most important measure taken.[41] Indeed, the I.B.R.D. (1951) report specifically criticised the attempt to combat labour turnover at the level of the firm by such non-monetary means (p. 148), and the U.N. publication *Manufacturing Industry in Turkey*, (1958, p. 88), considered high labour turnover to be itself a result of low wages. Moreover, average money wages in private establishments have not moved more slowly than those in state establishments (Table 7:3), as we should expect (bearing in mind the relatively greater effort exerted by state enterprises to reduce turnover), were the efforts to obtain a stable labour force decisive in raising money wages.

To conclude, the evidence concerning the reasons for the rural/urban population shift, of the urban labour supply position and of the methods used to obtain labour, stable or

TABLE 7:3
Turkey: Indices of Average Annual Money Wages in State and Private
Manufacturing Establishments, 1950-58 (1950 = 100)

	State	Private
1950	100	100
1951	105	114
1952	119	129
1953	139	142
1954	154	160
1955	165	183
1956	180	227
1957	202	282
1958	243	349

Source: Calculated from business survey figures from *Annuaire Statistique*, 1959.

unstable, cumulatively militates against any general explanation of the rise of money wages of unskilled urban labour
as being due either to attempts to obtain labour *per se* or
stable labour, and the methods used to obtain labour during
the war suggest that such scarcity of unskilled urban labour
as existed played a minor role in the rise of money wages
in this period.

Money Wage Changes—The Product Market

Turning to the relationship between money-wage changes
and industrial prosperity, we again observe from Table 7:4
that changes in industrial prosperity (as measured by the
changes of the gross surplus) in one year tend to be followed
by variations in the rate of rise of money wages in the same
direction (i.e. rises and/or accelerations, declines and/or
decelerations) in the following year (in 5 out of 6 cases). This
is again the kind of non-linear relationship we might expect
if bargaining power were partly but only partly a function of
industrial prosperity.

TABLE 7:4

Turkey: Percentage Changes in the Cost-of-Living Index, Average Money
Wages, Gross Surplus and Gross Margins in Manufacturing Industry,
1950-58

	Average Money Wages	Cost-of-Living Index	Gross Surplus
1950/51	—	−0.3	18.0
1951/52	10.1	5.8	34.8
1952/53	13.2	4.1	20.8
1953/54	10.2	10.2	8.3
1954/55	10.6	12.4	25.5
1955/56	18.6	114.0	11.9
1956/57	17.7	12.0	32.2
1957/58	21.9	16.3	13.8

Money Wage Changes and Industrial Pressures

Exactly the same kind of relationship between money-wage
changes and the cost-of-living index may be observed as was
observed between money-wage changes and changes in
industrial prosperity, except for the fact that the cost of
living appears to exert a greater influence on money wage

changes than do changes in prosperity. Thus, in Table 7:4 above, variations in the rate of change of the cost-of-living index in one year were in *every* case followed by variations in the rate of rise of money wages in the same direction in the following year, and taking the data for the period as a whole (Table 7:5), we observe this to have happened for 11 of the 14 years[43] for which we have figures. We may now use the data of Table 7:5 to obtain a broader perspective.

The war-time pattern is familiar, the cost-of-living index rising very steeply up to 1943, accelerating up to 1942 and with money wages doing the same at a somewhat slower pace. The rate of rise of money wages decelerated steadily from 1943, at least till 1946, as the cost-of-living index more or less ceased to rise.

However, consideration of the figures of Table 7:1, covering the post-war period up to 1951, suggests that the connection between the rate of rise of money wages and that of the cost-of-living index was rather weak in this period, since money wages rose considerably in the post-war years up to 1948, while the cost-of-living index was practically stable. Moreover, there is some suggestion that the rise of money wages may have begun to accelerate *before* the commencement of the inflation of the 1950's. The '50s, by and large, saw the link between the money-wage rise and the cost-of-living index rise still at work, i.e. with an irregularly accelerating rise of both money wages and the cost-of-living index.

The general movement of money wages, and the main divisions into which that movement falls, suggest a direct link between the rise of money wages and that of the cost-of-living index. It remains to be seen how, if at all, this link was established, and as a corollary, what explains the breaking or loosening of the link at certain times. 'In Egypt and Turkey . . . the function of adjusting the earnings of workers in relation to national income has been assumed chiefly by the Governments which have made extensive efforts in this respect,' and although 'strikes are illegal in Turkey. . . and instead labour disputes must be referred to a system of conciliation and arbitration,' nevertheless, 'such disputes appear as a rule to have been settled in favour of labour. . .'[44]

Other methods have been used by the state to regulate money wages. 'In the civil service and to some extent in state

TABLE 7:5[45]
Turkey: Percentage Annual Changes in Money Wages and the Cost-of-
Living Index, 1939-58

	Money Wages	Cost-of-Living Index
1939/40	8.0	9.8
1940/41	10.2	19.6
1941/42	16.0	66.4
1942/43	31.2	41.3
1943/44	18.2	3.2
1944/45	14.0	3.1
1945/46	4.5	−0.3
1946/47	—	−1.5
1947/48	—	2.4
1948/49	5.8	5.4
1949/50	5.7	−4.1
1950/51	9.1	−0.3
1951/52	11.0	5.8
1952/53	13.2	4.1
1953/54	10.2	10.2
1954/55	10.6	12.4
1955/56	23.9	11.4
1957/58	20.3	16.3

industrial plants, wage rates have been rising periodically, a bonus equivalent to several months' salary or wage is voted by the National Assembly for civil servants. Wage increases in these groups have the effect of bolstering the general wage level.'[46]

A wage-fixing system so dominated by the state cannot but have been strongly cost-of-living oriented: and even though the minimum wage system did not formally link wages with the cost-of-living index,[47] the minimum wage system was not in any case the principal form of state intervention, having been instituted only in 1951[48] and being 'limited to a few industries in Adana, Izmir, Istanbul and Ankara, principally tobacco processing, textile manufacture, cotton picking and ginning, food vending and entertainment.[49]

The break in the money-wage cost-of-living link in the immediate post-war period[50] was due to the trade union pressure of these years, stimulated by the drastic fall in real wages during the war and the changeover to peacetime political conditions. This pressure kept money wages rising irrespective of the stability of the cost-of-living index.

'Only a few months after the ban on the trade unions was

lifted in 1946 several hundred trade unions—and this without much prior experience—were established', and although 'most of the trade unions were dissolved in 1946 because supposedly they fell under the influence of the leftists'[51] nevertheless after 1947 (that is after the Trade Union Law was enacted) new trade unions were again formed throughout the country and made remarkable progress in the immediately succeeding years,[52] not to mention their subsequent even more rapid growth.

The crystallisation of the post-war industrial unrest[53] was no doubt catalysed by demobilisation, since the government in its army drafting had seriously reduced the numbers of experienced working class leaders.[54] Moreover, 'there have also been occasional rumours that industrial workers went on strike in various parts of the country during the period from 1946 to 1950 despite the prohibition of the law. . . although it is rather difficult to obtain information on the subject.'[55] Such were the pressures breaking the link between the movement of money wages and the cost-of-living index in the immediate post-war period.[56]

That money wages began to accelerate before the commencement of the rise of the cost-of-living index in the '50s is attributable to the continued rapid development of the trade union movement (so long suppressed)[57] in this period, to the pressures of the 1950 general election, in which the purely working class question of the right to strike became a major issue, and which resulted in a change of government; and to the change in the labour Code at the beginning of 1950, which permitted trade unions to engage directly in collective bargaining.[58]

These points are important also because they help to explain the generally substantial rate of money wage rise throughout the 1950's. '. . . In Turkey the growth of Trade Unionism since the Trade Union Act of 1947 has been most marked. While there existed in March 1949, under that Act, some 70 unions with 75,000 members, the numbers had risen by August 1952 to 211 unions with 173,000 members, i.e. 33 per cent of the total workers covered by the Labour Code or just over 25 per cent of all industrial workers—the highest percentage (Israel excepted) in any country in the Near and Middle East.'[59]

In the early '50s too, the trade unions benefited from a policy of governmental encouragement and from international trade union, mainly American, contacts. After 1953,

however, government policy changed and became more
restrictive.[60] The effect of this change can be seen in the
markedly reduced ability of the unions to keep money wages
rising ahead of prices between 1953 and 1955. Real wages,
indeed, were at a standstill from 1953 to 1955, in contrast to
the 14 per cent rise of the previous two years.

We need not stress the significance of elections in circumstances in which the state plays the major role in wage-
determination and in which problems of the rising cost of
living and trade union rights become major electoral issues,[61]
and there were three elections in this period (in 1950, 1954
and 1957). As regards the change in the Labour Code of 1950,
the point here is that the system of workers' representatives
detailed in the 1936 Labour Code had up till then precluded
trade unions from engaging in collective bargaining, although
the trade unions could represent the workers' interests in
other ways.[62] Although the growing strength of the trade
unions since the end of the war must have had its indirect
effect in strengthening labour's demands, the 1950 amendments to the Labour Code represented a major step forward
in permitting the influence of trade unions to be exercised
directly in the bargaining process.

We again consider the varying success in terms of real wage
movements of institutional forces raising money wages. Real
wages fell steeply from 1939 to 1943 and rose nearly continuously (except, as far as we know, for one year, 1948/49)
thereafter, although the rise halted between 1953 and 1955.

We have, in fact, already discussed most of the reasons for
the varying success of the efforts to maintain or improve real
wages. The total failure to raise money wages fast enough to
maintain real wages during the war is attributable to the
almost complete defencelessness of the working class due to
the banning of trade unions, the lack of properly institution-
alised government machinery for regulating money wages,[63]
the drafting to the army of the most experienced labour
leaders and the suspension during the war[64] of the inadequate
rights granted by the 1936 Labour Code. Real wages began
to rise only after 1943, when prices had almost ceased to
rise.

Quite different was the experience during the inflation of
the '50s which, although not such a steep inflation as that of
the early war years, was nevertheless substantial, the average
annual rate of rise of the cost-of-living index between 1951

and 1958 being 10.3 per cent, the lowest annual rise being 4.1 per cent. Whereas in the first four years of the wartime inflation, real wages declined to about 60 per cent of their original level, in the first four years of the inflation of the '50s, i.e. from 1951/52 to 1954/55, real wages rose by about 12 per cent.

We have already outlined the major changes[65] in the unionisation of the working class and in labour legislation which took place after the wartime inflation. We need only remind the reader, before turning to the question of employer resistance during the inflation of the '50s, that two more elections occurred in this period, in 1954 and 1957, that, albeit in a modest way, wage-fixing machinery was set up in 1951, together with the introduction of new regulations concerning conciliation and arbitration procedures,[66] and that the trade union movement continued to develop, forming its first national body in 1952,[67] the Turkish Confederation of Labour Syndicates. The trade union movement even succeeded in obtaining such revolutionary advances as closed shop agreements in 1951 and 1952.[68]

A further dimension of the role of institutional forces in the movement of real wages is that relating to employer resistance to wage demands. This is partly illumined by the moderate real-wage gains of the 1950's inflation as compared with the much more substantial gains of the non-inflationary immediate post-war period (whereas real wages were by 1951 over three quarters of their 1946 level, by 1958 they had risen by less than one third of their 1951 level). This contrast appears to have been principally the result of an increased degree of employer resistance in the 1950's. Taken overall, our evidence suggests that the inflationary period, 1951/52 to 1957/58, may well have witnessed more severe pressure of prime costs on gross margins than did the earlier non-inflationary period (at least in the years 1948-50, when raw material costs tended to decline). The importance of employer resistance is further indicated within the period of the 1950's by the ability to enforce real-wage gains up to 1953, contrasted with the stability of real wages between 1953 and 1955. As we have seen, the former was a period when the demand situation permitted employers easily to pass rising prime costs on to prices, whereas after 1953 market conditions became much more sticky. The pressure on margins after 1953 probably explains the switch to a more repressive government policy *vis-à-vis* the trade unions, which occurred at the same time.

We have the same picture, as in India and Peru, of money wages rising under the potential political pressure of the working class, with trade union industrial pressure as the sign of the Assyrians. This was brought out in the circumstances leading up to, and the debate in the National Assembly on, the 1947 Trade Union Act.

'The trade unions were freely formed in early 1946 following the amendment of the Association Law which permitted the establishment of associations based on class interests. Most of them were closed for having been influenced by leftists six months later. The Republican Government hurriedly introduced the Trade Union Act (5018) on February 20th 1947 because of international obligations and as a deputy expressed it, chiefly because "This Assembly which wants to avoid adventures cannot delay the organisation of the workers into associations which would protect them from having a black mark on their foreheads and which would remain pure, honest, nationalistic, patriotic and Turkish for ever" '.[69]

APPENDIX

Wage Relationships in Turkey

Earnings/price relationship

The hypothesis that earnings are related to prices was tested over the period 1939 to 1958 (19 observations, as earnings data for 1947 was missing).

The linear relationship showed evidence of autocorrelation, and this was not removed by taking first differences. The first order autoregressive coefficient (e) was estimated from the residuals of the linear relationship and the variables were transformed according to $X_t–lX_{t-1}$. Autocorrelation was still present, but on repeating the procedure above with the transformed data, the equation below estimated on the assumption of a second order autoregressive scheme, was obtained (15 observations).

$$E \quad = \quad 1.256\,p \quad + \quad 17.400$$
$$\quad\quad\quad (0.423) \quad\quad (24.220)$$
$$R^2 \quad = \quad 0.403 \quad\quad D.W. = 1.34$$

We would strictly reject the hypothesis of no autocorrelation at the 5 per cent level (the critical value of the Durbin Watson statistic is 1.36) but that would involve a slavish reliance on formal significance levels. The equation gives the price coefficient as being significant at the 5 per cent level, and the hypothesis that prices affect earnings in Turkey is confirmed.

Earnings/profits relationship

The linear relationship between earnings and profits, and between earnings and profits lagged a period, both showed evidence of autocorrelation. When this was removed by assuming a first order autoregressive scheme estimated from the residuals, the results were as follows (the untransformed data was nine observations for the period 1950-58)

$$E \quad = \quad 6.486\,ll \quad - \quad 282.4$$
$$\quad\quad\quad (1.038) \quad\quad (130.3)$$
$$R^2 \quad = \quad 0.867 \quad\quad D.W. = 2.265$$

$$E \quad = \quad 7.314\,ll\text{-}1 \quad - \quad 212.5$$
$$\quad\quad\quad (1.656) \quad\quad D.W. = 1.319$$

Where E is an index of money wages
ll is an index of gross surplus.

The profits terms are significant at the 5 per cent level, and of the two, the relationship linking earnings to profits in the current period looks slightly more strongly supported by the evidence.

Conclusion

There is evidence of relationships between earnings and prices and between earnings and profits.

NOTES

1.

TABLE 7:6

Turkey: Indices of Average Money Earnings, Prices of Manufactures and
Ratio of Average Money Earnings to Prices of Manufactures, 1939-58

	Average Money Earnings	Prices of Manufactures	Ratio of Money Wages over Prices of Manufactures (Index)
1939	100	100	100
1940	108	114	95
1941	119	139	86
1942	138	214	64
1943	181	290	62
1944	214	357	60
1945	244	373	65
1946	253	347	73
1947	—	344	—
1948	396	359	110
1949	419	394	106
1950	443	376	118
1951	483	410	118
1952	536	414	129
1953	607	406	150
1954	669	425	157
1955	740	459	161
1956	917	511	175
1957	1046	557	188
1958	1258	688	183

Notes: See chapter 6, note 7 for average money earnings index and
chapter 6, note 3 for price index of manufactures.

Our price index of manufactured articles is not reliable, but the
declining ratio of money wages to final prices it indicates during the
war is confirmed by the declining ratio index of wage bill to total value
of production shown in Table 6:4, in conjunction with declining
productivity during the war (Table 7:7).

2. This summary is based on the actual, not the smoothed figures.

3. In some individual years the rise of money wages had no effect on
the *direction* of income redistribution, i.e. although money wages rose
faster than final prices, the share of labour in gross value added
declined.

TABLE 7:7

Turkey: Indices of Production, Employment and Productivity, 1939-58

	Production	Employment	Productivity
1939	100	100	100
1940	108	112	96
1941	107	115	93
1942	94	—	—
1943	110	134	82
1944	116	137	85
1945	115	140	82
1946	117	147	80
1947	—	—	—
1948	—	—	—
1949	—	—	—
1950	122	157	78
1951	132	167	79
1952	142	176	81
1953	151	199	76
1954	178	209	85
1955	204	226	90
1956	206	232	89
1957	229	254	90
1958	—	279	—

Notes: See chapter 6, note 7.

4.   Of total manual workers (skilled and unskilled categories) in manufacturing industry in 1961, 60 per cent were unskilled (*First Five Year Plan*, 1963, p. 399).

5.   Parker and Smith, pp. 131-132. (*Cf.* Naval Intelligence Division, Geographical Handbook Series, *Turkey*, 1943, p. 197).

6.   Lingeman, 1947, p. 28 (*Cf.* U.N. Dept. of Economic Affairs, *Review of Economic Conditions in the Middle East, Supplement to World Economic Report, 1949-50,* New York, 1951, p. 147. Karpat, p. 91; Hershlag, p. 129. and U.N., *Manufacturing Industry in Turkey,* 1958, pp. 15 and 17).

7.   One estimate for 1950 is that the total numbers of both sexes over the age of 15 engaged in industrial occupations, including mining, utilities and construction and also including various categories of small-scale industry, account for only 8.3 per cent of the economically active population (U.N., *Manufacturing Industry in Turkey,* 1958, p. 92).

8.   I.L.O., *Labour Problems in Turkey,* Geneva, 1950, pp. 215-216. This inquiry, covering 1,638 establishments, found that workers between 14 and 22 years of age represented about 30 per cent of total manpower, those between 14 and 40 years of age about 80 per cent of total manpower, and those over 50 years of age only 5 per cent.

9. U.N., *Manufacturing Industry in Turkey*, p. 29.

10. Karpat, p. 101, mentions very high estimates of the number of landless peasants made in 1945, although he does not give figures.

11. Although we need not take its absolute figures very seriously, the steady rise of the applications figures in table 102 and the decline in the proportion of placings between 1946 and 1950 make it clear that the immediate post-war urban employment deficiency was more than a temporary phenomenon due to the change-over to peacetime conditions. The marked expansion in the field operations of the State Employment Service after 1950, and the extension of its activities in the later '50s to cover migratory workers (Rosen, pp. 276-277), render pre- and post-1950 comparisons valueless, especially since such expansion may have had a bigger effect in raising placings figures than application figures.

12. *Cf.* I.B.R.D., 1951, pp. 75 and 145; Thornburg, Spry and Soule, pp. 29, 48 and 127; U.N., *Economic Conditions, 1949-50*, p. 35; and U.N., *Economic Conditions, 1951-52*, p. 48.

13. *Cf. Manufacturing Industry in Turkey*, 1958, p. 85; O.E.E.C., 1958, p. 14; F.A.O., *Mediterranean Development Project*, 1959, p. 43; I.L.O., *Why Labour Leaves the Land: A Comparative Study of the Movement of Labour out of Agriculture*, 1960, p. 173.

14. I.B.R.D., 1951, p. 75.

15. I.L.O., *Movement of Labour*, 1960, p. 175. The I.B.R.D. report, 1951, also discusses the displacement of labour due to mechanisation on already cultivated land (p. 75).

16. U.N., *Economic Conditions, 1950-51*, p. 89.

17. U.N., *Economic Conditions, 1951-52*, p. 131.

18. Affecting women workers in the tobacco industry. I.L.O., *Report to the Government of Turkey on Possible Measures for Protection Against Unemployment*, Geneva, 1960, p. 7.

19. Thus, in 1951 the I.B.R.D. report noted that 'a permanent industrial force is conspicuously lacking in Turkey, where urbanisation has not yet occurred to any significant extent. Unskilled labour in particular is highly mobile, moving to and from agriculture with the seasons' (p. 118). Even in 1960, the I.L.O. report (*Expanded Programme*, p. 9) could remark that 'while many changes have taken place in the meantime since 1946 no evidence exists that the expansion of industry has been accompanied with any substantial improvement in respect of employment turnover.' For information on turnover rates and industries affected particularly badly, see Hershlag, 1958, *op. cit.*, p. 296; I.L.O., *Report 1, Regional Conference for the Near and Middle East, 1951. Manpower Problems; Vocational Training and Employment Service*, Geneva, 1951, p. 27; U.N., *Manufacturing Industry in Turkey*, p. 84;

U.N., *Economic Conditions,* 1951-52, p. 47; Thornburg *et al.* 1949, *op. cit.,* p. 128.

20. Most, if not all, efforts to overcome high turnover rates were made by state establishments. See U.N., *Manufacturing Industry in Turkey,* 1958, p. 38; U.N., *Economic Conditions,* 1951-52, p. 47; Thornburg *et al.* p. 116; I.L.O., *Expanded Programme,* 1960, p. 10. In 1953 the state employed about half of all workers employed in plants with 10 or more workers (A.P. Alexander, p. 141, cited in Rosen, p. 261). A good example, demonstrating the effectiveness of the state action taken in many places to stabilise the labour force, is provided by the Sumer Bank's Kayseri textile mill which, when established in 1935, had an annual turnover of 30 per cent, a rate which in the mid-'50s had been reduced to 3.5 per cent (U.S. Department of Commerce, *Investment in Turkey: Basic Information for U.S. Businessmen,* p. 92). The Sumer Bank has many factories in both light and heavy industry, including iron and steel, textiles, hide and footwear, cement, firebrick and ceramics. A.H. Hanson, pp. 120-121.

21. Thus '. . . the industrial labour force though small in proportion to the total population, is significant in numbers, and includes a high proportion of fully committed urban industrial workers,' S.M. Rosen, p. 261; and 'The percentage of permanent industrial workers has probably risen somewhat in recent years because farm mechanisation has resulted in some displacement,' U.N., *Manufacturing Industry in Turkey,* 1958, p. 85.

22. The 1960, I.L.O., *Movement of Labour,* report does not make this distinction, although it is concerned with the problem of a stable labour force for urban *industry.*

23. I.L.O., *Movement of Labour,* 1960, p. 175. The availability of industrial employment may be the crux of the matter, which would suggest a degree of stabilisation.

24. I.L.O., *Movement of Labour,* 1960, p. 173.

25. U.S., Department of Commerce, 1956.

26. I.L.O., *Expanded Programme,* 1960, p. 26.

27. U.S., Department of Commerce, 1956, pp. 92-93.

28. I.B.R.D., 1951, p. 159. Although managers may have evaded these restrictions to some extent. *Cf.* J. Parker & C. Smith, p. 132.

29. I am indebted to Mr. Karel Durman, Lecturer in Modern Middle Eastern History at Prague University, for the emphasis placed on direction of labour as the main method used to solve the wartime manpower problem.

30. Karpat, p. 91. 'Certain people' is a somewhat vague term—it apparently subsumes workers and qualified personnel.

31. A. Bonne, p. 130.

32. *Naval Handbook*, 1943, p. 197; J. Parker and C. Smith, p. 132. Parker & Smith also noted that not only did local supply and demand conditions vary, but also that the cost of living varied from place to place, and further remarked on the institutional influences of the People's Houses and People's Party branches on workers' conditions. These further points suggest quite different reasons for regional money wage variations (pp. 130-133).

33. Mr. F.M. Andic constitutes an exception. 'In face of the almost complete absence of collective bargaining, wages in Turkey are usually determined by economic conditions. The only bargaining power which workers possess in times of full employment is the threat to quit their jobs,' (Andic, p. 367). It is not clear how he would explain the rise of money wages and real wages in the post-war period.

34. Owing to the fact that 'Turkish private enterprise has a distinct trading complex,' I.B.R.D., 1951, p. 160.

35. Hershlag, p. 296. *Cf.* Hanson, pp. 450-451 for the case of a state enterprise (the Zonguldac coalmines) where the fear of unionisation has prevented any efforts to build up a stable labour force.

36. See I.L.O., *Movement of Labour*, 1960, p. 73.

37. I.B.R.D., 1951, p. 116.

38. U.S., Department of Commerce, 1956, p. 92.

39. I.L.O., *Expanded Programme*, 1960, p. 10.

40. U.N., *Economic Conditions*, 1051-52, p. 47.

41. U.N., *Manufacturing Industry in Turkey*, 1958, p. 85.

42. Sources as for Tables 6:5 and 7:1. Gross surplus defined as in Table 6:4. Average money wages include earnings of salaries workers.

43. Unlike Peru and India, the cost-of-living/money-wage link seems here to operate with a one-year lag.

44. U.N., *Manufacturing Industry in Turkey*, 1958, p. 47.

45. *Cost-of-living index* as for Table 6:1. For *money-wage index* see Chapter 6, note 7.

46. U.S., Department of Commerce, 1956, p. 92.

47. U.N., *Manufacturing Industry in Turkey*, 1958, p. 47.

48. J.A. Hallsworth, I.L.O., Geneva, 1955, p. 25.

49. U.S., Department of Commerce, 1956, pp. 91-92. *Cf.* J.A. Hallsworth, pp. 25-26.

50. The 'pause' in the rate of rise of money wages in 1945/46 was probably connected with the employment decline, due to the resumption of peace-time conditions, before industrial unrest had made itself properly felt.

51. K.H. Karpat, p. 110.

52. I.L.O., *Labour Problems*, 1950, p. 167.

53. See K.H. Karpat, 1959, *op. cit.*, p. 91, on the peasant discontent of this period. The link between peasantry and industrial workers was very strong, as we should expect with an urban labour force so close to the village (*Cf.* I.L.O., *Movement of Labour*, 1960, p. 173).

54. I am indebted to Mr. Durman for this point.

55. Karpat, p. 319. These legal prohibitions were enforced, as Karpat shows, and, indeed, subsequently became major electoral and social issues. *Cf.* Hershlag, p. 294.

56. The 1946 elections, the formation of the Democratic Party in that year, and its partial success in these elections, no doubt played some part in exerting pressure on the government. Prior to 1946, no opposition party existed (*Cf.* Hershlag, p. 294).

57. *Cf.* B. Lewis, pp. 219-290.

58. U.N., *Manufacturing Industry in Turkey*, 1958, p. 47.

59. J.A. Hallsworth, p. 7 ff. See also U.S., Department of Commerce, 1956, p. 95.

60. S.M. Rosen, pp. 267, 285 and 286.

61. The close connection of the urban workers with the peasantry should not be forgotten.

62. U.S., Department of Commerce, 1956, p. 94.

63. I.L.O., *Labour Problems*, 1950, p. 31. The arbitration and conciliation machinery which had been in existence since 1936 was rarely used for the first 10 years of its existence. Despite their formal exclusion from this machinery, it was the post-war strengthening of the trade unions which brought it into frequent use (Rosen, pp. 270-272).

64. Hershlag, p. 293.

65. Hershlag, p. 294, for a summary of the fundamental changes that took place in the position of labour in the late '40s and early '50s.

66. *Ibid.*, pp. 295-6.

67. U.S., Department of Commerce, 1956, p. 95.

68. Hallsworth, p. 24.

69. Karpat, pp. 312-3. Oral, the speaker for the Labour Committee, stressed the fact that it was necessary to organise the wokrers into trade unions to protect them against 'evil currents.'

CHAPTER 8

Inflation and Income Redistribution in The Modern Manufacturing Sector in Underdeveloped Economies — Some Conclusions

Our concern in this chapter is to consider what general conclusions emerge as to the determinants of income redistribution in the modern manufacturing sector during inflation in underdeveloped economies by comparing the experience of our three countries; and, finally, to consider some of the implications of the conclusions so reached.

(i) The Experience of Income Redistribution during Inflation

We have examined the experience of inflation in three countries between 1939 and the late 1950's. In all, this gives us eight distinct inflationary periods.[1] Of these eight inflations, only two witnessed an increase in the profit share of gross value added, i.e. those of India and Peru during the war. In the remaining six there were three inflationary periods of either relative stability of shares or of no clear overall direction of change (i.e. the Peruvian inflation of the 1950's, the Indian inflation of the Second Five Year Plan and the Turkish inflation of the 1950's). The remaining three inflations were periods of a rising share of labour in gross value added (i.e. the immediate post-war inflations in Peru and India and the wartime inflation in Turkey).

In view of the widespread belief that inflation in underdeveloped economies automatically increases income inequalities, especially by increasing profits at the expense of wages, this result is surprising enough. However, if we consider these periods more closely, it will be seen that the occurrence of an increasing share for labour in gross value added during inflation is even more pervasive than would at first sight appear.

This is apparent when we consider the three inflations of the 1950's (one in each country, that in India extending into the early 1960's), which we categorised as experiencing relative stability of shares or no clearly defined tendency for income to be redistributed in any one particular direction. Thus, although the Indian inflation of the Second Five Year Plan was not one in which there was a decisive increase in labour's share of manufacturing income, this inflationary period nevertheless succeeded in halting the tendency towards a steady increase in the share of profits which the previous non-inflationary period had been bringing about.

Again, if we turn to the Peruvian inflation of the 1950's and consider the period more closely, we can see that this period of apparent stability of shares really divided into three sub-periods (1949/50 to 1951/52, 1952/53 to 1955/56,a nd 1955/56 to 1957/58), during which the share of labour first rose, then fell, and rose again.[2] Thus, we now have two inflationary periods of a rising share for labour, as opposed to one of a falling share, and the sub-period in which labour's share fell was that sub-period when the price rise was at its mildest.

Much the same applies to the Turkish inflation of the 1950's. Between 1950/51 and 1957/58 labour's share first fell and then rose. But the period when labour's share fell might better be described as a proto-inflationary period, as a period of incipient inflation. As we have been, the rise in final prices was extremely mild, and the early rise in the profit share was in fact due to a decline in raw material costs. As soon as the inflationary process became thoroughly established, with significant percentage price rises extending to *all* major groups of commodities, then a decisive change in shares of value added took place—labour's share increased.

We may therefore, for the sake of argument, and for the time being, consider the case of a redistribution of gross value added away from profits and towards labour in the modern manufacturing sector to be the typical case. For convenience, we term this to be the case of an *un*successful defensive inflation.[3]

Taking this typical case, we have found the following price/cost characteristics to hold for all inflationary periods during which the share of profits declined.

1. The terms of trade between industry and agriculture moved in favour of the latter. For the agricultural sector this applied to both food products and agricultural raw materials.

2. Simultaneously, as the cost of living rose, especially food prices, money wages rose also, sometimes faster than the rise of prices of manufactures, partly owing to food prices rising faster than prices of manufactures.
3. Pressure on margins by rising raw material costs was, thus, never compensated by decline or stability of labour costs, and was sometimes supplemented by pressure from labour costs rising as fast as or faster than final prices. Even when labour costs lagged behind final prices, the squeeze on margins from rising material costs prevented the share of profits in value added from rising.

The underlying causal factors are thus, on the one hand, those associated with the movement of the terms of trade between the modern manufacturing sector and the agricultural sector; and on the other hand, those associated with the rise of money wages.[4] These two sets of factors are examined separately in sections *(ii)* and *(iii)* of this chapter. The overall view emerging is contrasted, in Section *(iv)*, with alternative views which have been advanced, and is finally summarised in Section *(v)*.

(ii) Causal Factors in Income Redistribution during Inflation— The Movements of the Terms of Trade Between Industry and Agriculture

The role of the movements of the terms of trade between industry and agriculture as a determinant of income re-distribution *within* the modern manufacturing sector is considered below in terms of the experience, first, of the 'typical' case of stable or rising labour shares and, second, of the 'untypical' case of declining labour shares.

A. The Typical Case—Stable or Rising Labour Shares

The movements of the agricultural/industrial terms of trade against industry during the typical inflation are the result of a process the principal elements of which are outlined in the paragraphs below.

Demand pressures, whether domestic or international, in the countries we have examined, have quickly resulted in rising prices of agricultural products, owing to the short-run supply inelasticity of the agricultural sector and the flexibility of agricultural prices.

Demand pressures on the modern manufacturing sector

have tended to have little or no direct effect on prices, owing to the flexible supply response of manufacturing industry (both as regards production with given capacity and as regards expansion of capacity) and the relative inflexibility of prices in response to demand in a predominantly oligopolistic market structure. Demand pressures have, thus, affected the modern manufacturing sector mainly indirectly, i.e. through their influence on the rate of rise of prime costs. The demand pressures referred to above which have raised agricultural prices have thereby raised industrial costs, i.e. of materials,[5] since the bulk of materials used in the organised sector are agricultural products[6] such as cotton, jute, sugar cane, unprocessed food products, tobacco, wool, etc. Consequently, industrial prices have risen to offset rising costs.

The market environment, or changes therein, has modified the extent to which rising prime costs per unit of output have been passed on to prices, with the result that, in the typical case under consideration, margins have been squeezed and, with rising money wages, the share of profit in gross value added has declined. This has been because the rise of agricultural prices has resulted in a greater rise of industrial costs than of rural demand per unit of industrial output from increasing agricultural money incomes. Whether or not total rural demand per unit of industrial output resulting from rising agricultural prices will exceed the rise in unit prime costs will depend on three principal sets of considerations:

1. The behaviour of the marketed agricultural surplus;
2. The expenditure and savings patterns of rural income recipients; and
3. The relative supply elasticities of the two sectors in the short run.

Thus, if the marketed surplus is reduced, the rise of industrial prime costs will be accompanied by a rise in rural money expenditure equal to the rise in prices of agricultural commodities less the decline in the quantity sold. Since the rise in prime costs to industry will tend to be roughly proportionate to the rise in the prices of agricultural commodities, assuming money wage costs to rise at a rate approximately determined by the rise in food prices,[7] then the organised manufacturing sector will find its cost curve rising faster than its demand curve, owing to the decline in the quantity of agricultural commodities sold, i.e. the decline in the marketed surplus. More generally, any factors tending to limit the rise of the marketed agricultural surplus will also act to limit the extent to which rural demand for industrial products can exceed the rise in prime costs of industrial products. In particular, factors encouraging increased self-consumption by the peasantry, or hindering the increase of agricultural production, will hinder the increase of the marketed surplus.

Further, even if the marketed agricultural surplus does increase, the proceeds may not be spent on the product of urban industry. There may be 'leakages' into imports, hoarding or investment in speculation, etc. To the extent that such leakages do occur, they tend to offset the effects of any increased marketed surplus in raising rural demand for urban products by a greater percentage than agricultural prices and, thus, industrial costs.[8] These effects may be compounded by the activities of middle-men, speculators, etc., who raise the price of agricultural products and, thus, industrial costs even higher, and whose expenditure will have a higher import content than that of the peasantry and agricultural labourers.

Finally, the relatively greater supply response of the industrial sector compared to the agricultural sector means that even if *total* money demand from agriculture for manufactures exactly matches the proportionate increase in manufacturers' unit prime costs transmitted from agriculture, the rise in unit manufacturing costs will be greater than the rise in demand per unit of industrial output, or, in certain cases, per unit of potential output (capacity), whichever (if not both) is relevant to the manufacturers' pricing policy.

In other words, the greater the elasticity of supply of manufactures relative to that of agricultural products in response to a given increment of demand, the higher will be the ratio of the rise in unit prime costs to the rise in money demand per unit of output (assuming, of course, that the increased marketed surplus is not sufficient to prevent agricultural commodity prices from rising) and this will tend to offset the effect of any increase in the marketed surplus in providing a favourable market environment for maintaining or improving margins.

Some caveats are, of course, required to the above argument, particularly to the extent that demand for urban manufactures is independent of rural demand, e.g. depends on export demand or depends on the growth of that portion of industrial production which is dependent in the short and medium run for its markets on the growth of the industrial sector itself. To the extent that this is so, then the lesser rate of rise of prime costs associated with an enlarged marketed surplus from agriculture will relieve pressure on margins, irrespective of whether or not the increased income of the rural sector is spent on urban manufactures. However, with specific exceptions noted in the Country Chapters, the outstanding determinant of the demand for urban products has been the growth of the agricultural sector. In all three countries the modern manufacturing sectors' output is sold mainly on the home market.[9]

The experience of the typical inflations which we have considered[10] in the Country Chapters illustrates the importance of the agricultural bottleneck (manifested in the three factors specified above), in raising labour's share by active pressure of raw material costs on gross profit margins.

Thus, as far as relative supply elasticities are concerned, we may note that in all seven inflations the supply response of the modern manufacturing sector was superior to that of the agricultural sector. In the Turkish wartime inflation, the immediate post-war inflation in India and the inflation of the late 1950's in Peru, agricultural production was not simply lagging but was either stationary or declining, with consequent restrictive effects on the market for expanding industrial production.

Furthermore, in all cases, the leakages mentioned above have aggravated what we may call the 'cost-demand transfer problem' from agriculture to industry, since expenditure on imported luxuries and investment in non-productive activities such as speculation and real estate were, to a greater or lesser degree, characteristic of the behaviour of the rural upper classes in all three countries.[11] Moreover, while these activities are likely to have been, to an extent, present in all periods, they are likely to have been particularly to the fore during inflation. This is partly the result of the conditions 'causing' inflation (insofar as inflation is the result of structural imbalances, e.g. the agricultural lag will discourage investment in manufacturing by large landowners, owing to the limitations imposed on the market for industrial products thereby) and partly the result of the inflation itself (e.g. the encouragement of speculative dealings, investment in real estate).

A further notable feature of the experience of inflation, and one linking the movement of the agricultural/industrial terms of trade firmly to changes in income distribution, has been the fact that, with the exception of the period of the

Indian Second Five Year Plan, every inflationary period in which raw material costs rose faster than final prices was also one in which labour's share of gross value added rose, despite the experience in some cases[12] of money wages lagging behind final prices of manufactures. This is in part due to the fact that the conditions causing raw material costs to rise faster than final prices were also those likely to raise labour costs and to limit the expansion of demand for manufactures from the agricultural population. These conditions related, of course, to the poor supply elasticity of agricultural production. Lagging agricultural output during inflation tended to bring about a rise of unit labour costs parallel with that of raw material costs, owing to the link between changes in money wages and changes in food prices and owing to the link between productivity changes in manufacturing industry and the rate of growth of agricultural output.

Lagging agricultural output has tended to raise food prices faster than prices of manufactures, at the same time as raw material prices have been rising faster than final prices,[13] and for the same reason. The result, with a cost-of-living oriented money wage rise in circumstances in which expenditure on food constitutes between half and two-thirds of working-class expenditure, has naturally been to create a tendency during inflation for money wages to rise faster than final prices. This, as we have seen, has not been a mechanical response, but one varying with the strength of various non-economic pressures. But even when money wages lagged behind prices they did not fail to rise substantially, so that if they were not actively exerting pressure on gross margins, they nevertheless provided an anvil to the hammer of raw material costs in reducing the share of profits.

The conditions which have tended to raise unit labour costs by stimulating money wage increases, viz. lagging agricultural output, have also been those tending to negate, wholly or partly, the possible stabilising effects on unit labour costs of increasing productivity. This is because productivity changes in manufacturing tend to be positively related to changes in total output, and total output in manufacturing tends to be strongly affected by the development of agricultural production. In particular, lagging agricultural production has tended to limit the growth of industrial production, by restricting the necessary expansion of the market, by physically limiting the availabilities of raw materials for manufacturing industry, or by limiting in one way or

another the foreign exchange available for purchase of
necessary imported raw materials and complementary goods
for manufacturing industry. These effects are obscured by
the fact that influences other than the growth of agricultural
output have affected the growth of manufacturing production.[15]

Finally, it is important to note that the normal trading
pattern of an underdeveloped economy, i.e. export of raw
materials (which compete for resources with production of
both food and raw materials for the home market) and
import of manufactures, is likely to reinforce the tendency
of inflation in underdeveloped economies to be associated
with pressure on profit margins in manufacturing industry,
because imports of foreign manufactures allowed into the
country will limit the upward adjustment of domestic prices
of manufactures to rising prime costs. Indeed, as we shall see
below, the disruption or modification of normal trade conditions was a crucial feature of the inflations in which,
untypically, the share of labour in manufacturing income fell.

B. The Untypical Case—Declining Labour Shares

The share of labour in gross value added declined during
the wartime inflation in Peru and India, in the inflationary
sub-period 1952-56 in Peru and during the proto-inflationary
period 1951-52 in Turkey. In all these cases, raw material
costs rose more slowly than final prices, so that gross margins
increased. The rise of money wages faster than final prices
during the Peruvian and Turkish inflationay sub-periods of the
early 1950's was unable to prevent the decline of labour's
relative share, brought about by the rise of gross profit
margins.

If we examine the particular features of these inflations
which have brought about this relatively slower (than final
prices) rise in prices of raw materials, we are in a position to
see more clearly the senses in which the *opposite* case, i.e.
that leading to a rise in labour's share, is the more typical.

These four exceptional cases divide naturally into the two
wartime inflations, in which the crux of the matter was the
disruption of the normal pricing conventions owing to the
exceptional wartime conditions; and the post-war inflations
in which, while normal, conventional, mark-up pricing policies
were maintained, there were particular 'unusual'[16] features of
these inflations which brought about a degree of upward

margin variation instead of the downward margin variation found in what we have characterised as our typical inflation.

The Indian and Peruvian wartime inflation brought about a declining share of labour in gross value added in factory industry. Most other inflations did not. Why the difference? And, more particularly, why the difference between these two inflations and the Turkish wartime inflation, during which labour's share of gross value added rose slightly? The wartime situation in India and Peru disrupted normal trade flows and simultaneously brought about much increased demand pressures on the economy as a whole. The result of the former was physically to reduce imports, mainly manufactures, and exports—mainly agricultural commodities.

The increased demand thus met with a greater relative response in terms of supplies of agricultural commodities available on the home market, as compared with industrial commodities, than was normally the case. Apart from the direct effect of the reduction of imported manufactured consumer goods, there was also the more indirect effect resulting from the fact that the expansion of capacity in the modern manufacturing sector was largely dependent on importation of capital goods. To a degree, also, the continuation of some current production was dependent on continued imports of semi-processed goods and raw materials. The implication of this situation was that the normal process, whereby increased aggregate demand in the economy comes up against the short-term limits of capacity of the primary producing sector sooner than the short-term limits of capacity of the modern manufacturing sector, was disrupted.

Furthermore, the attainment of full capacity and the magnitude of the demands on the manufacturing sector in both countries, were such as seriously to weaken such longer-term considerations relating to maintaining and expanding market shares as were conducive to a mark-up pricing policy. Clearly, the new wartime demands on manufacturing industry were much greater in the case of India than in that of Peru. On the other hand, Peru was much more dependent on imports for supplies of manufactured consumer and capital goods than was India,[17] and associated with this, the fast rise of prices of imported manufactures in Peru may have exerted an independent influence in bringing about the abandonment of the regulation of prices in relation to costs.

The net result of this combination of wartime circumstances was, on the one hand, that prices ceased to be regulated by a mark-up pricing policy based on conventional margins, and, on the other, that the rate of price rise determined by the changing excess of demand relative to supply, in the peculiar circumstances of the war in Peru and India, led to prices of manufactured articles rising faster than prices of raw materials.

Much the same foreign trade conditions held in Turkey—war conditions physically reduced both exports (agricultural commodities) and imports (manufactures), so that the volume of both exports and imports declined dramatically below pre-war levels. What, then, made Turkey different from India and Peru, so that raw material costs in Turkey rose faster than final prices? The answer to this question lies in the much poorer wartime agricultural performance in Turkey compared to India and Peru,[18] and in the governmental control over prices of manufactures in Turkey. The former situation ensured that the decline in the volume of exported agricultural commodities was more than offset by the steep decline of agricultural output, so that trade conditions brought about a much lesser alteration of the normal relative responses in terms of the flow of domestically available supplies, as between the industrial and agricultural sectors to the demand pressures upon them. The latter circumstance ensured that the greatly expanded demands upon the manufacturing sector, which raised capacity utilisation, did not succeed in breaking the link between prices and costs, i.e. did not disrupt normal pricing methods.

In the non-typical post-war inflations in Peru and Turkey, attention is focused on the conditions permitting upward margin variation with a mark-up pricing policy.

In the case of Peru, the decisive reason for the decline in the share of labour in the inflationary years between 1952 and 1956 was the lag of raw material costs behind final prices, together with the rise of productivity. Money wages actually rose faster than final prices. This occurred despite stagnating agricultural production. Why did raw material costs lag and productivity rise so that the share of profits rose?

What was happening in this period was that final prices were rising gently, but rather faster than prime costs (thanks to a slower rise of raw material costs and rising productivity), which were also rising (both raw material costs and unit labour costs), so that gross margins were increased somewhat.

The problem then is how were entrepreneurs, in responding
to rising prime costs by raising their prices, able to vary their
margins upwards? With agricultural production increasing
rather slowly in these years, and lagging behind the growth
of the rest of the economy, we should have expected the
familiar situation of declining margins. That this did not occur
was due to a circumstance which rarely obtains in underdeveloped economies, viz. complete liberalisation of trade.[19]
This had obtained since 1950, and its effect was, on the one
hand, to supplement domestic supplies of raw materials
(including food) so that their price rise was moderated and,
on the other, to prevent the diversion of money expenditures
towards agricultural products, especially food, which agricultural stagnation and price-inelastic demand for food would
normally have brought about. This latter effect, together
with the general growth of the economy, ensured manufacturers a market expanding sufficiently rapidly[20] to permit
margins to be raised while costs pushed up prices. Nor did the
unrestrained flow of imported manufactures prevent the
raising of margins,[21] since prices of manufactured imports
were tending to rise faster than prices of raw materials in
these years. The main adjustment of margins in manufacturing
following the freeing of imports had already taken place in
the previous period, 1949-52. Imports in these years covered
the deficiencies of the agricultural sector.

We need not dwell long on the proto-inflationary period of
1950/51 to 1952/53 in Turkey. The decline in labour's share
here was principally a product of the decline in raw material
costs in 1951/52, and the favourable demand situation,
which, initially, meant that manufacturers were on the whole
able to maintain high gross margins. Here, the essence of the
situation was the rapid expansion of agricultural output,
which raised demand for manufactures much more than raw
material costs were rising, so that the high margins could be
maintained despite pressure of rising unit labour costs. The
uniqueness of this situation was, of course, the rapid expansion of agricultural output. This expansion of agricultural
output was not sufficient, under the impact of rising home
and export demand, to prevent completely raw material costs
from rising (except in 1952). It did, however, mean that
increased rural demand (the result of rising prices of agricultural commodities plus the increase in the supply marketed)
was more than sufficient to permit increased prime costs to
industry to be absorbed by raising prices in such a way that

margins were maintained. It was, however, the very expansion of agricultural output which made this very much of a proto-inflation, with no more than a gentle and hesitant price rise.

C. The Typicality of Stable or Rising Labour Shares during Inflation

Before proceeding to consider some of the wider implications of the comparative experience of the three countries we have been considering, it is, perhaps, worth expanding slightly on the typicality of the tendency we have observed for inflation to witness a stable or rising share for labour. Leaving aside the cost-of-living orientation of money-wage changes, we have seen that this tendency rests upon the encroachment of rising raw material costs on gross margins, due to lagging agricultural production.

In a simple arithmetical sense, this type of inflation was, of course, the commonest in the underdeveloped countries over the years we have examined. Moreover, all the inflations during which gross margins rose and labour's share declined as a result of final prices rising faster than raw material costs took place in, and as a result of, circumstances which must be regarded as exceptional in the underdeveloped world. These exceptional circumstances were such as to emphasise, by way of contrast, the importance of lagging agricultural production as a causal factor in reducing the share of profit during other inflations. The unusual circumstances in which labour's share declined were the wartime disruption of trade flows in India and Peru; the complete liberalisation of trade, and the unusually adequate capacity to import in Peru between 1952 and 1956; and the hesitant, partial nature of the 1951-52 inflation in Turkey, caused by the remarkable increase in agricultural production. It is sufficient to pinpoint these features of the inflations in which labour's share declined, to suggest strongly that the circumstances associated with a rise in labour's share are likely to be the more common.

That the inflation with a rising labour share is likely to be typical, in the sense that the circumstances we have found to be concomitant with it are those most likely to give rise to inflation, is also suggested by the fact that the only period of price decline of any length, that of India in the period 1951-55, was one in which the ratio of raw material costs to final prices declined.[22]

The crux of the matter than, relates to the typicality of the conditions associated with defensive inflation in underdeveloped countries. We have seen these to be the greater short-run supply of manufactured products relative to agricultural products. There is no need to dwell at length on this point. The relative backwardness of the agricultural supply response throughout the underdeveloped world is well-known, and is signified by the post-war changeover of a number of underdeveloped countries from the category of food exporters to that of food importers, alongside a comparatively fast rate of growth of industrial production throughout the underdeveloped world.

The perhaps more surprising existence of excess capacity in manufacturing industry is attributable to three crucial considerations, considerations which are likely to hold for many underdeveloped countries:

1. The bulk (say two-thirds to three-quarters of the total) of modern manufacturing industry in underdeveloped countries in terms of employment or value added is concerned with the production of light consumer goods, processed foods, beverages, tobacco products, footwear, clothing, furniture, textiles, etc.[23] In other words, modern manufacturing enterprise displaces existing production units, and does so by utilising the benefits of more advanced techniques and the economies of scale. In particular, the economies of scale will acquire a long-run strategic significance in the attempt to expand sales. The very growth of large-scale manufacturing in fact signifies a situation, particularly in its earliest development, in which, in relation to effective demand, the overall position in the economy is one of excess capacity for certain broad categories of commodities.
2. Insofar as the development of large-scale manufacturing involves the introduction of new products, such as durable consumer goods, the producer will tend both to anticipate and to create the demand, with the result we saw in the case of Peru of extensive 'anticipatory' capacity.
3. Once established, an oligopolistic urban industry, with limited markets and with a limited capital market, which is reluctant to engage in price competition, will tend to rely more on reserves of capacity for long-run competi-

tive purposes than would be the case in a fiercer competitive situation. The tendency for demand for industrial products to undergo relatively wide fluctuations as a result of varying harvests and international trade conditions will accentuate the advantages of large capacity reserves.

Unless a rise in demand comes both very suddenly and is so large as to cause limits of capacity in manufacturing industry to be quickly reached, the same factors will tend to keep capacity somewhat ahead of demand. The logic of this argument is that such a large and sudden demand increase will occur in only exceptional circumstances. Such exceptional circumstances were found to be the case in our two non-defensive, wartime inflations, those of Peru and India. Moreover, in considering the existence of excess capacity we must also take note of the ability of manufacturing industry, when faced with a particularly favourable demand situation, to work beyond the 'normal' capacity limits by means of extending shift work, working machines beyond their normal limits, organising short-term training courses to make up for lack of skilled men, switching over to, or intensifying, incentive systems of work payment, and so on.

It is important to note in this general argument that the proportions or changing proportions of resources devoted to investment or consumtpion (other than food) will not necessarily affect directly, whether or not during an inflation rising prime costs encroach on profit margins. However, there may well be indirect effects, but these are likely to work in the opposite direction from that normally assumed, i.e. more resources devoted to investment relative to aggregate consumption may be *less* inflationary than the reverse situation (assuming the decline in aggregate consumption not to affect the volume of resources directed to food production), since labour costs will be a lower proportion of total costs in producer goods industry than in consumer goods industries, and since inputs in the former are less likely to originate in the agricultural sector and thus to be less synchronised with rising labour costs. However, after all the qualifications are made, it remains to be said, first, that rising money wages and agricultural inputs are likely to have some tendency to affect gross profit margins in producer goods industries; second, rising mineral and intermediate input costs are likely to synchronise to at least some extent with labour and agricultural input cost increases; and third, in any case, the bulk of manufacturing industry in underdeveloped countries is, and is likely to remain for some time, in the consumer goods sector, so that unless an increased proportion of resources is accompanied by a markedly increased marketed agricultural surplus, then there is likely to be a shift away from profits as a share of *aggregate* manufacturing income, owing to the increased pressure on margins in that part of manufacturing industry producing consumer goods. The point we have been concerned to emphasise, or rather to re-emphasise, here is that the basic conditions making the unsuccessful defensive inflation typical relate to the backward state of agriculture and its consequent poor supply response relative to that of manufacturing industry, itself a common feature of underdeveloped economies.

If to these considerations we add that there is some reason to believe that in the post-war underdeveloped world a successful response of rising money wages to rising prices is fairly likely, then it seems that the unsuccessful defensive inflation may well be the typical inflationary experience for the postwar underdeveloped world.

(iii) Causal Factors in Income Redistribution—Rising Money Wages

A. Rising Money Wages and Income Redistribution

We have seen that, in all our typical inflations, rising raw material costs exerted active pressure on gross margins and were even able, by so doing, to increase labour's share of value added at times when money wages lagged behind final prices. It is, however, necessary to emphasise at this point that for pressure on gross margins from rising raw material costs to raise the share of labour in value added while final prices are rising, it is also required that money wages should rise. As we have seen, this they did in every case, sometimes more, sometimes less than the rise of final prices and raw material costs, but nevertheless always substantially relative to the rise of final prices. That this was so was due to the fact that changes in money wages were very much a function of changes in the cost of living, even though they were a nonlinear function. The link, in other words, was not a mechanical one due to the interplay of impersonal economic forces or to the operation of institutional practices, the strength of whose response to the changing cost of living could be regarded as relatively stable; on the contrary, the institutional 'parameters' affecting money wages were themselves constantly being changed. Since this is so, i.e. since the relationship between rising food prices and rising money wages is not constant, but varies with the varying strength of institutional pressures operating on money wages, then the changing shares in gross value added during inflation cannot be solely ascribed to the lag or otherwise of the agricultural sector behind the rest of the economy,[24] of crucial importance though this is. Apart from the importance of the institutional pressures raising money wages in effecting the *direction* of income redistribution, the effect on the *extent* of such redistribution must also be borne in mind.

The importance of these institutional pressures in raising money wages and their varying effect on the relative rates of rise of money wages and final prices can be conveniently emphasised by an examination of the comparative movement of real wages[25] in our three countries.

B. *Real Wage Changes and Price Changes in India, Peru and Turkey—an Interpretation*

The rise of the cost-of-living index creates opposing pressures. On the one hand, it creates political and semi-political sources of strength upon which the trade unions are able to draw in attempting to raise money wages in line with or faster than the cost of living. On the other, the importance of food in the working class budget, and the tendency for food prices to rise faster than prices of manufactures during inflation, give rise to a situation in which the attempt to maintain or to raise real wages is likely to exert severe pressure on profit margins,[26] and thus arouse active opposition from employers. The interplay of these two effects on changes in real wages can be illustrated by a comparison of the changes in real wages in our three countries.

For all three countries real wages moved downwards in a roughly similar fashion during the war until 1943 or 1944; thereafter, they moved upwards more or less continuously, until the late 1940's or early 1950's; it is an ironic thought that when labour was at its scarcest, real wages fell, and when labour developed excess supply, real wages began to rise. The turning point for many underdeveloped countries came, of course, during the Second World War. In the 1950's, the real-wage movement of the three countries tended to diverge much more sharply than hitherto. Accordingly, we divide our discussion of the comparative movement of real wages in the three countries into the pre- and post-1950 periods (roughly), i.e. the period during which real wages moved in a roughly similar fashion in all three countries, and the period during which the real wage movement of the three countries tended to diverge.

In all three countries, real wages declined continuously and drastically during the first years of the war, until 1943 or 1944, by which date the cost-of-living index had either ceased to rise or had reached maximum acceleration, the decline being greatest in Turkey and least in Peru.

That such a decline should have taken place simultaneously in all three countries is attributable to the fact that the effects of the Second World War in all three countries were simultaneously to raise prices, including living costs, extremely steeply, in such a fashion as to raise the ratio of food to industrial prices; and in circumstances in all three countries such that the suddenness of the extremely steep rise in the cost of living 'took by surprise' the institutional forces operating to raise money wages. The importance of the non-mobilisation of these institutional forces in this period in permitting such a decline of real wages is illustrated by the experience of the immediate post-war inflationary periods in India and Peru, when institutional forces were more fully mobilised, and which were thus able to raise real wages despite the rise in the ratio of food to industrial prices which at that time took place in these countries,[27] and which then implied pressure of labour costs on margins, if wages were to keep pace with food prices.

The Country Chapters have dealt with the sense and the respect in which the institutional forces operating on money wages were weak or 'unmobilised' during the war, i.e. with the legal, administrative, political, industrial and trade union changes which marked their mobilisation and brought about the immediate post-war upsurge in real wages. All we need further remark on the wartime and immediate post-war similarities of these real-wage movements is that the steepness of the sudden rise in the cost of living was unprecedented for all three countries, at least since the First World War, and for all three countries the post-war period combined motive and opportunity to raise real wages, in the sense that the post-war social and industrial unrest took place in comparatively favourable political conditions, with behind it the stimulus of drastically-reduced living standards.

The role of the non-mobilisation of institutional forces in the wartime decline of real wages is emphasised by the varying fortunes of the working class in the modern manufacturing sector in the three countries, that of Peru suffering least and that of Turkey most. To explain the fact that real wages fell to as low as 49 per cent of the 1939 level in Turkey during the wartime inflation, whereas they dropped to only 75 per cent of the 1939 level in Peru,[28] we need only recollect a few institutional differences between Peru and Turkey in this period. In Peru, trade unions existed and, despite restrictions, even received some government encouragement during the war, and the Peruvian government was occupied right from the beginning of the war in developing and modifying the machinery to regulate money wages (in accordance generally with the movement of the cost of living) with minimum wage machinery, which, at least for some classes of workers, had been in existence before the war began.[29]

In Turkey, on the other hand, trade unions were banned during the war, the most experienced leaders were mobilised for the army, no properly organised machinery for wage regulation of government employees existed and, in particular, no regular money wage fixing machinery existed either before or during the war.[30]

In India and Peru, the effects of the movement of the ratio of food to industrial prices on the movement of real wages, were more or less constant in the immediate post-war, as compared with the wartime inflationary periods, at least in their accelerating phase.[31] The changes in real wages which took place were changes resulting from the varying pressures of institutional forces. This is not to say that the rise in the ration of food to industrial prices did not exert a retarding effect on the rise of real wages in these countries. The case of Turkey strongly suggests that it did. The post-war real wage rise in Turkey was steeper than in either India or Peru,[32] much steeper than in India, although the post-war unrest does not seem to have been notably greater and the conditions for its success in terms of real wage gains (other than the movements of the industrial/agricultural terms of trade) markedly better—if anything, the contrary. The crucial conditions, permitting real wages to rise faster in Turkey than in India and Peru, was that only in Turkey did the ratio of food to industrial prices remain comparatively stable (albeit fluctuat-

ing slightly from year to year) in this period, whereas in India
and Peru the ratio of food to non-food prices rose
considerably.[33]

As we have said, the movement of real wages in the 1950's
diverged in the three countries. This was most obvious in the
case of Turkey, compared with India and Peru. In Turkey,
not only did real wages not decline, but, in fact, they rose
nearly continuously and substantially throughout the considerable inflation of the 1950's,[34] whereas in this period
real wage gains took place in only a very irregular and halting
fashion, and much less substantially in India[35] and Peru. The
pronounced upward path followed by real wages in Turkey
must be partly attributed to the initial decline and later
relative stability in the ratio of food to industricl prices, a
circumstance which arose in no other inflation and which permitted employers to grant money-wage increases sufficient to
raise real wages with little pressure of labour costs on margins.[36] Analogously, the difficulties experienced in India and
Peru in raising real wages in the 1950's are, to a large extent,
attributable to the opposite situation, namely, the rise in the
ratio of food to non-food prices.

For example, during the 1955/56 to 1960/61 inflation in
India, the only post-war inflation to witness a nearly continuous decline in real wages, the ratio of food to industrial
prices rose steadily; and while in the period 1955-58 in Peru
the ratio of food to industrial prices declined and real wages
rose substantially, the previous three-year period in Peru saw
the ratio of food to industrial prices rise and real wages remain practically stable. The movement of the food to
industrial price ratio cannot, of course, alone explain the
difficulties in India and Peru in raising real wages in the
1950's, since in similar circumstances, i.e. with a rise in the
ratio of food to industrial prices, in the immediate post-war
period in these two countries more or less continuous real-
wage gains were made. And, of course, the relatively favourable position of Turkish industry for granting wage increases
did not automatically ensure that sufficient pressure would be
exerted to enforce wage increases. The necessary additional
consideration explaining the real-wage movement in the case
of Peru and India is the 'exhaustion' of the impetus to the
post-war rise in real wages in these countries. This exhaustion
was compounded of the return in the 1950's to a more
stable and less radical, industrial, social and political situa-

tion, and of the success of the previous period in restoring real-wage levels. In the case of Turkey, although, as in India and Peru, the immediate post-war period was one in which the change-over to peacetime conditions brought about a major impetus to the rise of money and, thus, of real wages, the 1950's did not witness, as happened in India and Peru, any exhaustion of this impetus. On the contrary, the beginning of the 1950's in Turkey was marked not only by a large-scale acceleration in the unionisation of the working class (which had occurred at an earlier date during the war and immediate post-war inflations in India and Peru), but also by a major advance in the rights of trade unions to bargain on behalf of their members, and by the first government minimum wage-fixing attempts; and the period of the 1950's in Turkey was also coterminous with a pronounced increase in the practice of electoral democracy.[37]

In short, the opposite, i.e. downward, movements of the ratio of food to industrial prices in Turkey to that of the ratio of food to industrial prices in India and Peru, and the fact that the institutional forces raising money wages in Turkey did not, as in India and Peru, lose their post-war impetus but, rather, were reinforced in the 1950's, were the reasons for the greater and more continuous real-wage gains in Turkey than in India and Peru in the 1950's.

(iv) Causal Factors in Income Redistribution—Alternative Views

It, thus, appears that the change in the share of wages in gross value added during inflation can be explained in terms of the movement of the agricultural/industrial terms of trade and in terms of the rise of money wages, as was suggested in Chapter 1. Except in exceptional circumstances, such as those arising from wartime conditions, the movement of the agricultural/industrial terms of trade has to be understood in the 'typical' case in terms of the effect on industrial prices of cost increases originating in demand pressures raising prices of primary agricultural commodities, with this effect modified by the extent to which these cost impulses are matched by increasing monetary demand from agriculture for manufactured products. Since money wage changes are strongly cost-of-living oriented, and since food is the most important item in the working class budget, rising money wages tend to supplement pressure of rising raw material

costs on margins. However, the rise of money wages is not
linked with the rise of food prices by market forces, but by
the direct action of institutional forces, the operation of
which is largely independent of conditions in the labour market or even of conditions in the product market. In consequence, whether or not inflation results in rising or falling
labour shares in industrial income depends both upon factors
influencing the movement of the agricultural/industrial terms
of trade, and on those influencing the varying strength of the
institutional forces operating to raise money wages.

It is convenient to discuss these conclusions by comparing
them with some of the strands of economic thought surveyed
in our Introductory Chapter. It will be recollected that the
alternative theories concerning the direction of income
redistribution of manufacturing value added (during inflation)
were based upon different suppositions concerning the relative
movements of final prices, money wages[38] and raw material
costs.

Turning first to theories predicated in a particular view of
the relationship between wages and final prices only, the most
straightforward and most widely accepted is that of Professor Lewis, that 'entrepreneurs benefit because of the tendency of the prices of what they sell to rise faster than
wages.'[39] Here, the lag of wages behind final prices has nothing to do with raw material costs pushing up final prices
faster than wages, but is the supposed result either of the
excess (unlimited) supply of labour (which means that
increased derived demand for labour raises employment
rather than wages) or of the weakness of the trade unions in
an environment of surplus labour alongside an aggregate
excess demand for manufactures. We have seen, however,
that our evidence, limited as it is, does not show wage-lag
to be the commonest case in our three countries—at least for
the post-war years.

Thus, of the eight post-war inflationary periods[40] —four in
Peru, two in Turkey and two in India—only two witnessed a
decline of real wages, i.e. that of the Second Five Year Plan
in India, and between 1949 and 1952 in Peru.[41] This un-
expected behaviour of real wages, this failure of money wages
to lag behind final prices as anticipated, is not due to the
disappearance of the elastic labour supply so much stressed
by Professor Lewis.[42] Moreover, in a sense, the trade union
movements of all three countries, despite very marked advances since 1939, remain in many respects weak, with their

bargaining positions enfeebled by a growing urban labour surplus, legal restrictions, divided leaderships and a host of other difficulties. The point is that money wages have not infrequently been able to keep pace with prices, not because the normal assumptions of the existence of an elastic supply of labour and of organisational and industrial weaknesses of the trade union do not hold, but because they are irrelevant. What is relevant is that the power of trade unions demands has been immensely reinforced by the political context in which they have been advanced, a context which itself has, on occasion, been more favourable to the trade unions the faster the price rise.

This latter point is of considerable significance, since it relates to a set of circumstances frequently found in the underdeveloped world. These circumstances are an urban working class in a strategic situation, whose demands are voiced in a political context which is generally unstable and rapidly changing. The effect of rapidly rising prices in these circumstances is to dramatise latent or existing feelings of exploitation[43] —even in circumstances in which money wages are rising faster than prices,[44] with the result that the *political* impetus to a rapid response of money wages to price increases is strengthened. There is some evidence that this has been a common phenomenon throughout the post-war underdeveloped world.[45]

The implications of the effectiveness of the response of money wages to cost-of-living increases[46] is that the inflation barrier theory which we noted in Chapter 1[47] apparently more closely corresponds to reality than does the profit inflation theory, even if the reasons for the ability of wages to keep pace with rising prices relate to institutional rather than efficiency factors, and even if, for that very reason, the relationship between rates of rise in wages and prices is less determinate than implied by the efficiency theory.

Turning from the relative movements of wages and final prices towards the relative movements of wages and raw material costs, we have the theory of relative cost changes during inflation associated with the name of Kalecki, according to which, assuming the degree of monopoly constant, labour's share in value added declines in the short run (or the upward phase of the cycle) when raw material prices are rising. The argument leading up to this result may be deployed as follows:

(a)   'Prices of raw materials undergo larger cyclical

fluctuations than wage rates' (p. 24).[48]

(b)   This is because changes in money wages can never 'catch up' with changes in raw material prices since changes in money wages cause a change in demand which brings about a further change in raw material prices (p. 24).[49]

(c)   This is in turn a result of the fact that changes in the prices of raw materials are demand-determined (p. 11).

(d)   Accordingly, 'the ratio of raw material prices to unit wage costs depends on the demand for raw materials, as determined by the level of economic activity in relation to their supply which is inelastic in the short run' (p. 29).

(e)   Thus, when demand is increasing, raw material costs will rise faster than unit wage costs.

(f)   Since all increases in prime costs result in proportionate increases in prices with a given degree of monopoly (p. 25), the result of increasing demand is that gross proceeds net of raw material costs rise faster than the wage bill, whose relative share of gross value added thus declines.[50]

Clearly, there is much in common between the view advanced by the present writer and that of Kalecki. Both views envisage prices of manufactures as being in some sense cost-determined, and both regard the supply inelasticities of raw material production in the short-run as a crucial determinant of relative income shares in the modern manufacturing sector. Moreover, both views hold that *if other things remain equal* 'a rise in. . . raw material prices in relation to unit wage costs causes a fall in the relative share of wages in the value added' (p. 29).

Despite these resemblances, however, the Kaleckian model envisages the share of wages as declining when raw material prices are rising, whereas in our view the opposite is more likely to happen.[51] These aspects of Kalecki's argument which bring about the difference in conclusions are (a) that increases in prime costs will be fully passed on to final prices, given that the degree of monopoly remains unchanged, and (b) that wage increases must lag behind increases in raw material prices. If *either* of these two propositions, *taken separately*, does not invariably hold, then neither does it invariably hold that the share of wages will decline as raw material prices rise.[52]

Thus, if pressure from rising raw material costs is able, in a hard market environment, to reduce gross margins,[53] this may raise labour's relative share even if money wages and, thus (ignoring productivity changes), unit labour costs rise more slowly than raw material costs. Rising raw material costs, in this case, are a causal factor in raising labour's share, i.e. the opposite case to Kalecki's. We should note, however, that the rise in labour's share due to the decline in gross margins is partly offset by the fall of labour's share in total prime costs due to the rise in the ratio of raw material costs to unit labour costs. However, as we have seen, when rising raw material costs have reduced gross margins and at the same time reduced the proportion of labour costs in total prime costs, the result has generally been to increase labour's share. The essential point remains that once downward margin variability is permitted, the rise in raw material costs, even in excess of the rise of unit labour costs, may well act as a causal factor in *raising* labour's share of manufacturing income.

The above argument does not depend on variation of margins due to a change in the degree of monopoly. Nor does it depend upon abandonment of a cost-based theory of pricing in the manufacturing sector. Kalecki's view of a cost-based pricing policy of oligopolistic manufacturers as an essential element in the theory of income redistribution can be retained if it is recognised that the conventional margin is likely to be variable within a certain range, even if the range is itself determined in the short-run by convention; and if it is further recognised that at certain critical periods particular circumstances may lead to a major 'displacement' of the conventional margins, i.e. to a change of conventions. The latter is likely to be the result of unusual difficulties due to the rise of prime costs in an unfavourable market environment for manufacturers[54] —and we have argued that small variations around the conventional margin are also explicable in terms of the demand situation faced by manufacturers during a period of rising costs.

There is likely to be a difference in the scale of income redistribution between these two cases. While periods of major displacements of margins are likely to be periods of substantial income redistribution, periods of limited variation around the conventional margin, as in 'normal' times, may well be periods in which the redistribution which does take place, although definite, is nevertheless slight. On the other hand, slight variations in margins year by year over a sufficient period may produce a cumulative change of some significance by means of a gradual revision of conventional margins.

The other condition, in the Kaleckian model, for rising raw material costs to bring about a reduction in labour's share of manufacturing income, is that raw material costs should rise faster than unit labour costs. However, this Kaleckian proposition depends upon the assumption: 1) that wage income constitutes the principal source of demand for the manufactures the production of which is in turn the principal source of derived demand for raw materials;[55] and 2) the assumption that money wages will be adjusted upwards more slowly than raw material prices. Clearly assumption (1) need not hold true in an underdeveloped economy, where the urban wage earners may constitute a small proportion of the market for urban manufactures. Nor is there any reason why raw material costs should rise faster than money wages, when the latter rise as the result of institutional pressure. The opposite result becomes the more possible insofar as the inflationary process itself has the effect of mobilising the institutional apparatus exerting pressure to raise money wages. Furthermore, these institutional pressures have tended to relate wage increases to cost-of-living changes, and since there can be no necessary assumption that food production will have a superior supply response to that of production of raw materials in general, a cost-of-living oriented money-wage rise may well keep pace with the rise of raw material costs, or even exceed it, as, indeed, it did on several occasions in the inflations under review.[56] Whether or not labour costs will lag behind, keep up with, or exceed rising raw material costs during inflation will depend upon the varying relationship of the money-wage rise to food price increases (assuming productivity constant) and upon the relative rate of rise of food prices and prices of raw materials. The answer cannot be determined *a priori.*

The Kaleckian model of rising raw material costs leading to declining relative labour shares in manufacturing income is, thus, seen to depend upon the proposition that margins will not be varied and that unit labour costs will invariably lag behind raw material costs. Both are necessary conditions for the argument to hold.

We have seen that, on the contrary, there is no element of inevitability about either proposition; that margins may vary; that unit labour costs may rise faster than raw material costs; and that, accordingly, the share of labour in manufacturing income may rise with rising raw material costs, and for a number of good reasons is quite likely to do so.

The differences between this conclusion and that of Kalecki, it may be remarked, do not depend upon the fact that our concern is with the manufacturing sector in the context of an underdeveloped economy,[57] whereas Kalecki is concerned with a manufacturing sector in the context of a developed industrial economy. While it is true that Kalecki's argument that money wages can never catch up with raw material prices applies specifically to the conditions of a developed economy (i.e. it is dependent upon urban labour income being the principal ultimate source of derived demand for raw materials), his assumption about the relative speed of adjustment of money wages and raw material prices is not—and the removal of this assumption alone is sufficient to destroy the inevitability of a rising ratio of raw material costs to unit labour costs during inflation. Nor is the assumption that margins will not vary affected by whether or not we are concerned with a developed or an underdeveloped economy.

(v) Causal Factors in Income Redistribution during Inflation—Summary of Conclusions

1. During the inflationary periods in the countries and years covered by our survey, the share of labour in gross value added in the modern manufacturing sector has risen more often than it has fallen.

2. Rising labour shares during inflation have been the result of declining gross profit margins in conjunction with rising money wages.

3. Declining gross profit margins during inflation have been in turn the result of unit prime costs rising faster than demand per unit of output, the effect of which has been to modify in a downward direction the extent to which the rise in prime costs has been passed on to prices. This has been possible since margins have not been completely inflexible, and have even at times undergone major 'displacements', despite the normal mark-up pricing policy prevailing in the modern industrial sector.

4. At the basis of the tendency for the rate of rise of unit prime costs to be faster than that of demand per unit of output during inflation, has been the relative short-run supply inelasticity of agriculture[58] in conjunction with the cost-of-living oriented rise of money wages.

5. Relative agricultural short-run supply inelasticity has tended to reduce gross profit margins in the modern manufacturing sector during inflation by the following process:

    (a)   Demand pressures have quickly raised prices of

agricultural products, owing to the short-run supply inelasticity of the agricultural sector and the flexibility of agricultural prices in response to demand.

(b) Demand pressures in the modern industrial sector have had little or no direct effect on prices, owing to the short-run supply elasticity of the modern manufacturing sector and the relative inflexibility of industrial prices in response to demand within a predominantly oligopolistic market structure.

(c) The demand pressures which have raised agricultural prices have thereby raised industrial prime costs—directly in the case of raw material costs, and indirectly in the case of labour costs, via the stimulus to rising money wages from rising food prices. In consequence, industrial prices have risen to offset rising prime costs.

(d) The rise in agricultural prices has not tended to raise rural demand per unit of industrial output to the same extent as it has raised unit prime costs to industry. With a declining marketed surplus this is because, while the rise of industry's unit prime costs is more or less closely related to the rise of agricultural prices, the rise of total rural demand for industrial products is related to the rise of agricultural prices less the decline in the quantity marketed. With a static or increasing marketed agricultural surplus, the rate of rise of rural demand per unit of industrial output will still tend to be less than the rate of rise of unit prime costs to industry[59] (resulting from the rise of agricultural prices) since, firstly, a proportion of the proceeds of the increased surplus will be 'leaked' away into savings or purchases outside the domestic manufacturing sector; and, secondly, even if *total* rural demand for industrial products rises at the same rate as unit prime costs due to a rising marketed agricultural surplus, the superior short-run supply elasticity of the industrial sector compared with the agricultural sector will mean that rural demand *per unit* of industrial output or potential output (capacity) will rise more slowly than unit prime costs.

6. Since money wages have been cost-of-living oriented, since food accounts for over 50 per cent of the working class budget and since food prices have risen alongside other agricultural commodity prices, rising money wages have tended to supplement the pressure of rising raw material costs on gross profit margins. This tendency has

been accentuated by the rise of food prices relative to prices of manufactures during inflation, the effect of which has been to tend to raise money wages faster than prices of manufactures and to divert urban demand away from industrial products. Even when the rise of money wages has lagged behind that of prices of manufactures it has tended to be sufficient, *in conjunction with pressure on gross profit margins from rising raw material costs,* to raise labour's share in value added.

7. The link between rising money wages and rising food prices has been the result of institutional pressures and not market forces. The varying success of institutional forces in raising money wages more or less in line with the rising cost of living has been closely related to the actual or potential political strength of organised labour, i.e. to the expected political consequences of a slower increase of money wages than that actually granted. Since money wages have not risen as a result of market mechanisms, and since the efficacy of institutional pressures has not been constant, money wages have sometimes risen more slowly than prices and sometimes faster. Consequently the rise of money wages relative to final prices has not been simply a function of the lag of the agricultural sector behind the rest of the economy. The institutional pressures raising money wages have thus been an independent factor affecting income redistribution during inflation.

8. The inflations during which the share of labour in gross value added in the modern manufacturing sector declined were not only fewer than those in which the reverse happened, they were also inflations which took place in rather exceptional circumstances. These exceptional circumstances have generally been associated with unusual trade conditions. Unusual trade conditions have led to increasing gross margins and a declining labour share in value added either by disrupting the normal mark-up pricing mechanism of manufacturing industry or by so mitigating or negating the more usual effects on industrial gross profit margins of a lagging agricultural sector as to permit gross.margins to rise without disrupting the normal pricing mechanism. The former case has been the result of the wartime disruption of trade flows and the latter case has been the result of an unusually favourable capacity to import, combined with the exceptional circumstance of complete liberalisation of trade.

9. Since declining labour shares have been associated with exceptional trade conditions, and rising labour shares with the lag of agriculture behind the rest of the economy, which itself has been a characteristic feature of inflation in the post-war underdeveloped world, it appears likely that stable or rising labour shares in the modern manufacturing sector during inflation may be the typical situation.

NOTES

1.   That is, dividing the continuous Peruvian inflation into three, a wartime inflation, an immediate post-war inflation and the inflation of the 1950's.

2.   These divisions correspond not only to the changing direction of income redistribution but also, as indeed might be expected, to other major changes in the economy which would have served to periodise the course of economic events.

3.   i.e. defensive because *reacting* to cost increases, and unsuccessful because the price rise was insufficient wholly to absorb the cost increases. Analogously, a *successful* defensive inflation may be defined as one in which prices rise in reaction to rise in prime costs but in which, owing to a favourable market environment, margins are increased in the process, as in Peru between 1952 and 1956. A *non-defensive* inflation would be one in which final prices are rising to take advantage of a favourable demand situation, without any pressure from rising prime costs, which lag behind final prices, so that profit margins increase.

4.   Strictly speaking, we are concerned with the rise of money wages relative to the rise of final prices, given the ratio of the rise of primary commodity prices to that of final prices, and given the division of total prime costs between labour costs incurred within the manufacturing sector and the materials purchased from outside it.

5.   These demand pressures have also tended to raise labour costs indirectly, by raising food prices. The rise in food prices has in turn stimulated the rise of money wages. Since the response of money wages to changes in food prices is brought about by institutional pressures, money wage increases, although connected with demand pressures on the agricultural sector, are not the result of demand pressures on the labour market.

6.   Of course non-agricultural industrial raw materials, such as minerals, also tend to have, relatively to the manufacturing sector, a short-run inelastic supply and a flexible response of price to demand changes.

7.   This is assumed in the argument throughout this section.

8.   Or aggravate the effects of a decline in the agricultural marketed surplus.

9. Thus, in 1955, about 14 per cent of Peru's total manufacturing production (i.e. covering registered and unregistered industry) was exported (U.N., *Development in Peru,* 1959, p. 57). In 1950, about 7 per cent of Turkey's domestic manufacturing output was exported (U.N., *Manufacturing Industry in Turkey,* 1958, p. 127); and in 1959/60 the total value of India's exports of manufactures was about 10 per cent of the total ex-factory value of the output of the organised manufacturing sector (from figures in *India, Industry and Trade,* 1961, published on the occasion of Indian Industries Fair and Afro-Asian Economic Conference, p. 141 and *Statistical Abstract of the Indian Union,* 1963 and 1964).

10. These were the Turkish wartime inflation and the Turkish inflation of 1953/54 to 1957/58; the Indian inflation of the immediate post-war years; and the three Peruvian inflationary periods—immediate post-war, 1949-52 and that of the late 1950's; with, less certainly, the Indian inflation during the Second Five Year Plan.

11. *Cf.* R.N. Tripathy, p. 209, G. Kazgan, pp. 154-5; and Pan American Union, 1950, p. 241, for the Indian Turkish and Peruvian economies respectively.

12. The Turkish wartime inflation and the Peruvian inflationary period of 1949/52.

13. Thus, in the seven typical inflations we are considering, food prices rose faster than prices of manufactures in all but one, the Turkish inflation of the late 1950's and, in this case, food prices appear to have risen at about the same rate as prices of manufactures.

14. Of the seven typical inflationary periods, four were periods when money wages rose faster than final prices.

15. In particular, during the war, the physical obstacles to importing supplies of capital goods, raw materials and spare parts limited the expansion of industrial output in all three countries. Industrial expansion under the Indian Second Five Year Plan was to some degree insulated from the effects of the agricultural lag by the enhanced importance of urban industry in the economy, which thus helped provide more of its own market.

16. We use the term 'unusual' in inverted commas to emphasise the limitations imposed by the small 'sample' we are considering.

17. Thus, more than a quarter of Peru's requirements of manufactures in 1955 were imported (U.N., *Development in Peru,* 1959, p. 57), whereas the equivalent proportion for India lies somewhere between 13 per cent and 20 per cent (U.N., E.C.A. *Industrial Growth in Africa,* New York, 1963, p. 14).

18. In Peru agricultural production increased, declined and rose again during the war, ending up rather lower in 1944 and 1945 than in 1938 and 1939. In India, agricultural production first fell and then rose

during the war, ending up at a rather higher level in 1944 and 1945 than in 1939/40. In Turkey, on the other hand, agricultural production declined in every wartime year   except 1941, ending up 30 per cent lower in 1944 than in 1939.

19. Backed up by a sufficiently adequate capacity to import based mainly, though not entirely, on the remarkable inflow of foreign assistance in the 1950's.

20. The rapid expansion of demand, together with the removal of sectoral domestic supply bottlenecks by imports, raised productivity and, thus, ameliorated the rise of unit labour costs.

21. Although it may have limited the extent of their rise.

22. The immediate post-war period in Turkey was one of the sporadic price rises and also of sporadic increases in the ratio of raw material costs to final prices. The Indian price pause of 1943-45 in the face of rising prime costs was due to the first rigorous and coordinated attempts of the Indian Government on a number of fronts to prevent inflation, and this represented a temporary, somewhat artificial, situation.

23. See, for India, M.K. Ghosh and S.C. Chaudhri, p. 735; for Turkey, *Manufacturing Industry in Turkey*, 1958, p. 11; and, for Peru, *Renta Nacional*, 1942-48, pp. 104-5.

24. As is particularly emphasised by the failure of labour's share decisively to improve during the inflation of the Indian Second Five Year Plan—and also, perhaps, by the slightness of the shift towards labour during the Turkish wartime inflation.

25. Although we are concerned with the rate of rise of money wages relative to final prices of *manufactures*, a comparative survey of real-wage changes (i.e. money-wage changes relative to price changes of all working class consumer goods, including food) permits a clearer appreciation of the role of institutional forces, since it is with real wages that trade unions are concerned.

26. Together with the pressure from rising raw material costs which is likely to be occurring at the same time.

27. The experience of Peru, in which the immediate post-war rise of the cost-of-living index was steeper than the wartime rise and accompanied an even faster money wage rise, particularly exemplified this.

28. Of course, there are statistical dangers in comparing the percentage fall in real wages of different countries. There is, however, no reason to assume in this case that our figures give a misleading comparative picture, particularly since the difference in the percentage fall of real wages in the two countries is so great. Although the existence of a black market probably means that we have under-estimated the rise of the cost-of-living index in Peru (Pan American Union, 1850, p. 233), the

same applies to Turkey (E.R. Lingeman, 1947, *op. cit.*, p. 162) and India (A.R. Prest, p. 49).

29. I.L.O., *Minimum Wages*, 1954, p. 148.

30. We have forborne to explain the difference in the extent of the wartime real wage decline in India and Peru, because the difference is not great enough to permit confidence that it is not due to weaknesses in the statistics. Such weaknesses, of course, are not likely to falsify our picture of the direction of change in real wages.

31. Leaving aside, that is, the relative stability of the ratio of food to industrial prices in the Indian price pause of 1943-45 and the decline of the ratio during the price deceleration of 1943-46 in Peru, which, no doubt, helped the real-wage rise taking place in those periods, permitting, as they did, money wages to pass food prices without exerting pressure on margins.

32. This remains true if we make the comparison with 1943 and 1944, the years when real wages reached their nadir.

33. Again, this remains true if we date the comparison from 1943 or 1944.

34. Although the rise was negligible between 1953 and 1955.

35. In the 1950's, real wages in India never rose during a year of price rise.

36. The rise of real wages slowed up after 1953, when the demand situation became stickier and margins came under pressure.

37. It may be that the failure of the Turkish post-war upsurge of trade union activity to die down was, in part, due to its partial suppression immediately after the war, when trade unions were banned for a time and the most militant leaders removed.

38. Assuming no sufficiently offsetting increase of productivity.

39. W.A. Lewis, 1961, p. 222. However, Professor Lewis has elsewhere qualified his model by specifying conditions under which money wages might keep pace with prices, (W.A. Lewis, May 1954, pp. 172-3). The wartime years correspond most closely to Lewis's picture, when prices soared while money wages lagged behind. It is a curious paradox that an orthodoxy should have been established, that real wages ought to decline during inflation since, under 'normal' assumptions, inflation should be the time when labour's bargaining power is greatest—so that money wages ought to exceed price rises.

40. i.e., distinguishing four sub-periods in the Peruvian inflation post-war, and two in that of Turkey in the 1950's.

41. If we take real wages in terms of manufactures alone, then the point is further emphasised.

42. An 'institutional' explanation of the rise of money wages is
a priori less likely to be associated with a view of declining labour
shares during inflation than is an explanation of the rise of money
wages, depending on the derived demand for labour (although, of
course, a demand-pull theory of the rise of money wages can be consistent with a rising share of labour in industrial income during
inflation).

43. Historically, rising prices have always been important catalysts and
sources of political discontent (*Cf.* E.P. Thompson, pp. 63-68, on the
pre-industrial primacy of bread prices over wages as 'the most sensitive
indicator of popular discontent' (p. 63). The post-war underdeveloped
context has combined a cost-of-living consciousness with a new
emphasis on state intervention to regulate money wages accordingly—
thus reintroducing elements of the old 'moral economy.'

44. The trade unions in Turkey were convinced that real wages were
declining in the early 1950's, as a result of the rise in the cost of living,
although the reverse was happening. There was practically no black
market in these years.

45. Turner has calculated, using I.L.O. figures, that between 1953 and
1960 real wages have risen alongside rising consumer prices in Arab
Africa, Black Africa, southern Latin America and Central America.
Moreover, real wages have risen most in those areas where prices have
risen most. Thus, the average annual rates of increase of the cost of
living and real wages in this period were, for South America, 50 per
cent and 6-7 per cent respectively; for Arab Africa; and for Central
America, a negligible rate of increase of prices and a 2 per cent annual
average rise of real wages (H.A. Turner, pp. 12-14).

46. Including what might be called an 'over-reaction.'

47. i.e. that theory which, applied to underdeveloped economies, holds
that, at a certain stage in the process of raising the level of investment,
the rise in prices forces the entrepreneurs themselves to grant higher
money wages, in order to maintain the efficiency of their labour force.
The resulting inflationary spiral in one way or another limits a further
shift of resources away from consumption and towards investment as
wages rise *pari passu* with prices (J. Robinson, pp. 48-49 and 356).

48. The discussion and the text references to Kalecki's views are based
on his *Theory of Economic Dynamics*, revised edition, 4th impression,
London 1965.

49. Kalecki's example of this process relates to the downswing of the
cycle only, i.e. when raw material prices are declining (*ibid.*, p. 24).

50. i.e., 'A rise in the degree of monopoly or in raw material prices in
relation to unit wage costs causes a fall of the relative share of wages in
value added' (*ibid.*, p. 29). In the work quoted, Kalecki nowhere
explicitly states that, when raw material prices are rising, labour's
share will decline with a given degree of monopoly. Only the reverse

case, i.e. falling raw material prices leading to rising labour shares, is argued out in full (pp. 24 and 31). It clearly follows, however, from the logic of his arguments, and Kalecki's own argumentation suggests that this is his own unstated conclusion. The following two quotations suffice to demonstrate this. Thus: 'A rise in the degree of monopoly or in raw material prices in relation to unit wage costs causes a fall of the relative share of wages in the value added.' 'It should be recalled in this connection that as distinguished from prices of finished goods, the prices of raw materials are "demand-determined". The ratio of raw material prices to unit wage costs depends on the demand for raw materials as determined by the level of economic activity in relation to their supply which is inelastic in the short run' (p. 29); and 'fluctuations of wages in the course of the business cycle are much smaller than those of prices of raw materials' (*ibid.*, p. 25).

51. The argument proceeds on the assumption that any marked and continuous rise of prices of raw materials is likely to take place in a period when the general price level is rising, i.e. during inflation.

52. It may be remarked that our argument is consistent with the possibility that the result envisaged by Kalecki *may* be brought about by the mechanism he envisages, as, indeed, happened in Peru at the beginning of the wartime inflation. The point advanced in the text is that, although a possible outcome, Kalecki's is not the only, nor indeed the most likely, outcome.

53. As we have seen them do, for example, in the immediate post-war Indian inflation, among others.

54. Just such a conjunction of trade union activity and a hard market environment we observed to have been instrumental in bringing about a major downward shift in conventional margins in India in the late 1940's. An analogous situation was brought about in Peru between 1949 and 1952, with the slight difference that the active factor in squeezing margins was not trade union activity in raising labour costs, but a rise in raw material costs during a period of transition from a protected domestic market to one open to unrestrained competition from imported manufacturers.

55. The effect of this assumption being that a rise in wage costs following a rise in raw material costs is 'cancelled out' by a further rise in raw material costs, owing to the resulting increase in demand.

56. In the immediate post-war inflation in Peru, unit labour costs rose slightly faster than raw material costs, and this also happened during the later inflationary years of the war in the same country. Between 1952 and 1956, in Peru, the ratio fluctuated without moving decisively in either direction. In the Turkish inflation of 1953/54 to 1957/58, after an initial decline in the ratio, unit labour costs tended to rise slightly faster than raw material costs.

57. Although it might be argued that, because urban labour income is a small proportion of total demand for manufactured products in an

underdeveloped economy, Kalecki's theory is even less likely to be the only possible outcome in an underdeveloped economy than it is in a developed economy.

58. i.e. the short-run supply response of agricultural output to demand relative to that of industry, the relative steepness of the supply curve in the agricultural as compared with the industrial sector. In the longer run, the relative rates of shift of the two curves to the right may be such that agriculture becomes a drag on the growth of the industrial sector.

59. It must be borne in mind that this argument rests on the assumption that, in some sense, the growth of the marketed agricultural surplus is lagging behind the demands for that surplus promoted by the growth of modern industry, assuming a two-sector economy.

CHAPTER 9

SOME IMPLICATIONS

Inflation, Industrial Expansion and Real Wages

The kind of picture we have drawn of the characteristics of the typical inflation in underdeveloped countries suggests certain reflections on the relationship of inflation to industrial expansion. This relationship has often been posed in terms of the favourableness or otherwise of inflation to industrial expansion. We have earlier distinguished between inflation considered as an independent phenomenon and as the net result in the field of prices of all the economic phenomena at work in the economy and, following this, we consider it useful to distinguish between the effects of inflation *per se* and the effects of the economic conditions typically giving rise to inflation. It is with the latter that we are for the moment concerned. The conditions typically causing inflation we have found to be those associated with the unsuccessful defensive inflation. It is, therefore, this case that we now discuss and, again, our discussion is not intended to imply that no other case exists. A further limitation of our discussion is that it relates only to market economies[1] in which the bulk of manufacturing industry is in private hands (as in India, Peru and Turkey).

It is immediately apparent that, if an inflation is unsuccessfully defensive, there is no question of a shift to profits as a proportion of industrial income, and that a view of inflation as an 'engine of development' by means of forced savings is thereby precluded. Insofar as such forced savings are those supposed to accrue directly to the entrepreneur in manufacturing industry from the postulated rise in prices above prime costs, this will be true whether interpreted financially or in real terms. In financial terms, the relevant causal connection is likely to be that relating the rate of investment to the volume of internally-generated funds via the risk factor—and here the result is clearly negative, with a decline in the profit share in gross income.[2] In real terms, the situation is less clear. If investment in modern industry is conceived of as a matter of extracting food from agriculture to feed newly employed industrial workers (and/or to permit higher consumption levels for industrial employees in general),[3] then the movement of income shares within the modern manufacturing sector may have little relevance to this problem.[4] In this case, a modified version of the forced savings argument might suggest that the rise in agricultural prices would benefit the rural upper classes relative to the peasantry, and that this would limit the extent of self-consumption by the agricultural population, and improve the flow of food to the towns.

How likely is such an outcome in our typical, i.e. unsuccessfully defensive, inflation? Granted that the basic condition of such an inflation is a lagging agricultural sector, such a redistribution might well reduce the extent of the lag, insofar as this manifested itself in a short-fall in the marketed surplus. However, there can be no *a priori* assumption that a rise in the price of food, even if it benefits the agricultural sector as a whole by turning the terms of trade against industry, will result in a more unequal distribution of agricultural income. This depends, among other things, on a wide range of institutional factors, whose effects will vary from country to country and from time to time. If there is, on the contrary, a shift towards a more equal distribution of agricultural income, increased self-consumption by the peasantry is likely to *reduce* the marketed surplus. Moreover, in either case, the turn in the terms of trade against industry will tend to limit the size of the marketed food surplus. Further, even if there does take place, as a result of a rise in food prices, a decline in the peasantry's share of rural income, this need not result in an increased marketed surplus. The gains from rising food prices may be used by the rural upper classes to finance peasant consumption in return for the acquisition of claims to property, e.g. land, implements, bullocks, etc.

In short, in the inflations of the type we have found to be most common, the forced savings view does not apply if interpreted in financial terms. In real terms, a typical inflation is likely to signify an already existing situation in which it is difficult to increase resources (food and raw materials) for the expansion of the industrial sector,[5] and it is impossible to generalise on whether or not the price rise helps to modify this situation in one direction or the other.

A more crucial consideration militating against the view that inflation will encourage economic development by raising the proportion of resources which can be devoted to investments, is that the obstacle to industrial development lies in the limitations set by effective demand, rather than the competition for resources between investment and consumption. We have noted evidence for this view in the excess capacity which characterised defensive inflations in manufacturing industry, and our discussion of the role of agriculture in the typical inflation has indicated the source of the constraints limiting expansion of markets for industrial production. From another angle, the terms of our discussion have been such as to suggest that any counterposing of consumption to investment in the fashion required by the forced savings theory is liable to meet with serious difficulties when agriculture tends to lag so much behind the development of the rest of the economy. In such a situation, the imbalance appears as a sectoral imbalance, and not as an overall disproportion between planned saving and planned investment. Resources of manpower, plant and materials may be in sufficient supply to meet the needs of the non-food consumer goods industries, while resources of capital and land are inadequate or insufficiently well-organised to meet the demands on the food producing sector. In this situation, *ex ante* aggregate savings and investment may be in balance, but the distribution of consumption expenditure may be such as to exert pressure on limited food supplies, so that the resulting rise in prime costs, with its supporting rise in demand, leads to a general price rise. For both consumption goods and investment goods sectors of manufacturing industry there need be no aggregate excess demand during the price rise.[6] In short, the conditions typically underlying inflation are more likely to hinder industrialisation, by restricting the necessary expansion of the market for industrial products, rather than to help it, via forced savings. It seems likely that the necessary prerequisite for any increase in the proportion of resources devoted to investment is a prior, or at least simultaneous, increase in agricultural production or the marketed surplus.

As we noted in an earlier chapter, the same kind of limitations as regards the counterposing of investment and consumption apply to the 'inflation barrier' view.[7] However, as we have found inflation more generally to limit the proportion of profits in industrial income than to raise it, the inflation barrier view fits the facts of underdeveloped countries as we have found them[8] more closely than does the forced savings view. This limitation of the proportion of profits, as we have seen, springs from the same source as the narrowness of the market, *viz.* the difficulties of expanding agricultural production. In Mr. Kaldor's words, 'the reason why the growth of manufacturing industry has not proceeded further must be sought, therefore, not in any lack of capabilities for manufacturing, but in the inability of these (underdeveloped) countries to supply food for larger industrial and urban populations. This inability may manifest itself in a lack of capital for industrial expansion or in a lack of markets; in both cases, however, the fundamental cause is the inability or unwillingness of the agricultural sector to supply more food to the towns.'[9]

This is not, of course, to say that it is immaterial which manifestation of the short-fall in food supply (or agricultural output generally) is the operative constraint on industrial expansion, since the mechanism at work will be different in the two cases, with correspondingly different, albeit similarly negative, consequences. This is well illustrated by the different *modus operandi* of the food bottle-neck in its role as an obstacle to industrial expansion in a centrally planned, as compared to a market, economy.

It is important, however, to stress that the inflationary spiral, of which the rise in money wages is the 'backbone', will have favourable as well as unfavourable effects on development. The first of these lies in the tendency we have already mentioned for a rise in real wages to stimulate an increase in productivity, although this effect may be achieved in an underdeveloped economy without a rise in real wages in terms of food. What is relevant here is that there should be a rise of real wages in terms of the product of manufacturing industry. 'The real cost of labour to each employer is the cost in terms of his own product. From the point of view of the worker it is the price of his labour in terms of the commodities he consumes that matters. The divergence between the two may be very great especially when productivity is altering differently in manufactures and in agriculture.'[10] Possibly, here lies the explanation for the introduction of labour-saving machinery in countries where the workers' standard of living is extremly low and the labour supply abundant.[11] The rise in raw material costs also stimulates innovation in the directin of the development of substitute raw materials and the better utilisation of known raw materials,[12] and, indeed, if labour-saving innovation is easier, a rise in raw material costs may, of course, stimulate more actively in this direction—or, indeed, a rise in labour costs may stimulate innovation in the use of raw materials.

Besides this long-run favourable effect as a result, in a typical inflation, of prime cost pressure on margins in encouraging innovation, there is a sense in which the inflationary process is beneficial, in the short run, to growth. This effect is linked with the lack of effective demand we have remarked upon as being the principal obstacle to a more rapid development of industry. The point here is that, although the general conditions typically giving rise to inflation will be such as to restrict the market, the inflationary process itself, in particular the rise of money wages associated therewith, may be the necessary support of a certain minimum rate of increase of production.[13] Unless money wages rise sufficiently fast in relation to food prices, the diversion of demand towards agriculture may have the effect of preventing the permissive demand rise necessary to maintain existing rates of increase of production. The practical importance of this point has been cogently illustrated by the recent experience of a number of Latin American countries, where attempts to halt inflation, by halting, in particular, the rise of money wages either directly or indirectly, have caused a halt or even a serious decline in industrial production.[14]

To conclude, in the conditions typically giving rise to inflation in underdeveloped economies, in particular in backward agriculture with a poor supply response, the inflationary process is likely to permit existing rates of increase of industrial production to continue which, indeed, would not be able to do so without the inflationary process, in particular, without the rise in money wages associated with it. The inflationary process, in fact, helps to counteract the negative effect on growth of agricultural stagnation. This it does by maintaining a rise in demand sufficient to permit the rise in prime costs to be more or less passed on to prices. In effect, the rise of money wages here (which is both a causal factor in and stimulated by the general rise of the price level) has a positive effect on industrial expansion, by limiting the redistribution of income towards agriculture in a situation where agricultural production is lagging. The inflationary process itself, however, is the product of conditions which, on balance, retard the growth of industrial production by their

effect in restricting markets. To some extent also, the inflationary process compounds this unfavourable effect on development by restricting the proportion of profits in industrial
income and thereby limiting development, insofar as it
depends upon internally-financed[15] and/or autonomous
investment. Counterbalancing this, the prime cost pressure
of the typical inflation will have a long-run favourable effect
on development by stimulating labour-saving innovation and
the development of raw material substitutes, and by improving
labour and raw-material utilisation.[16]

Institutional Wage Determination and Real-Wage Changes

The emphasis placed in the foregoing discussion on the role
of institutional forces in the movement of real wages (and,
indeed, the failure of the expectation of declining real wages
during inflation generated by the Lewis model) naturally
suggests two questions:
  1. How are real wages able to rise at all, given our emphasis
  on some form of cost-plus pricing and a relatively inelastic
  food supply?
  2. In principle, given strong enough institutional forces
  raising money wages, what, if anything, is the limit to the
  rise of real wages or the rate of rise of real wages?
How can real wages rise during inflation? The crux of the
matter is the behaviour of real wages in terms of food. Although
food supply is relatively inelastic, it is not always completely
inelastic in the short run. Particularly when fovernmental
attempts to increase food supply are taken into account, there
is likely to be a shift to the right of the food supply curve over
time. Such a shift may be insufficient to feed the growing
population as a whole. If, however, workers in manufacturing
industry are able to increase their money wages faster than
urban food prices, they will be able to increase their real
wages at the expense of other urban dwellers, of the urban
middle classes, the mass of semi-employed, civil servants at all
levels, etc. There is no reason in principle why this should not
happen. Moreover, real wage gains at the expense of other
urban groups need not depend upon an increased marketed
supply of food, although they would doubtless be greatly
facilitated by it. Further, real wages in terms of manufactures
will tend to be rising as productivity is increasing and if gross
margins are declining—a distinct possibility, as we have seen,
during the typical inflation.[17]

Finally, even if the agricultural sector as a whole is gaining at the expense of the urban sector through a favourable movement of the terms of trade for agriculture, the urban employees may nevertheless be gaining at the expense of the rural sector, if their average money earnings are rising faster than average agricultural incomes. In particular, urban employees would be likely to gain at the expense of those sections of rural society who have to purchase foodstuffs on the market, such as landless labourers, some plantation workers, etc.

What limits the rise of real wages during inflation?[18] There are two separate questions involved here: What limit is there, in principle, to the rate at which real wages can rise as a result of institutional forces over a given period? Is there any limit in principle, to the length of time over which real wages can rise owing to institutional forces?

Concerning our first question, there is, of course, in principle, a limit to the rise of real wages over a given period of time. The limit, in principle, is reflected in the fact that, having specified institutional forces external to the firm as being the operational forces raising money wages (and thus, given the rate of price rise, real wages), we have, by implication, assumed the existence of forces of resistance to the rise of money wages, forces which have given rise to the need for, and existence of, institutional forces to break down that resistance. The limits set by this resistance, although not susceptible to mathematical formulation or precise statistical measurement, are, nevertheless, real. This resistance, on the one hand, takes the form of passing a rise of labour costs on to prices and, on the other hand, of counter-pressure of one form or another to the rise of money wages by the employer.

As regards the first method of employer resistance, the same process which causes real wages to rise necessarily sets a partial limit to that rate of rise, by strengthening the ability to resist via raising prices when demand rises as a result of increased wage incomes.

As regards the second method of employer resistance, although there are competitive forces in a oligopolistic economy which mitigate for the worker the frustrating effect of the defensive price rise via downward margin variation, and which create the possibility of real wages rising faster than productivity, the existence of such helpful circumstances does not mean that, even in an inflationary situation, there is no limit to the extent to which real wages can rise faster than the rise in productivity. Here again, the process causing real wages to rise faster than productivity creates its own obstacles. The very competitive conditions which prevent costs being fully passed on to prices mean that the more intense the pressure to raise real wages after a certain point (the point at which real wages begin to rise faster than productivity) the progressively greater the resistance to that attempt is likely to be.

What we have said does not imply, however, that the rate of rise of productivity determines the rate of rise of real wages, or that it sets an upper limit to the rate of rise of real wages in a mechanistic sense. The rate of rise of real wages may well lag behind that of productivity, if institutional forces are not strong enough to raise money wages at the appropriate rate.

That the rate of rise of productivity does not set an upper limit to the rate of rise of real wages appears less obvious. There are two senses in which this is true. The first relates to the difference between a mechanistic relationship between the upper limit of the rate of rise of real wages and the increase in productivity, and to an institutional relationship between the maximum rate of rise of real wages and the rate of increase of productivity. The mechanistic view of the relationship of the rate of rise of productivity to the upper limit of the rate of rise of real wages may be predicated either on the assumption of compensating price rises by the entrepreneur, or of unemployment halting the rise of money wages and, therefore, of real wages. However, if for competitive reasons already discussed it is considered unsuitable to raise prices to the full extent of the rise in labour costs, firms may be more inclined to resist the wage demands rather than to reduce their production and/or labour force. If the entrepreneur loses the struggle, and if he has to take a long-term view-point, he may simply take the decline in margins as given. Over the economy as a whole, the rate of rise of productivity will tend to set a limit to the rate of rise of real wages via the resistance to money wage increases. However, given a reluctance to reduce production and employment, the possibility of increased real wages via the downward variability of margins becomes more likely than in the case of the postulated mechanistic relationship between the maximum rate of rise of real wages and the rate of rise of productivity. All this amounts to saying that to raise the rate of rise of real wages faster than that of productivity becomes progressively more difficult after the break-even point (at which real wages are rising at the same rate as productivity) has been reached.

Our second reason for believing that the rate of rise of productivity does not set an upper limit to the rate of rise of real wages, is that the rate of rise of productivity itself is likely to be partly a function of the rate of rise of real wages. In other words, the more the rise of real wages in terms of output tends to exceed that of productivity, the more, given a competitive economy, will be the tendency to mechanisation,[19] and the introduction of innovations raising productivity.

'A higher rate of increase in *real* wages not only increases the rate of turnover of equipment, but it tends to enhance the rate of improvement of design of new equipment since it gives stronger incentive for making the new equipment more labour-saving.'[20]

In the condition of an underdeveloped economy this means that real wages in the modern sector may rise at the expense of employment or the rate of growth of employment in that sector.

The effect of the rise of real wages upon productivity gives us our answer, a negative one, to the second question we asked about the limits to the rise of real wages, i.e. whether or not there is, in principle, a limit to the length of time over which real wages can rise owing to institutional forces.

To sum up, institutional forces external to the firm are the operational forces raising money and, thus, real wages, and up to the point at which real wages are rising at the same rate as productivity, it is nothing more or less than the strength *or weakness* of such forces which determines the rate of rise of real wages. In the short run, the rate of rise of productivity tends to set a broad and very elastic limit to the rate of rise of real wages, but this maximum rate of rise of productivity is itself raised the more the rate of rise of real wages presses against it in the long run. Moreover, since the nature of the mechanism whereby the rate of rise of productivity limits the rate of rise of real wages is dependent upon primarily institutional and non-mechanistic factors (e.g. the conventional profit margin, price leadership, the political influence of trade unions, etc.) then in the long run institutional forces are able to exert a continuous upward pressure on real wages, by institutional as well as economic means, e.g. by enforcing a displacement of the conventional margin.

NOTES

1. Despite the importance of planning in India, the Indian economy, and within it the manufacturing sector, remains basically a market economy.

2. This may be offset by an expanding sales volume—but the 'forced savings' view relates to the effects of the relative movement of prices and prime costs only.

3. With, presumably, indirect favourable effect on industrial expansion.

4. It might, however, be argued that a decline in the wage share of value added in factory industry releases a larger supply of manufactured goods for sale to the rural population, thus swelling the marketed food surplus received in exchange, and so permitting increased investment in the modern sector. If, however, the most important obstacle to the expansion of the industrial sector is the limitation of the market, a decline in the labour share cannot exert more than a minor favourable influence on investment by this route.

5. Difficult, that is, without government intervention—and, perhaps, even then.

6. G. Maynard, June 1961, pp. 195-6.

7. However, the same caveat has to be made here as was made earlier in discussing the forced savings view, *viz.* that insofar as the volume of internal savings limits the rate of investment by private firms, then the proportion of profits in industrial income becomes financially relevant to industrial expansion.

8. With the exception that the inflation barrier will be set by the strength of the institutional forces external to the firm operating on entrepreneurs and not by considerations of efficiency, so that it is likely to set in at a somewhat higher real wage than is envisaged. *Cf.* J. Robinson, p. 49.

9. N. Kaldor, 1960, pp. 39-42.

10. J. Robinson, p. 356.

11. See M. Dobb on the paradox of the apparent abundance and cheapness of labour and the introduction of labour-saving machinery during the industrial revolution in the 18th century in Britain. M. Dobb, 1954, p. 276). As Felix notes (D. Felix, August 1956, pp. 445-57), this is a period when food prices were outstripping industrial prices.

12. On this point, in the context of early British industrial development see D. Felix (1956, 8 ff.) and E.J. Hobsbawm, 1960, p. 124.

13. In this context the effect of inflation *per se* on development emerges via its effect in stimulating the institutional forces operating to raise

money wages, in such a way that whatever subsequent weakening of them takes place, nevertheless the net long-run effect is likely to be permanently to strengthen them.

14. *Cf.* G. Maynard, 1961, pp. 192-3. On the other hand, if there is a 'leakage' of effective demand from money-wage income into imports, then rising real wages could well have an adverse effect on continued expansion—certainly the effect would not be ambiguously favourable.

15. The inflationary effect of the rise in food prices will tend to cause government restrictions on bank credit, etc. (*Cf.* N. Kaldor, 1960, p. 241).

16. We must re-emphasise that the unsuccessful defensive inflation is not the only type of inflation, and these reflections on development do not apply to other types of inflation.

17. Although, since raw materials constitute a significant proportion of total prime costs, it might be argued that wage increases will, with full cost pricing, bring about smaller percentage increases in final prices, realism demands that we assume raw-material costs to be rising also.

18. This discussion is conducted, for the sake of convenience, in terms of a homogeneous business economy. The main qualifications necessitated by the fact that we are considering underdeveloped economies have, in effect, been dealt with in our earlier discussion.

19. Mechanisation itself, it has been argued, may create more favourable conditions for innovation, since 'the technical possibilities are richest at the capital-intensive end of the spectrum,' Habakkuk, p. 50 ff. Habakkuk has stressed the point that, if the cost of labour rises in all sectors of industry, including the machine-making sectors, and if prices rise in proportion, in a closed system and in the long run, 'there would be no inducement to shift towards more capital-intensive methods' (p. 18). He points out that in practice there would be considerable time lags, that in any case prices might not be fully adjusted upwards, and that he is not considering a closed system. In the context of our own argument, we may recall that we have been concerned particularly to show that prices have often not been fully adjusted upwards and to explain the reasons for this. For the introduction of labour-saving machinery in the modern sector in Turkey see I.L.O., *Protection Against Unemployment*, 1960, p. 7. For the marked rise in the degree of capital intensity in the modern sector in Peru see U.N., *Development of Peru*, 1959, p. 39; and for rising capital intensity in India during the Second Five Year Plan following the extreme pressure on margins of the immediate post-war years, see S.A. Palekar, 1962, pp. 101-3 and P.C. Jain, pp. 344-354.

20. N. Kaldor, August 1959, p. 298.

Bibliography

Non-official

W.R. Ackroyd, 'The Nutritive Value of Indian Foods and the Planning of Satisfactory Diets', G.O.I. *Health Bulletin*, Delhi, No. 23, 4th edition, 1951.

A.P. Alexander, *Turkey*, in E. Pepelasis, L. Mears and I. Edelman, ed., *Economic Development: Analysis and Case Studies*, New York, 1964.

R.J. Alexander, *Communism in Latin America*, New York, 1957.

P.M. Andic, *'Development of labour legislation in Turkey'*, *Middle Eastern Affairs*, Vol. VIII, No. 11, November, 1957.

E.M. Bernstein and I.G. Patel, 'Inflation in Relation to Economic Development', *I.M.F. Staff Paper*, 1952.

A. Bonné, *State and Economies in the Middle East*, London, 1948.

E.W. Burgess and F.H. Harbison, *Casa Grace in Peru* (National Planning Association, United States Business Performance Abroad, Case Studies, No. 2), Washington, 1954.

T.J. Byres, 'Indian Planning on the Eve of the Fourth Five-Year Plan', *The World Today*, Vol. 22, No. 3, March 1966.

H. Chenery, G. Brandon and E. Cohn, *Turkish Investment and Economic Development*, Foreign Operations Administration, Ankara, 1953 (restricted circulation).

A.J. Coale and E.M. Hoover, *Population Growth and Economic Development in Low-Income Countries: A Case Study of India's Prospects*, Bombay, 1959.

S.A. Dange, 'Prices and Wages', *New Age*, Vol. X, No. 2, February, 1961.

L.A. Dicks-Mireaux, *Cost or Demand Inflation?* Woolwich Economic Papers, No. 6, London, 1965.

M. Dobb, *Studies in the Development of Capitalism*, 6th Impression, London, 1954.

M. Dobb, *Wages*, Revised Edition, Cambridge, 1956.

G.S. Dorrance, 'Inflation and Growth: The Statistical Evidence', *I.M.F. Staff Papers*, March, 1961.

Eastern Economist, Annual Number, various issues. *Records and Statistics*, various issues.

V. Eldem, 'Les Progrès de l'Industrialisation en Turquie', *Revue de la Faculté de Sciences Economiques de l'Université d'Istanbul,* Eighth Year, 1946-47.

V. Eldem, 'Le revue national de la Turquie', *Revue de la Faculté de Sciences Economiques de l'Université d'Istanbul,* Ninth year, 1947-48.

V. Eldem, 'Changements survenus depuis la guerre dans le niveau de vie des fonctionnaires et des salaries de l'Etat', *Revue de la Faculté de Sciences Economiques de l'Université d'Istanbul,* Thirteenth year, Nos. 1-4, October 1951-July 1952.

D. Felix, 'Profit Inflation and Industrial Growth', *Q.J.E.,* Vol. LXX, No. 3, August 1956.

A.J. Fonseca, *Wage Determination and Organised Labour in India,* 1964.

T.R. Ford, *Man and Land in Peru,* Gainsville, Florida, 1955.

M. Geyda, 'Balance of Payments', *Turkish Economic Review,* Vol. 1, No. 1, May 1960.

P. Geren, *Impact of Rising Prices on Various Strate in Punjab,* Lahore, 1944.

M.K. Ghosh and S.C. Chaudhri, *Statistics: Theory and Practice,* Seventh edition, Allahabad, 1955.

K.S. Gulati, 'Under-Utilisation of Capacity, Chemical Industries', *The Economic Weekly,* Vol. XI, No. 47, November 21, 1959.

M.L. Gupta, *Problems of Unemployment in India,* New Delhi, 1956.

J.A. Habakkuk, *American and British Technology in the Nineteenth Century,* Cambridge University Press, 1962.

J.A. Hallsworth, *Freedom of Association and Industrial Relations in the Countries of the Near and Middle East,* I.L.O., Geneva, 1955.

E.J. Hamilton, 'American Treasure and the Rise of Capitalism', *Economica,* IX, 1929.

E.J. Hamilton, 'Profit Inflation in the Industrial Revolution', *Quarterly Journal,* 1942.

E.J. Hamilton, 'Prices and Progress', *Journal of Economic History,* 1952.

A.H. Hanson, *Public Enterprise and Economic Development,* London, 1959.

R.E. Harris, ed., *Economic Problems of Latin America,* 1st edition, New York, 1944.

Z.Y. Hershlag, *Turkey: An Economy in Transition*, The Hague, 1958.

E.J. Hobsbawm, 'Custom, Wages and Work-Load in Industry', in A. Briggs and J. Saville, eds., *Essays in Labour History in Memory of G.D.H. Cole*, London, 1960.

E.M. Hoover, *Population Growth and Economic Development in Low Income Countries*, Bombay, 1959.

P.C. Jain, *Problems of Indian Economics*, Allahabad, 1956.

R.C. James, *Labour and Technical Change*, unpublished Ph.D. dissertation, Cornell University, 1957.

D.K. Jameson, *Overseas Economic Survey: Economic and Commercial Conditions in Peru*, London, July 1955.

N. Kaldor, 'Economic Growth and the Problem of Inflation Part 2', *Economica* (New Series), Vol. XXVI, No. 103, August, 1959.

N. Kaldor, *Essays on Economic Stability and Growth*, London, 1960, Duckworth.

M. Kalecki, *Theory of Economic Dynamics*, Revised Edition, London, 1965, Unwin.

V.B. Karnick, *Indian Trade Unions: A Survey*, Bombay, 1960.

K.H. Karpat, *Turkey's Politics: The Transition to a Multi-Party System*, Princeton, N.J., 1959.

G. Kazgan, 'Structural Changes in Turkish National Income, 1950-60,' in T.M. Kahn, ed., *Middle Eastern Studies in Income and Welath*, London, 1965.

J.M. Keynes, *Treatise on Money*, 1930, London, Macmillan, Vol. II.

Sir Henry Knight, *Food Administration in India, 1939-47*, Stanford, California, 1954.

P. Kotler, *Problems of Industrial Wage Policy in India*, unpublished doctoral dissertation, Cambridge, massachusetts Institute of Technology, 1956.

B. Lewis, *The Emergence of Modern Turkey*, Oxford, 1961.

W.A. Lewis, 'Economic Development with Unlimited Supplies of Labour', *Manchester School*, Vol. XXII, No. 2, May 1954.

W.A. Lewis, *The Theory of Economic Growth*, 5th Impression, London, 1961.

I.M.D. Little, 'The Strategy of Indian Development', *National Institute Economic Review*, No. 19, May 1960.

W. Malenbaum, *Prospects for Indian Development,* London, 1962.

S.W. Maranjan, 'Public and Private Sector—the Rationale', *Indian Economic Journal,* Vol. 5, No. 2, October, 1957.

G. Maynard, 'Inflation and Growth: Some Lessons to be Drawn from Latin American Experience,' *O.E.P.* (N.S.), Vol. 13, No. 2, June 1961.

G. Maynard, *Economic Development and the Price Level,* 1962.

D. Mazumdar, 'Underemployment in Agriculture and the Industrial Wage Rate', *Economica,* (New Series), Vol. XXVI, No. 104, November 1959.

E.H. McDonald, *Latin American Politics and Government,* 2nd edition, New York, 1954.

E.J. Meyer, *Middle Eastern Capitalism,* Cambridge, Mass., 1958.

W.E. Moore, *Industrialisation and Labour,* Ithaca, 1951.

M.D. Morris, 'Labour Discipline, Trade Unions and the State in India', *J.P.E.,* Vol. LXIII, No. 4, August 1955.

M.D. Morris, *The Emergence of an Industrial Labour Force in India (A Study of the Bombay Cotton Mills, 1854-1947),* University of California Press, Berkeley and Los Angeles, 1965.

K. Mukerji, *Levels of Economic Activity and Public Expenditure in India,* Bombay, 1965.

C.A. Myers, *Labour Problems in the Industrialisation of India,* Cambridge, Mass., 1958.

G. Myrdal, *Asian Drama,* 1968, Penguin.

O. Okyar, *'Yatirimlarin Sektarler Itibarili Dagilisi',* Forum i Sunbat, 1962.

S.A. Palekar, *Problems of Wage Policy for Economic Development (with Special Reference to India),* London, 1962.

C.M. Palvis, *An Econometric Model for Development Planning (with Special Reference to India),* Dissertation, Rotterdam School of Economics, The Hague, 1953.

J. Parker and C. Smith, *Modern Turkey,* London, 1940.

E.H. Phelps Brown and M.H. Browne, 'Distribution and Productivity Under Inflation', *Economic Journal,* December, 1960.

E.H. Phelps Brown, 'The Long-term Movement of Real Wages', in J.T. Dunlop, ed., *The Theory of Wage Determination*, London, 1964.

A.R. Prest, *War Economies of Primary Producing Countries*, Cambridge, 1948.

R. Radhakamae, *Indian Working Class*, Bombay, 1945.

T.N. Ramaswamy, *Full Employment for India*, Benares, 1946.

R.I.I.A., *Peru: A Background Note*, London, 1955.

J. Robinson, *The Accumulation of Capital*, London, 1956, Macmillan.

S.M. Rosen, 'Turkey' in W. Galenson, ed., *Labour in Developing Economies*, Berkeley and Los Angeles, 1962.

P. Sanghvi, *Surplus Labour in Indian Agriculture*, 1969.

D.N. Sastri, 'Idle Capacity in the Metallurgical Industries', *Applied Economic Papers*, Vol. 1, No. 1, 1961.

D.B. Singh, *Inflationary Price Trends in India*, Bombay, 1957.

A.D. Smith, ed., *Wage Policy Issues in Economic Development*, 1969.

P. Thomas, 'Towards a General Theory of Industrial Relations', *The Economic Weekly*, Vol. XI, Nos. 51 and 52, December 19, 1959.

E.P. Thompson, *The Making of the English Working Class*, London, 1963.

R.W. Thornburg, G. Spry and C. Soule, *Turkey: An Economic Appraisal*, New York, 1949.

D. Thorner, 'Casual Employment of a Factory Labour Force', *The Economic Weekly Annual*, Vol. IX, Nos. 3, 4 and 5, January 1957.

V.R.K. Tilak, 'Unemployment Statistics in India', *The Economic Weekly*, Vol. XVII, No. 1, January 2, 1965.

R.N. Tripathy, *Fiscal Policies and Economic Development in India*, Calcutta, 1958.

H.A. Turner, *Wage Trends, Wage Policies and Collective Bargaining: The Problem for Underdeveloped Countries*, University of Cambridge, Department of Applied Economics, Occasional Paper 6, Cambridge, 1965.

Union of Chambers of Commerce and Industry and Commodity Exchanges of Turkey, *Problems of Industrialisation and Investment in Turkey*, Ankara, 1957.

Official

(a) International Official

F.A.O., *Mediterranean Development Project,* Rome, 1959.

F.A.O. and I.B.R.D., *The Agricultural Development of Peru, Part i, General Report,* Washington, 1954.

I.B.R.D., *The Economy of Turkey,* Baltimore, 1951.

I.L.O., *International Labour Review,* various issues.

I.L.O., *Yearbook of Labour Statistics,* various issues.

I.L.O., *I.L.O. Yearbook,* 1939-40, Geneva, 1940.

I.L.O., *Labour Courts in Latin America,* Geneva, 1949.

I.L.O., *Labour Problems in Turkey,* Geneva, 1950.

I.L.O., *Report of the Director General to the Fourth Conference of American States Members of the I.L.O. 1949. Report 1,* Geneva, 1951.

I.L.O., Fourth Conference of American States Members of the I.L.O. 1949, *Record of Proceedings,* Geneva, 1951.

I.L.O., I.L.O. Regional Conference for the Near and Middle East, 1951. *Report 1. Manpower Problems: Vocational Training and Employment Service,* Geneva, 1951.

I.L.O., *Methods of Remuneration of Salaries Employees,* Third Item on the Agenda. Conference of American States Members of the I.L.O. Rio de Janeiro, 1952.

I.L.O., *Minimum Wages in Latin America,* Geneva, 1954.

I.L.O., *Why Labour Leaves the Land: A Comparative Study of the Movement of Labour out of Agriculture,* Geneva, 1960.

I.L.O., *Report to the Government of Turkey on Possible Measures against Unemployment,* Geneva, 1960.

O.E.E.C., *Statistical Bulletins. Definitions and Methods, Part 1. Industrial Production,* 2nd edition. Paris, 1953.

O.E.C.D., *Statistical Bulletins. Industrial Statistics, 1900-1959,* Paris, 1960.

O.E.C.D., *Economic Surveys by the O.E.C.D.,* Turkey, Paris, 1963.

Pan American Union, *The Peruvian Economy,* Washington D.C., 1950.

U.N., Department of Economic Affairs and Department of Economic and Social Affairs:

Economic Survey of Asia and the Far East, various issues.

Economic Bulletin for Latin America, various issues.

Economic Survey of Latin America, various issues.

Review of Economic Conditions in the Middle East, Supplement to World Economic Report, various issues.

Survey of Current Inflationary and Deflationary Tendencies, New York, 1947.

Inflationary and Deflationary Tendencies, 1946-48, New York, 1949.

Processes and Problems of Industrialisation in Underdeveloped Countries, New York, 1955.

E.C.A.F.E./F.A.O. Agricultural Division, *Food and Agricultural Price Policies in Asia and the Far East,* Bangkok, 1958.

E.C.L.A. *Analysis and Projections of Development VI: The Industrial Development of Peru,* Mexico, D.F., 1959.

The Development of Manufacturing Industry in Egypt, Israel and Turkey, New York, 1958.

E.C.A., *Industrial Growth in Africa,* New York, 1963.

E.C.E., *Economic Survey of Europe in 1961. Part 2. Some Trends in Economic Growth during the 1950s,* Geneva, 1964.

(b) National Official
India

G.O.I., Labour Bureau, *Indian Labour Gazette,* various issues.

G.O.I., Labour Bureau, *Indian Labour Statistics,* various issues.

G.O.I., Central Statistical Organisation, *Statistical Abstract,* various issues.

Reserve Bank of India, *Bulletin,* various issues.

G.O.I., Royal Commission on Labour in India, *Report,* Calcutta, 1931.

G.O.I., Principal Information Office, *Indian Information,* Vol. 10, No. 161, June 1, 1945.

G.O.I., Labour Investigation Committee, *Main Report,* Delhi, 1940.

G.O.I., Ministry of Industry and Supply, *First Census of Manufactures, India—1946,* New Delhi, 1949.

G.O.I., Ministry of Information and Broadcasting, *Labour in India,* New Delhi, 1949.

G.O.I., Manager of Publications, *India: Guide to Current Official Statistics. Volume 1—Production and Prices,* Fourth Edition, New Delhi, 1949.

G.O.I., Planning Commission, *The First Five Year Plan,* New Delhi, 1952.

G.O.I., Taxation Enquiry Commission, *Report of the Taxation Enquiry Commission, Vol. 1, 1953/54,* New Delhi, 1955.

G.O.I., Planning Commission, *Papers Relating to the Formulation of the Second Five Year Plan,* New Delhi, 1955.

G.O.I., Planning Commission, *Second Five Year Plan,* New Delhi, 1956.

G.O.I., Planning Commission, *Review of the First Five Year Plan,* New Delhi, 1957.

G.O.I., Ministry of Commerce and Industry, *Report of the Textile Enquiry Committee, 1958.* Yeravda Prison Press, 1958.

G.O.I., Central Statistical Organisation, *Estimates of the National Income, 1948-49 to 1958-59,* New Delhi, 1960.

India, Industry and Trade 1961. Published on the occasion of Indian Industries Fair and Afro-Asian Economic Conference.

G.O.I., Ministry of Food and Agriculture, *Growth Rates in Agriculture,* Delhi, 1965.

R.B.I., *Report on Commerce and Finance for the Year 1955-56,* Bombay, 1956.

R.B.I., *Banking and Monetary Statistics of India. Part Two Supplement,* Bombay, 1964.

Peru

Banco Central de Reserva del Peru, *Renta Nacional del Peru,* various issues.

R.P., Contraloria General, *Balance y Cuenta General de la Republica,* various issues.

R.P., Ministerio de Fomento y Obras Publicas, *Estadistica Industrial,* various issues.

R.P., Ministerio de Hacienda y Comercio, *Annuario Estadistica del Peru*, various issues.

Banco Central de Reserva del Peru, *Balanza de Operaciones Internacionales de Peru*, 1938-52, 1954.

Peruvian Embassy (London), *Peru: Statistical and Economic Review*, B. de la Torre, London, 1953 and 1958.

R.P., Institute Nacional de Planificacion, *Estimaciones del Producto e Ingreso Real*, Lima, 1965.

Turkey

R.O.T., Central Statistical Office, *Annuaire Statistique*, various issues.

R.O.T., Central Statistical Office, *Monthly Bulletin of Statistics*, various issues.

R.O.T., Central Statistical Office, *National Income of Turkey (and Family Expenses in Country and Towns): Estimates (1927-45), Forecasts (1948-52)*, S. Bilkur, Ankara, 1949.

R.O.T., Central Statistical Office, *Small Statistical Abstract of Turkey, 1949*, Ankara, 1952.

R.O.T., Central Statistical Office, *National Income of Turkey, 1938, 1948-54*, Ankara, 1955.

R.O.T., Ministry of Economy and Commerce, *Conjoncture*, Nos. 10-12, October-December, Ankara, 1955.

R.O.T., Ministry of Finance, *Budget Speech*, 1957, Istanbul, 1957-58.

R.O.T., State Planning Organisation, *First Five Year Plan, Development Plan 1963-67*. Ankara, 1963.

United Kingdom

Naval Intelligence Division, Geographical Handbook Series, *Turkey*, 1943.

Department of Overseas Trade, *Peru: Review of Commercial Conditions*, London, 1944.

Department of Overseas Trade, *Turkey: Review of Economic Conditions*, London, 1945.

Board of Trade, *Overseas Economic Surveys: Turkey*, E.R. Lingeman, London, 1947.

Board of Trade, *Overseas Economic Surveys, Economic and Commercial Conditions in Peru*, D.K. Jamieson, London, 1955.

United States

U.S. Department of Commerce, *Foreign Commerce Weekly*, Vol. 39, No. 75, June 9, 1948.

U.S. Foreign Commerce Bureau, *Investment in Turkey: Basic Information for U.S. Businessmen*, Washington, 1956.

U.S. Foreign Commerce Bureau, *Investment in Peru, Basic Information for U.S. Businessmen*, Washington, 1957.

INDEX
(Numbers referring to tables are italicized)

For Product Safety Concerns and Information please contact our EU
representative GPSR@taylorandfrancis.com
Taylor & Francis Verlag GmbH, Kaufingerstraße 24, 80331 München, Germany

 www.ingramcontent.com/pod-product-compliance
Ingram Content Group UK Ltd.
Pitfield, Milton Keynes, MK11 3LW, UK
UKHW040927180425
457613UK00010B/271